The Orpheum Theater, Memphis, Tennessee

Cherry Mansion, Shiloh, Tennessee

Enjoy!

Arthur M. Barbour

# Fine Dining
# Tennessee Style

*by John M. Bailey*

**The Iris, Tennessee's State Flower**

Garden of Dr. & Mrs. Frank Osborn

**Recipes from one hundred and twenty
of the most outstanding chefs
at some of the finest restaurants
and bed and breakfast inns in Tennessee**

John M. Bailey

About the author:

Author of FINE DINING, MISSISSIPPI STYLE
Graduate of the University of Mississippi
Associate Member of the American Culinary Federation
Member of the Southern Foodways Alliance
John and his wife Ann reside in Germantown, Tennessee

Copyright 2000 John M. Bailey

ISBN 0-942249-19-4
Library of Congress: 00-134730
First Printing September 2000

**Cover photograph by John M. Bailey**
**Cover design by Herschel Wells**

Published by
**Toof Cookbook Division**
**STARR ★ TOOF**
670 South Cooper Street
Memphis, Tennessee 38104
800-722-4772

**This book is dedicated to:**

*My wonderful wife Ann for her continued love and support for my projects and to Marcia, Phillip, John Jr., Laura and David for their inspiration and to my seven grandchildren: John III (Trey), Emilie, Andrew, Mimi, Ann, & twins Joseph Cassidy & James Bailey Osborn.*

# Introduction

Let this book be your guide to talented chefs, great restaurants and bed & breakfast inns across the state of Tennessee. As expected, the food was wonderful and the chefs were anxious to share their signature recipes for this project. If we missed a couple of your favorite restaurants, please forgive us. Because of space availability in the book, we were unable to use recipes from all of the fine dining restaurants and bed & breakfast inns in the state. We are, however, extremely pleased with the recipes that we have and think that these recipes represent a good sampling of the fine food that is available across Tennessee.

This is the second in a series of cookbooks to showcase the fine chefs, restaurants and bed & breakfast establishments that abound in the Southern states. The South has always been known for its graciousness and hospitality. This cookbook contains many recipes that are popular in our region.

In this book, we have divided the state into three distinctly different and beautiful areas: West, Middle and East Tennessee; separated geographically by the way the Tennessee River meanders across the state. Tennessee is certainly blessed to have such beautiful scenery, friendly people and wonderful food! From Memphis to Mountain City, Tennessee has it all! These recipes have been tested over the years in restaurants and bed & breakfast inns throughout Tennessee. Now enjoy them in your home. They are on the house, compliments of the Chef!

John M. Bailey

### Acknowledgments:

**I would like to thank the following people:**

- **The Chefs of Tennessee for all of their great recipes.**
- **The local chapters of the Tennessee Chamber of Commerce for all their help.**
- **Bill Williams Jr. AIA for the use of his wonderful pen & ink drawings.**
- **Jan Maurer, artist, for the use of her beautiful pen & ink drawings of East Tennessee.**
- **Mary Stodola and Colleen DePete of the Viking Culinary Art Centers for their assistance.**
- **Frank Grisanti, former President of the Tennessee Restaurant Association for his help.**
- **I would also like to thank the following for their help on this project:**
  **W. Jett Wilson, attorney & Ed Neal, CPA**

**JMB**

# TABLE OF CONTENTS

Please note all recipes were written and contributed by the finest chefs, restaurants and bed and breakfast establishments in Tennessee. These recipes are not written for the inexperienced cook. If there are any questions about cooking terms, please refer to the extensive glossary beginning on page 178. Some minor editing was done for added clarity on each recipe.

John M. Bailey

Riverside Drive, Memphis, Tennessee – PHOTO BY JOHN BAILEY

Pyramid, Memphis, Tennessee – PHOTO BY JOHN BAILEY

Goldsmith Civic Garden Center, Memphis, Tennessee – PHOTO BY JOHN BAILEY

Dixon Gallery & Gardens, Memphis, Tennessee – PHOTO BY JOHN BAILEY

Shiloh National Park – PHOTO BY JOHN BAILEY

The Hermitage, Home of Andrew Jackson, Nashville, Tennessee – PHOTO BY JOHN BAILEY

Cheekwood, Nashville's Home of Art & Gardens – Photo by John M. Bailey

Opryland Hotel, Cascades Restaurant, Nashville, Tennessee – photo by John Bailey

Fall Creek Falls, Tennessee State Park – PHOTO BY JOHN BAILEY

Bluff View Art District, Chattanooga – PHOTO COURTESY OF BLUFF VIEW ART DISTRICT

Ann Bailey with the Chattanooga Choo Choo – PHOTO BY JOHN BAILEY

Tennessee Aquarium, Chattanooga, Tennessee – PHOTO BY JOHN BAILEY

Rural East Tennessee Scene – PHOTO BY JOHN BAILEY

Cades Cove Smokehouse, Smoky Mountains National Park – PHOTO BY JOHN BAILEY

Smoky Mountain National Park Creek, Gatlinburg – PHOTO BY JOHN BAILEY

Knoxville, Tennessee Dogwood Arts Festival – PHOTO BY JOHN BAILEY

1882 Doe River Covered Bridge, Elizabethton, Tennessee – PHOTO BY JOHN BAILEY

1788 Home of Andrew Jackson, Jonesborough, Tennessee – PHOTO BY JOHN BAILEY

Jonesborough, Oldest Town in Tennessee – PHOTO BY JOHN BAILEY

MEMPHIS is Tennessee's largest city. It is situated on the Chickasaw bluffs that overlook the fertile Mississippi and Arkansas Delta. The Mississippi River forms the western boundary of the city. Memphis took its name from the ancient city on the Nile River that means "place of good abode." From the blues to rock-n-roll, Memphians are proud of their musical heritage. Beale Street and Graceland are major destination points for visitors to the city. Memphis is also a leading distribution center for rail, truck and air deliveries across the United States. It is one of the busiest ports on the Mississippi River. Memphis is a world-class medical center. The world-renowned St. Jude Children's Research Hospital and the University of Tennessee-Memphis medical school are located here. The University of Memphis is the second largest university in Tennessee.

GERMANTOWN is an upscale city east of Memphis, and is one of the fastest growing communities in the Mid-South. Germantown's educational, cultural and recreational opportunities make it a premier residential community. The acoustically superior Germantown Performing Arts Center brings world-class artists to the area. Nearly 1,000 horses are brought to town each June for competition in the Germantown Charity Horse Show.

COLLIERVILLE is situated east of Germantown. Even though its population has more than quadrupled in the past 20 years, Collierville has maintained its small-town charm. The renovated town square has been in existence since the 1870s, as have many of the businesses still operating around it. Numerous parks and churches, plus a community center, enrich the community, while its homes represent some of the finest residential construction in the Mid-South.

BARTLETT is located northeast of Memphis and offers quality residential development, safe schools and educational opportunities for its citizens. The city recently completed the beautiful Bartlett Performing Arts Center. Bartlett is one of the fastest growing cities in the Memphis metropolitan area. The city also has a strong industrial base.

DYERSBURG is one of the largest cities in northwest Tennessee, located in the middle of rich farm lands. The Dr. Walter E. David Wildlife Museum is located at Dyersburg State Community College. It contains a species of every known duck on the Mississippi Flyway.

REELFOOT LAKE is located in the northwest corner of the state. The lake was formed as a result of an earthquake that rocked the area in the early 19th century. On December 16, 1811, the ground rose and then sank, causing the Mississippi River nearby to flow backward and pour into the open fault. This rare geological event formed the 15,000-acre, cypress-lined Reelfoot Lake. Bald eagles nest in the area during the winter months. The town of Tiptonville is nearby.

PARIS is the home of The World's Biggest Fish Fry! This event is held each April. Kentucky Lake is located just minutes east of downtown Paris. This recreational wonderland is the largest reservoir in the TVA system. Paris Landing State Resort Park & Convention Center is located 16 miles northeast of the town on Kentucky Lake. A 60-foot-tall replica of the Eiffel Tower is located in Memorial Park. It is the tallest one outside of Paris, France.

JACKSON is the second largest city in West Tennessee. It was named for President Andrew Jackson because many of his wife's relatives lived in the area. Folk hero and railroad engineer, Casey Jones, lived in Jackson. The house he was living in at the time of his death in 1900 is now in the Casey Jones Village complex in Jackson. The 165-acre Cypress Grove Nature Park is located west of Jackson. A two-mile-long elevated boardwalk winds through the cypress grove where wildlife such as deer, egrets and many other animals are commonly spotted.

SHILOH was one of the bloodiest battles in the Civil War. As a result of this long skirmish, 13,047 Union men and 10,699 Confederate soldiers were lost, wounded or dead. This Civil War battlefield is operated year-round by the National Park Service. Pickwick Dam is located nearby on the Tennessee River.

# WHITE CHURCH TEA ROOM

### *196 North Main Collierville, TN 38017*

*Built in 1873, White Church was the home of the Collierville Christian Church. In 1992, it was sold to Jim & Cher Foth who paired the restaurant with an antique shop. This one-of-a-kind church is listed on the National Historical Register and features a fine example of late 19th century stained glass valued in excess of $100,000. The classic Victorian woodwork adds additional splendor. Some of the original pews are in the tea room which allow diners to literally sit on the past. Seasonally decorated, the mismatched period table settings and flatware add to the cozy congeniality.*

**Michael Fink, Executive Chef**

*Chef Michael Fink is a Collierville native and a 1996 graduate of the Memphis Culinary Academy. His previous cooking stints include Café Society, Bonne Terre and the University Club. Michael joined White Church in June 1999.*

## TAPIOCA CRÈME BRÛLÉE

| | | | |
|---|---|---|---|
| 6 | egg yolks | 1⅝ | cups half-and-half |
| 1¼ | teaspoons vanilla | 1⅝ | cups heavy |
| 1¼ | teaspoons brandy | | whipping cream |
| ¾ | cup sugar | ⅓ | cup tapioca |

Place egg yolks, vanilla, brandy and ½ of sugar in large bowl and place to the side. In a saucepan, bring half-and-half, heavy whipping cream and remainder of sugar to a boil. Once at a steady boil, slowly add tapioca while stirring with a wire whip. Continue stirring for 20 minutes. Whip the egg mixture vigorously while slowly adding the hot cream mixture in a steady stream. Put custard mixture into 6-ounce ramekins and bake in a bain marie at 325 degrees for 30 minutes. Let cool for 20 minutes. Dust the top of each custard with ½ teaspoon of white sugar and caramelize with a torch. Serve with whipped cream or fresh berries.

Serves 4.

## ARTICHOKE SALAD

| | | | |
|---|---|---|---|
| 2 | tablespoons grenadine | ½ | teaspoon cracked black pepper |
| 1 | tablespoon Dijon mustard | ⅓ | cup extra virgin olive oil |
| 2 | tablespoons red wine vinegar | 1 | red onion, sliced |
| 1 | teaspoon sugar | 1 | tablespoon fresh cilantro, chopped |
| 1 | dash garlic, minced | 2 | cans artichoke hearts, drained |
| 1 | pinch kosher salt | 1 | head bibb lettuce |

In small saucepan put grenadine, Dijon mustard, red wine vinegar, sugar and garlic and bring to a boil. Stir in kosher salt and cracked black pepper and turn the flame to medium. While stirring vigorously, slowly add olive oil until completely incorporated. Remove from heat immediately. Place red onion, fresh cilantro and artichoke hearts in metal bowl. Pour hot vinaigrette onto vegetables and turn lightly with a spoon. Cover and chill overnight. Serve on bibb lettuce leaves.

Serves 8.

## LAMB EMPANADA

| | | | |
|---|---|---|---|
| 1½ | pounds ground lamb, browned and drained | 1 | teaspoon kosher salt |
| ¼ | cup yellow onion, minced | ½ | teaspoon cracked black pepper |
| 1 | teaspoon garlic, minced | ½ | teaspoon cayenne pepper |
| 1 | teaspoon paprika | 1 | can tomato sauce |
| 1 | teaspoon cumin | ½ | cup pine nuts (pignolia) |
| 1 | teaspoon oregano | ½ | cup feta cheese, crumbled |
| 1 | teaspoon basil | | |
| 1 | teaspoon chili powder | 4 | each frozen pie crusts, thawed |

Once the lamb meat is browned and drained, add all ingredients except feta cheese and pie crusts. Cook on medium heat for 20 minutes stirring often. Let cool then fold in feta cheese. Place ¼ of the meat mixture on each pie crust in a mound to 1 side of the center. Fold pie dough over the meat mixture to form a half circle. Crimp edges to seal in the meat. Place on parchment paper and bake at 350 degrees for 20 minutes or until crust is golden brown. Serve hot and garnish with chopped cilantro, chopped mint and lemon zest.

Serves 4.

## BOSCO'S PIZZA KITCHEN & BREWERY

*7615 West Farmington Germantown, TN 38138*

*2120 Madison Avenue Memphis, TN 38104*

*1805 21st Avenue South Nashville, TN 39212*

*Bosco's is Tennessee's first restaurant brewery and home of world-class Famous Flaming Stone Beer. Famous Flaming Stone is featured in* **Ultimate Beer,** *a new book by beer critic and author, Michael Jackson. Bosco's has been voted one of the top 2 for beer and top three for pizza in the reader's poll in* **Memphis Magazine.**

**Andrew Feinstone, Regional Manager**

## APPLEWOOD SMOKED BACON PIZZA

| | | | |
|---|---|---|---|
| ½ | tablespoon olive oil | 3 | strips applewood |
| 1 | ounce whole milk mozzarella | | smoked bacon |
| 2 | ounces roma tomato | 1 | ounce fontina cheese |
| 2 | artichoke hearts, quartered | ½ | teaspoon fresh thyme |

Place a pizza brick, baking tiles or baking sheet in the oven and preheat the oven to 500 degrees F. Place a 6-ounce ball of dough on a work surface sprinkled with semolina. Using the heels of your hands, press down to flatten the dough. Lift and gently pull the dough to stretch it into a circle 8 inches in diameter. Brush crust with olive oil; then distribute the mozzarella, roma tomato, artichoke hearts, bacon and fontina. Bake until crust browns and cheese is bubbly. Before serving, sprinkle with fresh thyme.
Serves 2.

## CRAB CAKES & CRAWFISH

| | | | |
|---|---|---|---|
| 1½ | cups bread crumbs | 2 | tablespoons fresh corn |
| ½ | pound lump crabmeat | 1 | egg |
| 2 | tablespoons white wine | 1 | teaspoon Tabasco sauce |
| 1 | red bell pepper, seeded and chopped | 1 | teaspoon salt |
| | | 2 | teaspoons pepper |
| 2 | ribs of celery, finely diced | ½ | pound crawfish |

Mix all ingredients, form cakes and sauté.
Serves 2.

## PIZZA DOUGH

| | | | |
|---|---|---|---|
| 1 | tablespoon active dry yeast | 2 | teaspoons olive oil |
| 2 | teaspoons sugar | 2 | cups high gluten flour |
| 1 | cup warm water | ½ | cup semolina |
| ½ | cup light beer | 1 | teaspoon salt |

In a small bowl, dissolve the yeast and sugar in ½ cup water. Let sit until it begins to foam, 3 to 5 minutes. Next, add the remaining ingredients to the mixing bowl until it forms a smooth dough. Transfer the dough to a large bowl that has been oiled. Cover the bowl with a damp kitchen towel and let the dough rise for 30 minutes. Remove the dough from the bowl and cut in into 4 equal portions about 6 ounces each.
Serves 4 to 6.

**The Restaurant For Beer Lovers™**

## CALIFORNIA PIZZA

| 2 | ounces goat cheese | ½ | ounce pine nuts |
| 1½ | ounces sun-dried tomatoes | 3 | ounces whole milk mozzarella |
| 1 | ounce fresh basil | ½ | tablespoon olive oil |

Place a pizza brick, baking tiles or baking sheet in the oven and preheat the oven to 500 degrees F. Place a 6-ounce ball of dough on a work surface sprinkled with semolina. Using the heels of your hands, press down to flatten the dough. Lift and gently pull the dough to stretch it into a circle 8 inches in diameter. Brush crust with olive oil; then distribute the goat cheese, sun-dried tomatoes, mozzarella and pine nuts. Bake until crust browns and cheese is bubbly. Garnish with basil.

Serves 2.

## OSSO BUCO À LA BOSCO'S

| ½ | cup olive oil | 2 | onions, diced |
| ¼ | cup butter | 2 | cups beef broth |
| 1 | cup flour | ¼ | cup orange juice from frozen concentrate |
| 6 | lamb shanks | | |
| 2 | cups red wine | | |
| 2 | carrots, diced | 2 | pinches salt and pepper |
| 2 | stalks celery, diced | | |

Preheat oven to 300 degrees F. Heat the oil and butter in a skillet. Next, flour lamb and season with salt and pepper. Brown in a pan and deglace with the red wine. Remove the lamb and reserve the sauce. Add carrots, celery, onion and garlic to a braising pan, place the lamb on top of the vegetables and add beef broth, orange juice and sauce from deglazing sauce. Bake in a 300 degree F oven for 3 hours or until meat pulls away from the bone.

Serves 6.

## FORMOSA*

### 2060 West Street
### Germantown, TN 38138

*Perennial winner of the Reader's Poll in* **Memphis Magazine** *for "Best Chinese Cuisine". In fact, Formosa has won this award every year since 1990! *Formosa has three locations in the Memphis-Germantown area.*

**Tony Leong, Chef/Manager**

## EGG DROP SOUP

| 8 | cups chicken broth (64 ounces) | 1 | teaspoon salt |
| | | ½ | teaspoon sugar |
| 2 | drops egg shade (yellow food coloring) | 1 | teaspoon MSG |
| | | 2 | whole eggs |

Beat the eggs and drizzle into above mixture of broth, coloring and seasonings. Bring the above mixture to a boil (do not overcook). After it boils, add cornstarch to thicken mixture. Boil again.

Serves 8.

## GARLIC EGGPLANT

| 1 | whole eggplant, skinless and ½-inch slices | 1 | teaspoon oyster sauce |
| | | 3 | teaspoons sugar |
| 2 | teaspoons vegetable oil | 1 | teaspoon white vinegar |
| 3 | cloves garlic, diced | 1 | teaspoon cooking wine |
| 1 | teaspoon soy sauce | ½ | cup water |

Sauté garlic and scallions in hot oil until the mixture becomes translucent. Add eggplant slices, ½ cup water, wine, oyster sauce, sugar, vinegar and soy sauce to mixture. Cook on low heat for 10 minutes and stir as needed.

Serves 2.

## MR. B'S

### 6655 Poplar Avenue
### Germantown, TN 38138

*Mr. B's began at Winchester and Perkins in 1975 as a hobby for Dick Baker, "Mr. B", upon his retirement as Vice-President of Dobbs House. Begun as a gathering place for all of his old airline pals, it soon became a crowd favorite, known for its Cajun fare, seafood and colossal steaks. Included free with dinner was a taste of "Mr. B's" sarcastic sense of humor (some say he was the original Archie Bunker). He once was overheard telling a customer complaining that she had been waiting for well over an hour, "THAT'S NO RECORD!' In 1995, Mr. B's was placed in the hands of his two sons and their wives and moved to its present location at Poplar and Kirby. The restaurants' success is owed to its two adored cooks, "Miss Ernestine" and "Miss Essie". They began with "Mr. B" at Dobbs House in 1947 and are still going strong!) Once again retired, "Mr. B", can be seen there faithfully every Wednesday at lunch, dining with his old Dobbs House pals.*

**Dick Baker, Founder**

## CRABMEAT IMPERIAL
*(Appetizer)*

| | | | |
|---|---|---|---|
| 2 | pounds fresh lump crabmeat | 1 | teaspoon white pepper |
| 4 | ribs of celery | 1⅓ | teaspoons salt |
| 2 | green bell peppers | | Accent for flavor |
| 1⅓ | yellow onions | 1⅓ | cups mayonnaise |
| 8 | hardboiled eggs | | Paprika |
| 1⅓ | tablespoons Tabasco sauce | | Lemon wedges |
| ½ | cup horseradish | | Your favorite hollandaise sauce |

Chop celery, green bell peppers, onions and eggs very fine. Fold in Tabasco, horseradish, pepper, salt and a dash of Accent for flavor. Next fold in mayonnaise and crabmeat. Spoon into individual shell baking dish and top with a dollop of your favorite hollandaise sauce and sprinkle with a dash of paprika. Run into microwave for 1½ to 2 minutes. Serve with lemon wedge on top.

Serves 12.

## CHOCOLATE ICE BOX PIE

| | | | |
|---|---|---|---|
| ¾ | cup sugar | 3 | egg yolks |
| 2 | tablespoons flour (slightly heaped) | 1½ | cups milk |
| 2 | tablespoons cocoa (very slightly heaped) | 3 | tablespoons butter Graham cracker crust Real whipped cream |
| | Shake of salt | | |

Warm milk. Mix sugar, cocoa, flour and salt. Add warmed milk. Cook this mixture just a few minutes. Take 4 tablespoons of this out and mix with the egg yolks that have been beaten. Put all ingredients in pan on medium heat and stir constantly till thick and coats wooden spoon. Remove from heat and beat with a wire whip. Pour into graham cracker crust and cover with real whipped cream. Garnish with shaved chocolate.

Serves 8.

# YIA YIA'S EUROCAFE

## 7615 West Farmington Germantown, TN 38138

### Jeffrey A. Winat, Executive Chef

*Jeff is a native of New Jersey and just recently moved to Memphis after living in Kansas City for 14 years. A graduate of the Culinary Institute of Washington, D.C., with over 15 years culinary experience in fine hotels and private country clubs. Jeff has been with Yia Yia's Eurocafe for the past 5 years. When he is not in the kitchen cooking, Jeff is a husband to Kathy and a father to his 2½ year old daughter, Katie.*

## YIA YIA'S SHRIMP LINGUINI

| | | | |
|---|---|---|---|
| 2 | pounds cooked linguini noodles | 2 | cups julienne fresh spinach |
| 24 | pieces 16/20 ct. peeled, deveined black tiger shrimp | 2 | cups oven dried tomatoes |
| 1 | cup brown butter (recipe below) | 1½ | cups roasted garlic cloves |
| 1 | quart sweet vermouth chicken stock (recipe below) | 1 | cup whole unsalted butter |
| | | ¾ | cup chopped sage Salt and pepper to taste |

### BROWN BUTTER

Simmer 2 pounds of unsalted butter over medium heat until the milk solids have separated and caramelized on the bottom of the pan and the butterfat has a rich golden brown color and a sweet, nutty aroma. Strain through a fine sieve or cheesecloth.

### SWEET VERMOUTH CHICKEN STOCK

| | | | |
|---|---|---|---|
| 1 | gallon chicken stock | 1 | quart sweet Vermouth |

Combine both items in a large stockpot over high heat. Reduce to 1 quart.

Heat a large sauté pan over medium-high flame. Add brown butter, shrimp and garlic cloves. Toss

together and sauté for 1 minute. Add vermouth stock and reduce by ½. Add spinach and dried tomatoes and cook until both are slightly wilted. Reduce heat, add whole butter and sage. Season to taste with salt and pepper. Pour evenly over hot pasta noodles.

Serves 4.

*Note: Extra dried tomatoes are excellent for a salad topping.*

## YIA YIA'S SPINACH SALAD

| | | | |
|---|---|---|---|
| 8 | cups stemmed and washed spinach | ½ | cup blue cheese, crumbled |
| ¾ | to 1 cup roasted pear vinaigrette (recipe below) | 1 | fresh pear (sliced thinly) Salt and pepper to taste |
| 1 | cup spiced walnuts (recipe below) | | |

In a large mixing bowl, toss spinach with vinaigrette, coating leaves evenly. Season to taste with salt and pepper, tossing again. Arrange dressed spinach on 4 plates. Sprinkle with walnuts, cheese, and garnish with spiced pears.

Serves 4.

### ROASTED PEAR VINAIGRETTE

| | | | |
|---|---|---|---|
| 2 | fresh pears, stemmed and cored | 1 | teaspoon minced garlic |
| ½ | cup red wine vinegar | 1 | cup walnut oil |
| ½ | cup sugar | ½ | cup vegetable oil |

Brush pears with a little of the walnut oil and roast in oven until very tender. Purée roasted pears in blender. Combine all ingredients and refrigerate before using.

### SPICED WALNUTS

| | | | |
|---|---|---|---|
| 1 | cup walnut halves | 2 | teaspoons sugar |
| 1 | tablespoon olive oil | 1 | teaspoon kosher salt |
| 1 | teaspoon chili powder | | |

Toss all ingredients together and spread onto a sheet pan. Toast in a 350 degree F oven for 10 to 12 minutes until evenly browned. Allow to cool completely.

## YIA YIA'S EUROCAFE

**Jessica Cosner-Lowe**
**Executive Pastry Chef**

*Jessica has just recently joined the Yia Yia's Eurocafe organization. Until recently, Jessica was the pastry chef for the Charleston Grill in Charleston, South Carolina. The Charleston Grill is the only restaurant in the state of South Carolina to earn the coveted Mobil Four Stars designation. Jessica is a native of Florida and a graduate of the Johnson & Wales Culinary School in Charleston, S.C.*

## LUSCIOUS BROWNIES

| | | | |
|---|---|---|---|
| 3 | sticks soft butter | 2 | teaspoons salt |
| 6 | cups granulated sugar | 1¼ | cups cocoa powder |
| 5 | whole eggs | 1½ | cups all-purpose flour |
| 2 | tablespoons vanilla extract | 2 | cups walnuts (if desired) |

Cream butter and sugar. Add eggs, vanilla and salt. Sift cocoa powder and flour and add to butter mixture. Line a 9x9-inch pan with parchment paper and spray. Spread mixture into pan and bake until a toothpick comes out clean (350 degrees F for 25 to 35 minutes). You want these to be gooey.

Servings: 1 pan

## CHOCOLATE GANACHE TO ICE BROWNIES

| | | | |
|---|---|---|---|
| 2 | pounds semisweet chocolate (good quality, such as giradelli, callebaut, etc.) | 1 | pint heavy cream |
| | | 1 | cup light corn syrup |

In a saucepan, heat cream to boil. Place chocolate in a large bowl. When cream reaches a boil, pour over chocolate. Shake bowl to cover all chocolate with cream. Let stand for 1 minute. Then whisk until smooth and velvety. This takes a good 3 to 5 minutes. Whisk in corn syrup. Let stand for 3 hours at room temperature. Ice brownies, refrigerate. When ganache is hard, cut brownies to desired size.

## WHITE CHOCOLATE PEAR BREAD PUDDING

| | | | |
|---|---|---|---|
| 8 | large chopped croissants | 2 | cups granulated sugar |
| 1 | cup white chocolate | 1 | quart heavy cream |
| 1 | cup heavy cream | 1 | pint whole milk |
| 10 | egg yolks | 2 | pears (peeled, cored and chopped fine) |
| 1 | vanilla bean, scraped | | |

In a medium saucepan, heat 1 cup of cream. Bring to a boil and pour over white chocolate. In a bowl whisk until smooth. In a large bowl combine yolks, sugar and the vanilla bean. Add remaining cream and milk to white chocolate mixture — whisking constantly to combine. Add a small amount of milk to egg to thin out by whisking, then add all and pour over chopped croissants. Mix in pears and bake in ovenproof bowls with desired amounts at 350 degrees for 25 to 35 minutes.

Serves 8.

## CASHEW PRALINES

| | | | |
|---|---|---|---|
| 2 | cups granulated sugar | 1 | stick butter (cut into small pieces) |
| 1 | cup heavy cream | 16 | ounces salted cashews |
| 1 | shot Frangelico | | |
| 2 | cups firmly packed brown sugar | | |

In a medium sized, heavy bottomed saucepan, combine all ingredients except cashews. Mix with wooden spoon to combine, then heat on medium high heat to the soft ball stage about 240 degrees. (Use a candy thermometer.) Remove from heat and stir in cashews. Scoop out with a mini scoop or tablespoon and drop onto parchment paper. Let sit for at least 30 minutes to set. Store in an airtight container.

## THREE OAKS GRILL

### 2285 Germantown Road S. Germantown, TN 38138

*"Best Kept Secret"* – *'98* **Memphis Magazine** *poll. "Best Restaurant in Germantown"* – **Memphis Flyer** *Poll. Three Oaks offers very tender filet mignon, rack of lamb, famous ginger-roasted salmon plus daily specials. Restaurant is located just across from the old train depot in historic Germantown. "Service efficient, friendly and polite,"* **Memphis Business Journal.**

## PAN-ROASTED SALMON WITH GINGER CRUST

| | | | |
|---|---|---|---|
| 1 | (8 ounce) salmon fillet, skinless | 1 | ounce olive oil |
| ¼ | teaspoon kosher salt | ¼ | cup ginger bread crumb mixture |
| ⅛ | teaspoon black pepper, regular grind | | |

Season both sides of salmon fillet with kosher salt and black pepper. Place skillet over high heat. After skillet is very hot, add the olive oil. Heat oil until almost smoking. Place salmon fillet in skillet top side down. Sear the fillet until golden brown, approximately 1 minute; turn fillet and sear the other side. Remove from heat. Lightly press ginger bread crumb mixture on to the salmon fillet until the top is completely covered. Place skillet in 350 degree oven until cooked medium, unless another temperature is specified. Line round dinner plate with 2 ounces of soy beurre blanc sauce; place salmon fillet in center of plate, crusted side up. Garnish with black sesame seeds sprinkled over the sauce and a sprig of fresh cilantro on the fillet.

Serves 1.

## GINGER CRUST FOR SALMON

| | | | |
|---|---|---|---|
| 2 | cups bread crumbs, dry | 2 | tablespoons fresh cilantro, chopped fine |
| ¼ | cup fresh ginger, chopped fine | ¼ | cup soft butter |

Mix bread crumbs, ginger and cilantro well. Add soft butter and knead well until crust holds it's shape when squeezed together. Keep at cool room temperature. Do not refrigerate. Make fresh daily.

Yield: 3 cups

## SOY CREAM SAUCE FOR SALMON

| | | | |
|---|---|---|---|
| ½ | cup soy sauce | ¼ | cup white wine (dry) |
| 1 | tablespoon fresh ginger, chopped fine | 1 | quart heavy cream |
| | | 1 | tablespoon soft, unsalted butter |

Melt 1 tablespoon butter in heavy 1-quart saucepan. Add ginger and cook 10 seconds. Add white wine and simmer until wine is nearly evaporated. Add cream. Reduce cream until thick. Add soy sauce; mix well. Label container with name of product and date. Refrigerate.

Yield: 1 quart

## THE BAILEY HOUSE

*8755 Monte Carlo Cove*
*Germantown, TN 38139*

**Ann Freeman Bailey, Executive Chef**
**John M. Bailey, Sous Chef & Author**

## ROTISSERIE 1000 ISLAND DRESSING

| | | | |
|---|---|---|---|
| 4 | cloves grated garlic | 1 | teaspoon black |
| 1 | cup mayonnaise | | pepper |
| ½ | cup chili sauce or | 1 | teaspoon paprika |
| | ketchup | ¼ | small onion, grated |
| 1 | teaspoon mustard | | Juice of 1 lemon |
| ½ | cup vegetable oil | 1 | tablespoon water |
| 1 | teaspoon | | Dash of Tabasco |
| | Worcestershire | | sauce |
| | sauce | | Salt to taste |

Combine all of the above ingredients and mix in a blender.

Yield: 1½ pints

## COCONUT POUND CAKE

| | | | |
|---|---|---|---|
| 3 | sticks softened | ¼ | teaspoon salt |
| | butter | 1 | cup sour cream |
| 3 | cups sugar | 1 | teaspoon vanilla |
| 6 | eggs | 1 | (6 ounce) package |
| 3 | cups all-purpose | | frozen coconut, |
| | flour | | thawed |
| ¼ | teaspoon baking | | |
| | soda | | |

Prepare a tube pan by rubbing with vegetable shortening. Add flour and shake to cover. Place 3 sticks of butter in bowl and cream. Add sugar slowly as you mix. Add eggs, one at a time, and beat. Sift flour with soda and salt. Alternate adding flour mixture and sour cream in thirds until well mixed. Add vanilla. Fold in coconut. Pour into prepared pan and bake at 350 degrees for approximately 1 hour, 15 minutes to 1 hour, 30 minutes.

Yield: 1 cake

## POTATO CASSEROLE

| | | | |
|---|---|---|---|
| 6 | or 8 large potatoes | | Salt to taste |
| 2 | cups sour cream | ¼ | cup whole milk |
| 2 | cups grated Kraft | 1 | stick butter |
| | Old English cheese | | |
| 1 | bunch chopped | | |
| | green onions (tops | | |
| | and bottoms) | | |

Boil potatoes in jackets in salted water and chill. Peel when cold and grate potatoes. Melt 1 stick of butter and cheese in skillet with a little milk. Add onions and sour cream. Mix in potatoes. Put in large buttered casserole dish. If possible, chill several hours or overnight. Bake about 45 minutes or until hot at 350 degrees.

Serves 6.

## ITALIAN SPINACH

| | | | |
|---|---|---|---|
| 3 | boxes frozen leaf | ¼ | cup olive oil |
| | spinach | | Salt to taste |
| 3 | eggs | | Parmesan cheese |
| | Fresh garlic | | Mozzarella cheese |
| | (2 or 3 cloves) | | (2 slices or to taste) |

Cook spinach (salt to taste) and drain very well (press the water out with a paper towel). Heat ¼ cup olive oil in skillet with garlic (don't burn the garlic). Add spinach and three beaten eggs to oil. Stir until the eggs are cooked (over low heat). Add Parmesan and mozzarella cheese to spinach. Stir until cheese melts. Ready to serve. Great as side dish with pasta or steak.

Serves 4.

## GRAM'S PECAN PIE

| | | | |
|---|---|---|---|
| 2 | eggs, beaten | 2 | tablespoons flour |
| ½ | cup sugar | 1 | teaspoon vanilla |
| 1 | cup white Karo | 1 | cup chopped |
| | syrup | | pecans |
| ¾ | cup melted butter | 1 | unbaked piecrust |

Beat eggs, add sugar and mix in the other ingredients. Pour into unbaked piecrust. Bake at 350 degrees for approximately 1 hour or until a knife comes out clean.

# AUBERGINE

## 5007 Black Road
## Memphis, TN 38117

**Brice Graziano, Owner**
**Jean Christophe Blanc, Chef**

*Chef Jean Christophe Blanc studied with Paul Bocuse and was sous chef de cuisine at the Restaurant Les Pres d'Eugenie owned by famous French chef Michel Guerard.*

*This unique restaurant offers contemporary French cuisine in an elegant atmosphere. French Chef Jean Christophe Blanc incorporates the finest local produce and organic meats as well as other selected ingredients to create innovative dishes that have garnered national praise. The impeccable wine list complements the menu beautifully. It has been rated as one of the top French/Continental restaurants in the city by the* **Memphis Magazine's** *Readers Choice poll.*

## PORTABELLO ROTI EN SALADE

| | | | |
|---|---|---|---|
| 4 | large portabello mushrooms | 2 | teaspoons of herb mix (chives and parsley) |
| 2 | shallots, peeled and diced | 12 | green onions |
| 2 | tomatoes, peeled and diced | 12 | thinly sliced pieces of prosciutto ham |

### PARMESAN DRESSING

| | | | |
|---|---|---|---|
| 1 | soup spoon of Dijon mustard | 1 | clove of garlic, peeled and chopped |
| 3 | soup spoons of sherry vinegar | | Juice of 1 lemon |
| 8 | ounces extra virgin olive oil | | Salt and pepper to taste |
| 100 | grams Parmesan | | |

### PARMESAN TUILE

| | | | |
|---|---|---|---|
| 200 | grams Parmesan (approx. 7 ounces) | 20 | grams flour (⅔ ounce) |

**Preparation of portabello:** Remove caps from mushroom and cut into ½-inch slices. Cut the stems into a small dice. In a sauté pan with olive oil, sauté the caps, seasoning with salt and pepper, until a nice golden color and strain on a paper towel. In the same pan, cook the diced stems until crispy and golden, seasoning as well with some salt and pepper, and strain. When finished clean sauté pan and add some more olive oil. When hot, add green onions and prosciutto, cooking until a nice crispy brown color. Remove from heat.

**Preparation of dressing:** In a mixer, add mustard, sherry vinegar, lemon juice, garlic, Parmesan, salt and pepper. With the machine on a medium speed, slowly add in the olive oil. Emulsify. Taste and check for correct seasoning.

**Preparation of Parmesan tuile:** In a small bowl, mix flour and Parmesan. Using a strainer, pass the mixer through into a non-greased sauté pan on medium heat. When coloration begins, flip the tuile and finish to color on the opposite side. Remove from pan.

**Preparation of the plate:** In a small bowl, mix diced shallots, diced tomatoes, portabello stems and herbs with some of the Parmesan dressing until nicely coated. Spoon half of the mix into the center of the plate. Arrange the cooked slices of portabello caps on top of the mixture to create the original shape of the portabello. Spoon the remaining mixture in the bowl around and on top of the portabello. Place 3 green onions and 3 pieces of prosciutto irregularly around the plate. Breaking the tuile into large pieces, arrange 3 pieces on the plate. Garnish with chopped parsley or chives.

Serves 4.

## TURBOT ROTI AU LA RAGOUT DES LEGUMES SAFRANE & SAUCE MARINERE

| | | | |
|---|---|---|---|
| 4 | pieces of turbot on the bone about 250 grams each (9 oz. each) | 4 | thick slices of pancetta (Italian bacon) |

### FOR STEW VEGETABLES

| | | | |
|---|---|---|---|
| 3 | large potatoes, peeled | 200 | grams (7 ounces) black olives |
| 1 | onion | 5 | grams curry paste (1 oz. = 30 grams) |
| 5 | carrots | | |
| 2 | branches of celery, peeled | 10 | grams cumin |
| 200 | grams (7 ounces) shiitake mushrooms | 5 | grams saffron |
| | | 10 | grams sugar |
| | | 250 | grams white wine |
| 2 | green bell peppers | 50 | grams olive oil |
| 3 | red bell peppers | | Salt and pepper to taste |

**Preparation of turbot:** Remove dark skin. Season fish with salt and pepper. In a skillet on medium-high, heat ½ olive oil and ½ butter. Add pancetta to skillet. Place turbot skinless side down and cook until a golden brown color. After coloration, turn the turbot and pancetta and place in a 350 degree oven for about 7 minutes. When cooked remove the white skin and the bone from the turbot.

**Preparation of stew vegetables:** Cut vegetables into a medium sized irregular cut. In a large pot, add olive oil and put on medium-high heat. When hot, add onions, celery and carrots. Sweat. After, add mushrooms and bell peppers. Finish to sweat the vegetables and then add potatoes and white wine. Reduce some and cover vegetables with water and boil. Boil 8-10 minutes or until potatoes are cooked. Check seasoning when cooked.

**Preparation of sauce marinere:** In a saucepan, reduce mussel jus and diced shallots until there is no liquid. When reduced, add crème and bring to a small boil. When boiling, while whisking constantly, add small pieces of butter slowly until emulsification is complete. Remove from heat and season with salt, pepper and lemon juice. Taste.

**Preparation of the plate:** In a serving bowl add the stewed vegetables and some of the juice. Spread the 2 pieces of the turbot out on the top. Place the piece of pancetta on the top of the turbot. Spoon the sauce around the edge of the inside of the bowl covering generously the vegetables. Garnish with chives, fresh parsley and a few pieces of rock salt on the turbot.

Serves 4.

## SALADE DE FRUITS ET SON SABAYON AU CHAMPAGNE

| | | | |
|---|---|---|---|
| 3⅓ | ounces champagne | 4 | yolks |
| 3 | ounces sugar | | |

### FRESH FRUIT SALAD

| | |
|---|---|
| Apple | Pineapple |
| Banana | Strawberry |
| Mango | Mint (julienne) |
| Orange | Grand Marnier |
| Pear | Sugar |

Cut fruit and marinate in a bowl with some sugar, Grand Marnier and the mint for 30 minutes to 1 hour. In a medium pot, add champagne, sugar and yolks. Put over medium heat and whisk constantly while cooking in a figure eight motion. Sabayon should rise and be a mousse-like consistency. To check if finished to cook, the mix should be thick, mousse-like and should stick to the whisk when lifted from the mixture.

**To serve:** In a serving bowl, add the fruit salad and some of the marinating juices. Top the fruit evenly with the sabayon. With a pastry blowtorch in a salamander oven, brown the top until a nice golden color. Garnish with mint. (To complement the dessert you can serve with a quenelle of vanilla ice cream on the top of the sabayon.)

Serves 2.

## BRONTE RESTAURANT

*Davis-Kidd Booksellers*
*387 Perkins Road Ext.*
*Memphis, TN 38117*

**Shelley Hodges, General Manager**
**Cliff Milam, Executive Chef**

## DOUBLE SALMON PASTA

| | | | |
|---|---|---|---|
| 1 | cup heavy cream | | Salt and pepper to |
| 1 | cup butter | | taste |
| 1 | teaspoon tarragon | 2 | tablespoons flour |
| | leaves | 2 | pounds linguini |
| ½ | pound bleu cheese | 2 | (8 ounce) salmon |
| | crumbles | | fillets |
| ¼ | cup white wine | 4 | ounces smoked |
| 2 | tablespoons honey | | salmon |

Cook linguini al dente according to package instructions. Set aside. Marinate salmon fillets in equal parts olive oil, soy sauce, salt and pepper for 15 minutes. Grill or broil until medium rare to medium. Make 4 equal portions with smoked salmon. Melt butter in pot. Add cream and tarragon until boiling. Whisk in bleu cheese, white wine and honey. Incorporate until smooth. Add flour, salt and pepper. To serve, add sauce, salmon and linguini. Add a splash of white wine if needed to thin.

Serves 4.

## TOMATO BLEU CHEESE SOUP

| | | | |
|---|---|---|---|
| ¼ | ounce butter | ½ | pound bleu cheese |
| 1 | yellow onion | 1 | to 2 tablespoons |
| 1 | tablespoon minced | | salt |
| | garlic | 1 | teaspoon white |
| 1 | cup flour | | pepper |
| 1½ | quarts water | 1 | cup heavy cream |
| 2 | (32 ounce) cans | | |
| | diced tomatoes | | |

Melt butter, dice onions and sauté until translucent along with garlic. Add flour to make roux. (be careful not to burn). Whisk water into roux until smooth. Add diced tomatoes, bleu cheese, salt and pepper. Bring to boil and turn off heat. Add cream. Purée with hand blender or food processor.

Serves 6 to 8.

## SPINACH-ROSEMARY QUICHE

| | | | |
|---|---|---|---|
| 8 | eggs | 2 | cups cheddar |
| 2 | cups heavy | | cheese |
| | whipping cream | 1 | cup Swiss cheese |
| 4 | tablespoons | 1 | cup Parmesan |
| | rosemary | | cheese |
| 2 | (8 ounce) packages | 2 | (9 inch) pie crusts |
| | chopped spinach | | |

Pre-bake pie crust while poking holes with fork on bottom of crust. Cook rosemary in 1 cup of water. Drain and chop. Thaw spinach and squeeze out excess water. Whisk eggs in a bowl and then combine remaining ingredients unto thoroughly incorporated. Ladle into pie crust and bake at 295 degrees for 35 to 40 minutes or until it is set.

Makes 2 pies (quarter cuts per pie) = 8 total servings.

# BUCKLEY'S FINE FILET GRILL

### East Location
### 5355 Poplar Avenue
### Memphis, TN 38119

### Downtown Location
### 117 Union Avenue
### Memphis, TN 38103

*Buckley's Fine Filet Grill owners, Kenneth Dick and Jeff Fioranelli ,began their foray into the restaurant world at the ripe old age of twenty-four. Six years later, their two locations in Memphis boast fine dining at a value price. Consistently winning "best meal for the money" in **Memphis Magazine** Readers' Poll 1997 & 1998. Ken and Jeff went on to win in the "best steak category" of the **Memphis Magazine** Readers' Poll in 1999 and again in 2000. They, along with Chef Yorbi Caoba are proud and pleased to share a small sampling of their cuisine with all Tennessee — and with the rest of the world!*

## CAJUN SALMON PASTA

| | | | |
|---|---|---|---|
| 16 | ounces heavy whipping cream | ½ | cup shredded Parmesan cheese |
| 1 | tablespoon chopped basil | ¼ | stick butter |
| 4 | tablespoons chopped parsley | ½ | cup Cajun spice* Salt to taste |
| 2 | tablespoons minced garlic | ½ | teaspoon white pepper to taste |
| 1 | tablespoon lemon juice | 2 | pounds linguini pasta |
| ⅓ | cup grated Parmesan-Romano blended cheese | 4 | (6 ounce) portions skinless salmon |

**Cream Sauce:** Sauté minced garlic with butter until garlic is light brown. Add heavy cream, basil, lemon juice, grated cheese blend and white pepper. Bring to a boil on medium-high heat, stirring often. Place on low heat after boiling and salt to taste.

**Cajun Salmon:** Preheat oven to 375 degrees. Lightly coat salmon filets with Cajun spice.

*Remember, the amount of spice will determine the degree of spice and heat. Bake salmon at 375 degrees for 8 to 15 minutes depending on desired doneness.

**Presentation:** Toss cooked pasta with the cream sauce. Portion 8 ounces of pasta per serving. Place the cooked salmon filets atop the portions. Garnish with parsley and shredded Parmesan cheese. A slice of garlic toast and a lemon wedge will further complement this dish.

Serves 4.

## ARTICHOKE DIP

| | | | |
|---|---|---|---|
| 3 | (14 ounce) cans artichoke hearts | 1 | tablespoon minced garlic |
| 1½ | cup ranch dressing | 1 | tablespoon paprika |
| 1½ | cups Italian bread crumbs | 1 | (24 inch) loaf French baguette |
| 1¼ | cups grated Parmesan-Romano cheese blend | | Salt and pepper to taste |
| | | ½ | stick butter – optional |

**Toast Chips:** Slice baguette into ¼-inch slices. Butter the tops if desired. Place on a cookie sheet and toast in oven at 350 degrees for 10 to 15 minutes—or until desired crunchiness.

**Artichoke Dip:** Strain artichoke hearts and place in a mixing bowl. Break up the hearts with hands or spoon. Add ranch dressing, bread crumbs, grated cheeses, and minced garlic. Mix well. Salt and pepper to taste. Place dip in a shallow baking dish. Sprinkle paprika on top. Bake 15 to 20 minutes. Top should brown nicely. Remove and let cool 5 minutes before serving.

## LEMON SPINACH

| | |
|---|---|
| 2 | shallots, finely chopped |
| 2 | garlic cloves, finely chopped |
| 2 | lemons (roll along counter and cut in half for easy juicing) |
| 1½ | pounds fresh spinach, cleaned and de-veined if necessary |
| 1 | tablespoon olive oil |

Begin only after every other part of meal is prepared. This takes only 3 minutes to sauté and serve. Heat skillet. Heat oil. Sauté shallots until translucent. Add garlic and spinach. Squeeze lemon juice on top. Season with salt and pepper. Turn over spinach in sauté pan. Voila! Serve.

Serves 4.

## MUSHROOM GORGONZOLA BEEF TENDERLOIN ROULADE

| | | | |
|---|---|---|---|
| 1½ | pounds beef tenderloin, trimmed and cleaned | 2 | sprigs fresh thyme |
| 1 | pound portabello mushrooms, rough chop | 4 | ounces gorgonzola cheese (or any blue veined cheese), crumbled |
| 3 | shallots, cleaned and finely chopped | ¼ | cup Jack Daniel's whiskey |
| 2 | garlic cloves, minced | | Salt and black pepper to taste |
| | | ¼ | cup olive oil |

### KITCHEN TOOLS

| | |
|---|---|
| Twine | Skillet |
| Meat mallet or tenderizer | |

Preheat oven to 375 degrees F. Butterfly tenderloin lengthwise. Best method is to cut lengthwise making ½-inch cut. Roll body of tenderloin out. Continue with next cut maintaining ½-inch width until beef is flat. Tenderize with mallet for even width. This method cuts down amount of mallet tenderizing needed. Heat skillet on medium-high. Heat 1 tablespoon of oil in skillet. Sauté shallots until translucent. Add garlic and fresh thyme and sauté one minute. Add chopped portabellos and sauté until almost cooked (approximately 10 minutes). Season with salt and pepper. Deglaze with ¼-cup of Jack Daniel's whiskey. Continue to sauté until liquor evaporates. Take off heat.

Mix crumbled blue cheese with mushrooms. Season inside of meat with salt and pepper. Place cheese mushroom mixture on ¾ of meat leaving the last ¼ furthest from you empty of the mixture. Tightly roll the tenderloin, beginning with the mushroom covered portion, until the roulade is complete. Tie with twine to ensure that it stays together. Season the outside with salt, pepper and olive oil. Place on grill or in sauté pan on high heat until all sides are golden brown. Finish in 375 degree F oven for 10 minutes or until desired temperature is reached. Best served medium rare. Let rest on counter a few minutes. Cut into 4 equal portions and serve with cut side up. Any remaining mushroom mixture may be used to garnish the serving plate.

Serves 4.

## GARLIC SHALLOT MASHED POTATOES

| | | | |
|---|---|---|---|
| 4 | potatoes, peeled and cubed | 2 | shallots, thinly sliced |
| 4 | tablespoons unsalted butter, cubed and room temperature | 4 | cloves of garlic, minced |
| 4 | tablespoons crème fraiche (heavy cream) | 1 | sprig fresh thyme Salt and black pepper to taste |

In pot with salted water, bring potatoes to a boil until fork tender. Heat skillet. Sauté shallot rings, garlic and thyme until tender. Deglaze with a splash of white wine if browning too quickly. Warm the crème fraiche. Place cooked and drained potatoes in ricer with butter. Fold in crème fraiche, shallot and garlic mixture (with thyme sprig removed). Season to taste.

Serves 4.

## RASPBERRY CLAFOUTI (PUDDING)

| | | | |
|---|---|---|---|
| 1 | tablespoon unsalted butter | 6 | tablespoons flour |
| ½ | cup plus 1 tablespoon sugar | 1½ | cups heavy cream |
| 3 | cups raspberries | 1 | pinch white pepper |
| 3 | large eggs | 1 | tablespoon brandy, preferably fruit brandy |
| 2 | teaspoons vanilla extract | 4 | scoops vanilla bean ice cream |

Preheat oven to 375 degrees F. Grease 10" baking dish with butter. Sprinkle with 1 tablespoon sugar. Arrange raspberries in pan. Beat eggs until fluffy. Add vanilla, sugar, flour, cream, white pepper and brandy. Whisk together. Let rest. Pour over fruit and bake for 40 minutes until firm. Serve with vanilla bean ice cream.

Serves 8.

## CRAB CAKES

| | | | |
|---|---|---|---|
| 3 | pounds jumbo lump crab meat | 1 | teaspoon Tabasco sauce |
| 2 | loaves sliced white bread (crust removed and diced) | 2 | tablespoons season salt |
| 2 | tablespoons Cajun seasoning | 1 | tablespoon lemon pepper seasoning |
| 3 | tablespoons fresh chopped chives | 1½ | cups mayonnaise (premium brand or homemade) |
| 3 | tablespoons parsley (minced) | 2 | cups whipping cream |
| 3 | tablespoons Dijon mustard | 1 | teaspoon whole leaf thyme |
| 2 | dashes Worcestershire sauce | 4 | eggs |
| | | 1 | teaspoon baking powder Plain bread crumbs (as needed to coat) |

Pick through crab meat to remove any shells. Place all ingredients in a large mixing bowl and mix well with hands. Be careful not to break up crab meat too much. Use an ice cream scoop mixture and roll in bread crumbs and pat out. Place cakes on a lined pan until ready to cook, keep refrigerated. Sauté cakes in a little melted butter until browned. Place in a preheated 425-degree oven for 8 to 10 minutes. Cakes will rise and crack on top when done. (They freeze extremely well.)

Yield: 30 2½-ounce cakes

## ERLING JENSEN'S, THE RESTAURANT

### 1044 South Yates
### Memphis, TN 38119

*This upscale restaurant features the freshest, most seasonal ingredients to produce a meal of the highest quality and caliber. Erling Jensen was voted "Best Memphis Chef" in 1999 and 2000 by the Readers Poll,* **Memphis Magazine.** *"Erling Jensen's, The Restaurant" was voted "Best Restaurant" by the Readers Poll,* **Memphis Magazine** *in 1999 and 2000!*

**Erling Jensen, Chef/Owner**

## BRAZILNUT ENCRUSTED RABBIT LOIN

### FOR THE RABBIT

| | | | |
|---|---|---|---|
| 4 | (4 ounce) pieces rabbit loin, boneless Salt, pepper, garlic and thyme to taste | ⅓ | cup chopped brazilnuts, scented with vanilla beans |

### FOR THE SAUCE

| | | |
|---|---|---|
| ½ | cup port wine | Rabbit Demi Glace: |
| ⅓ | cup golden raisins | Rabbit bones (roasted), |
| | Cinnamon to taste | tomato paste, celery, |
| 1 | tablespoon sugar | carrots, onions, parsley, |
| | Cream as necessary | garlic, peppercorns, bay leaves and dry thyme, water |

### FOR THE POTATOES

| | | | |
|---|---|---|---|
| 1 | pound sweet potatoes | 2 | tablespoons honey Salt and pepper to taste |
| ¼ | cup chopped brazilnuts, scented with vanilla beans | | |

### FOR THE GARNISH

**Fried Sweet Potato Hay**

**To make the sauce:** Roast rabbit bones and make 1 quart of rabbit stock. Strain and reduce to nappe. Rehydrate golden raisins in port wine. Add cinnamon and sugar and 8 ounces rabbit demi, add cream to desired consistency. For the potatoes, peel and cube sweet potatoes, boil in water until tender. Strain and in food processor, purée potatoes. Place in bowl and add honey and nuts, season to taste. For the rabbit, roll loins into round pieces and sear off in butter, remove from heat. Egg wash loins and roll in chopped brazilnuts. Toast of under broiler. To assemble, pipe sweet potatoes onto center of plate, slice loin into medallions and fan around potatoes, ladle sauce around meat. Finish with fried sweet potato hay.

Serves 4.

## BEET-HORSERADISH ENCRUSTED SALMON

### FOR THE SALMON

| | | | |
|---|---|---|---|
| 4 | (4 ounce) salmon fillets Salt and pepper to taste | | Garlic and chopped thyme to taste |

### FOR CRUST

| | | | |
|---|---|---|---|
| 1 | cup bread crumbs | ¼ | cup puréed beets |
| ⅓ | cup horseradish | | |

### FOR THE SAUCE

| | | | |
|---|---|---|---|
| 1 | ounce shallots, chopped | ¼ | pound butter Salt and pepper to taste |
| ½ | cup red wine | | |
| ½ | cup beet purée | | |

### FOR THE GARNISH

| | |
|---|---|
| Beet curls, done on mandoline | Yellow pepper, julienne |

**For the salmon:** Season fillet with salt, pepper, thyme and garlic to taste. Shallow poach fish to desired doneness in white wine.

**For the sauce:** Place chopped shallots in red wine and reduce by ½. Add beet purée and continue cooking. Add a little butter to enrich sauce.

**For the crust:** Peel beets and place in water with red vinegar and salt and pepper. Cook until tender. Remove from heat and purée using small amount of the cooking liquid. Combine horseradish and bread crumbs until moistened. Add beet purée to achieve desired color.

**To serve:** Place horseradish crust on top of salmon fillet and place under salamander to warm. Place fillet on plate and ladle sauce around. Garnish with beet curls and yellow pepper.

Serves 4.

## LOBSTER CROQUETTES

### FOR THE SAUCE

| | | | |
|---|---|---|---|
| 1 | quart lobster stock: Lobster bodies, carrots, celery, onion, garlic, tomato paste, parsley, black peppercorns, bay leaves, dry thyme, water | 1 | cup heavy cream |
| | | ¼ | pound butter Lemon grass Salt and pepper to taste |

### FOR THE CROQUETTES

| | | | |
|---|---|---|---|
| 2 | ounces butter | 10 | ounces of lobster meat, diced |
| 8 | ounces flour | | Flour, eggwash and shredded filo dough and bread crumbs for breading |
| 1 | cup heavy cream | | |
| 1 | tablespoon brandy Salt, pepper and nutmeg to taste | | |
| ⅓ | cup scallions, sliced | | |

### FOR MUSHROOMS

| | | | |
|---|---|---|---|
| 4 | ounces Enoki mushrooms | | Salt, pepper and garlic to taste |
| 4 | ounces Chanterelle mushrooms | | Olive oil |
| 2 | ounces carrots, julienne | | |

### FOR THE GARNISH

**Italian parsley, fried**

**To assemble croquettes:** In saucepan, melt butter and combine with flour to create a pale roux. Incorporate cream to make a béchamel; season with salt, pepper and nutmeg. Stir in lobster meat and scallions, finish with brandy. Let mixture cool to room temperature, roll into cylinder shapes using parchment paper. Once firm, cut cylinder into 2-inch long pieces. Bread croquettes using flour, then eggwash, and finishing with filo dough and bread crumbs.

**For sauce:** Make a lobster stock, using lobster bodies, mirepoix and tomato paste. Let simmer for 2 hours and strain, reserving liquid. Combine liquid with chopped with lemon grass, reduce liquid until nappe, add cream and monte au beurre. For mushroom salad, sauté julienne carrots and sliced chanterelle mushrooms, season with garlic, salt and pepper. Combine chanterelles and carrots with enokis. To serve, place breaded croquettes in 350 degree fryer and cook until golden brown. Place mushroom salad in center of plate, ladle sauce around and stand two lobster croquettes leaning on mushroom salad. Finish with fried Italian parsley on top of croquettes. Serves 4.

## POTATO WRAPPED SWEETBREADS

### FOR THE SWEETBREADS

| | | | |
|---|---|---|---|
| 4 | (2 ounce) pieces of sweetbreads | 4 | bay leaves |
| 1 | onion | 1 | quart water |
| ½ | cup red wine vinegar | | Flour to dredge |
| 1 | bunch parsley | | Olive oil |
| 1 | teaspoon black peppercorns | | Salt and pepper to taste |

### FOR THE SPINACH

| | | |
|---|---|---|
| ½ | pound baby spinach Olive oil | Salt, pepper and garlic to taste Dash white truffle oil |

### FOR THE POTATO

| | | |
|---|---|---|
| 1 | large russet potato, peeled | Eggwash |

### FOR THE GARNISH

| | | |
|---|---|---|
| 4 | bunches lolla rossa greens | Raspberry purée Julienne red and green peppers |
| 8 | slices fresh black truffle | |

**For the sweetbreads:** Rinse sweetbreads in cool water. Place in saucepan with water and vinegar, diced onion, peppercorns and bay leaves. Bring to a boil and remove from heat, let cool to room temperature. Remove from cooking liquid and dry. Dredge in seasoned flour and panfry to golden brown in small amount of olive.

**For the spinach:** Heat sauté pan with olive oil; add spinach and wilt. Season with salt, pepper and garlic, finish with white truffle oil, reserve. On mandoline, slice potatoes paper thin, you will need four slices for each portion.

**To assemble:** Overlap 3 slices of potato and brush with eggwash. Place 1 tablespoon of wilted spinach on top of potatoes, followed by the sweetbread. Pull up the 2 ends of the potato and secure with toothpick and proceed to bring up sides of potato to completely enclose sweetbread. In 350 degree fryer, cook until potatoes are golden brown, remove and reserve.

**To assemble:** Place bunch of lolla rossa greens and place fresh truffles on top of greens. Cut sweetbread on a bias to achieve two pieces. Place in center of plate. Garnish plate with dots of raspberry purée and julienne red and green peppers.
Serves 4.

# FOLK'S FOLLY PRIME STEAK HOUSE

## 551 S. Mendenhall Road Memphis, TN 38117

### Humphrey Folk, Jr., Founder

*Folk's Folly Prime Steak House is a Memphis tradition for the finest prime steaks and fresh seafood. Consistently voted "Best Steak" by Memphians in virtually every restaurant poll, Folk's Folly pairs fine dining with a cozy, comfortable atmosphere. Folk's Folly also features one of the city's most extensive wine lists, which recently received **Wine Spectator** magazine's Award of Excellence. Affectionately named Folk's Folly, the restaurant was the result of construction businessman Humphrey Folk, Jr.'s desire for a genuine steakhouse in his hometown of Memphis. Although well known throughout the Mid-South construction community, Mr. Folk's dream of opening a steakhouse raised quite a few eyebrows. However, Folk's Folly, established in 1977, continues to reign as one of Memphis' most loved restaurants.*

## BLEU CHEESE FILET MIGNON

1   (16 ounce) prime filet mignon
    Salt and pepper, to taste

2   ounces premium bleu cheese

Lightly salt and pepper filet. Broil for 15 to 20 minutes depending on desired doneness. Remove from grill and cut pocket in side of filet. Stuff bleu cheese in center of filet and return to grill for a few minutes, until cheese melts.

Serves 1.

## CRABMEAT CHRISTOPHER

1   cup fresh jumbo lump crab meat

1   hard boiled egg (grated)

2   teaspoons Christian Brothers Cream Sherry

½   cup real butter

½   tablespoon fresh lemon juice

1½   cups hollandaise sauce

2   slices white bread (lightly toasted, crust removed)

1   generous dash Tabasco sauce

Melt butter in large sauté skillet. Over medium heat, add crab meat, grated egg, lemon juice, sherry and Tabasco sauce – stirring constantly. Heat mixture thoroughly, approximately 5 minutes (do not overcook!) Place 2 toasted bread slices in a small casserole dish; or if you wish to separate into 2 orders to share between 2 people each, place them in separate dishes approximately 8 to 10 ounces in size. Cover bread with crab meat mixture. Top with hollandaise sauce and brown for 1 to 2 minutes in broiler.

Serves 4.

## HOLLANDAISE SAUCE

1   cup egg yolks

3   cups butter, softened

1   teaspoon salt

1   teaspoon cayenne pepper

2   teaspoons fresh lemon juice

Pour eggs into a blender and slowly mix in butter until it becomes creamy. Pour mixture into a large mixing bowl and add remaining ingredients. Mix thoroughly with rubber spatula. Use immediately.

## IRISH BREAD PUDDING

| | | | |
|---|---|---|---|
| ¼ | cup raisins | 2 | loaves French |
| 1¼ | cups sugar | | bread (tear into |
| 1¼ | cups butter | | approximately |
| | (softened) | | 1-inch pieces) |
| 4 | eggs | 2 | tablespoons |
| 1 | quart milk | | ground cinnamon |

Place the milk, bread and raisins in a 9x13-inch baking pan and let soak for approximately 5 minutes or until milk is almost completely absorbed into bread. In a separate mixing bowl, mix the eggs, butter, cinnamon and sugar. Pour mixture into the bread and fold until mixed well. Bake at 325 degrees for 40 to 45 minutes until top is golden brown. Let cool for 5 minutes. Cut into 8 pieces. Serve warmed, topped with *Irish Whiskey Sauce.*

Serves 8.

## IRISH WHISKEY SAUCE

| | | | |
|---|---|---|---|
| 1¼ | cups sugar | 3 | ounces Irish |
| ¾ | cup unsalted butter | | whiskey |
| ¾ | cup heavy whipping | | |
| | cream | | |

Combine sugar, butter and heavy cream in a saucepan over medium heat. Bring mixture to a boil, stirring constantly. Reduce the heat to low and cook for approximately 5 minutes, stirring occasionally. Slowly stir in whiskey and cook for an additional 5 minutes. Remove from heat. Let cool at room temperature.

## FRANK GRISANTI'S AT THE EMBASSY SUITE HOTEL

### 1022 Shady Grove Memphis, TN 38120

*"Since 1909, there has never been a day that a Grisanti hasn't been in the restaurant business here in Memphis." So declares Frank Grisanti, FMP, CEC, a third-generation Memphis, TN, restaurant owner and now executive chef of Frank Grisanti's, an upscale Italian eatery located in the city's Embassy Suites Hotel. In addition to traditional Italian favorites, Grisanti's menu also includes popular items such as veal, Angus steaks and seafood. Frank Grisanti is the past president of the Tennessee Restaurant Association. His restaurant has been voted by the Reader's Poll,* **Memphis Magazine,** *as one of the top two Italian restaurants in Memphis. Chef Grisanti, along with his sons, Frank, Jr. and Larkin also own a two-unit chain of "suburban family restaurants" called Bol a' Pasta.*

## CRABMEAT LARKIN

| | | | |
|---|---|---|---|
| 8 | ounces fresh lump crab meat (picked/ cleaned) | 2 | dashes Tabasco sauce |
| ½ | cup heavy whipping cream | 2 | dashes Worcestershire sauce |
| 2 | tablespoons sherry | | Juice from ½ fresh lemon |

In a saucepan, add the butter, crab meat and whipping cream. Over medium heat, allow the butter to melt down and cook the ingredients for 2 to 3 minutes. Add in the sherry, Tabasco sauce, Worcestershire and lemon juice. With all the ingredients now in the pan, cook for 2 to 3 more minutes until the mixture is hot. Place the ingredients into a ramekin and top with bread crumbs. Place a small amount of béarnaise sauce on top of the dish and run in the oven until the bread crumbs begin to turn brown.

Serves 1.

## OYSTERS ROCKEFELLER

| | | | |
|---|---|---|---|
| 12 | large fresh oysters in the shells | 3 | tablespoons finely crumbled, cooked bacon |
| 1 | cup butter | ½ | teaspoon MSG (optional) |
| 1 | cup chopped celery | | |
| 1 | cup chopped onion | ½ | teaspoon salt |
| ½ | cup chopped parsley | 3 | dashes hot pepper sauce |
| 1 | cup freshly cooked spinach, thoroughly drained | ⅓ | cup freshly grated imported Parmesan cheese |
| 1 | cup dry bread crumbs | | Rock salt |
| 2 | tablespoons Pernod liqueur | | Lemon wedges |

Scrub oyster shells thoroughly. Shuck oysters, leaving oysters and liquid in bottom shells (the deeper shells). Melt butter in a saucepan over medium heat and sauté celery, onion and parsley until soft. Add spinach, bread crumbs, liqueur, bacon and seasoning. When very hot, transfer mixture to a blender or food processor fitted with a fine blade. Process for 1 minute. (At this point the mixture can be refrigerated overnight, if you wish to prepare it ahead.) Spread over oysters so that entire oyster and top of shell are covered. Sprinkle with Parmesan. Arrange oysters on a bed of rock salt on an ovenproof platter and bake in a 425-degree oven for 4 to 5 minutes until topping is hot and bubbly. Run under a broiler long enough to brown Parmesan, if you like. Serve with lemon wedges.

Serves 4.

## ELFO SPECIAL

| | | | |
|---|---|---|---|
| ½ | cup butter | 4 | ounces spaghettini, cooked al dente |
| 4 | jumbo shrimp, diced | ¼ | cup freshly grated imported Romano cheese |
| 3 | large mushrooms, diced | | |
| 1 | clove garlic, minced | | Salt and freshly ground pepper |

Heat butter in a large, heavy skillet over moderate heat. Sauté shrimp and mushrooms for 1 minute, add garlic and sauté 1 or 2 minutes more. Add hot, drained spaghettini to the skillet along with 3 tablespoons of the cheese, salt and pepper. Toss carefully until very hot, but do not allow butter to brown. Place in warm serving bowl and sprinkle with remaining cheese. Serve immediately.

Serves 2.

## GRISANTI'S SPINACH & EGGS

*(Italian Spinach)*

| | | | |
|---|---|---|---|
| 2 | pounds chopped spinach | 12 | eggs |
| ½ | cup olive oil | ½ | cup Parmesan cheese |
| ½ | tablespoon minced garlic | | Salt and pepper to taste |

Heat olive oil in a large skillet. Add garlic and sauté until brown. Add spinach and salt and pepper to taste. Sauté. Add eggs and Parmesan cheese. Keep turning until eggs are cooked. Serve immediately.

Serves 6.

## VIVIAN'S CHOCOLATE CHEESECAKE

| | | | |
|---|---|---|---|
| 1 | cup butter | 2 | cups sugar |
| 3 | cups graham cracker crumbs | 4 | eggs |
| | | 1 | tablespoon cocoa |
| 1 | (12 ounce) package semi-sweet chocolate pieces | 2 | teaspoons vanilla extract |
| | | 2 | cups sour cream |
| 2 | pounds cream cheese, at room temperature | 1 | cup whipping cream |
| | | 1 | teaspoon sugar |

Remove cream cheese from refrigerator about 2 hours before mixing cake. Melt butter in a medium saucepan over low heat. Add cracker crumbs and stir until crumbs are moistened, then press crumbs onto bottom and sides of a 10-inch springform pan. (Add more butter if mixture is too crumbly.) Chill. Melt chocolate in top of a double boiler over simmering water. Remove from heat. Place softened cheese in a large mixing bowl and beat with mixer set at medium speed, until cheese is smooth. With mixer still on medium, beat in sugar gradually, then add cocoa, beating until well combined and smooth. Add eggs, 1 at a time, beating well after each addition. Beat in melted chocolate and vanilla, then stir in sour cream and pour into chilled crust. Bake in a 290-degree oven for 1½ hours. Cool at room temperature, then chill at least 5 hours before serving. (Cooked cake will be slightly runny, but will become firm as it chills.) Whip cream with 1 teaspoon of sugar until very thick.

Spoon into a pastry bag and decorate cake. Garnish with grated chocolate or pecans and maraschino cherries. Slice thinly. *NOTE: This cake freezes well.*

Serves 16.

## THE GROVE GRILL

### 4550 Poplar Avenue
### Memphis, TN 38117

*This upscale relatively new restaurant in the Laurelwood shopping center has quickly gained a loyal following with its variety of steaks, chops, fresh seafood and oysters complemented by an excellent wine list. The cooking team is skillfully led by Chef Jeff Dunham, a Culinary Institute of America graduate. Chip Apperson is general manager.*

## CHOCOLATE PRALINE CHEESECAKE

### CHEESECAKE FILLING

| | | | |
|---|---|---|---|
| 2 | pounds cream cheese | 2 | tablespoons maple |
| 1 | cup packed light | | syrup |
| | brown sugar | 1½ | teaspoons vanilla |
| ⅓ | cup granulated sugar | 1 | tablespoon lemon |
| 4 | eggs | | zest |
| 1 | cup pure sour | 1 | teaspoon orange |
| | cream grade A | | zest |

Place cream cheese and brown and granulated sugars in bowl and process for 30 seconds. Scrape bowl well and process for 10 seconds more. Add eggs 1 at a time and process 10 seconds for each egg. Add sour cream, maple syrup, vanilla, lemon and orange zest. Process 10 seconds. Do not overprocess! Preheat oven to 350 degrees. Place baked shell* and springform pan on a large enough piece of foil so the foil comes above the top of the pan. Place springform pan in another larger baking dish and place in the oven. Pour hot water in baking dish so it comes up to the halfway point of the springform pan. Bake at 350 degrees for 70 minutes. When done, turn off the oven and allow the cake to sit for 30 minutes in the oven. Remove and chill 8 to 24 hours.

### *CRUST

| | | | |
|---|---|---|---|
| ¼ | cup roughly chopped pecan pieces | 1 | teaspoon ground cinnamon |
| 8¼ | ounces Oreo cookie crumbs | 6 | tablespoons unsalted USDA AA butter |
| ¼ | cup granulated sugar | | Pinch kosher salt |

Lightly butter and line the bottom of a 9-inch springform pan with parchment. Butter parchment. In the bowl of an electric food processor fitted with a metal blade, grind cookies into a moderately fine mixture. Add sugar, cinnamon and salt. Process briefly. Transfer to a mixing bowl and toss in melted butter with a fork to moisten evenly. Gently press crumbs evenly over the bottom and sides of the prepared pan. Bake in 350 degree oven for 10 minutes to set crust.

### CHOCOLATE PRALINES

| | | | |
|---|---|---|---|
| 3 | cups granulated sugar | 1 | teaspoon baking soda |
| ½ | cup margarine | 1 | cup buttermilk |
| 3 | tablespoons light corn syrup | 2 | tablespoons sifted cocoa powder |
| | Pinch kosher salt | 1 | teaspoon vanilla |
| | | 1 | cup pecan pieces |

Mix sugar, margarine, corn syrup and salt in heavy saucepan. Place baking soda in 1 cup measure and stir in enough water to liquefy the baking soda, then stir in the buttermilk to blend. Add to saucepan and stir well. Cook over medium heat for 15 minutes, stirring constantly. Check mixture at this time for the soft ball stage (234 degrees). If ready, remove from heat. If not ready, continue cooking until the soft ball stage is reached on a candy thermometer. (A few drops of the hot syrup dropped into cold water forms a ball that flattens when removed from the water.) Add cocoa powder, vanilla and pecans. Stir well. Using a tablespoon, portion onto was paper or cookie sheet. Allow to cool. After the filling is placed in the crust, top with the chocolate pralines. Serves 12.

## OYSTER & ARTICHOKE SOUP

| | | | |
|---|---|---|---|
| 3 | slices smoked bacon | 4 | ounces flour |
| ¼ | cup whole butter | 3 | cups chicken stock |
| 1 | cup diced onion | 1 | (10 ounce) can fresh oysters |
| 1 | ounce diced celery | | |
| 1 | ounce diced leeks | 1 | cup heavy cream |
| 1 | can of artichoke bottoms (rinse well) 5 ounce hold back (2 bottoms for garnish) | 1 | teaspoon Cajun seasoning Salt and pepper to taste |

Melt butter in a heavy bottom saucepan at medium-high heat. Slice bacon into ¼-inch pieces and add to pan. Render bacon, add vegetables holding back on the artichokes. Sauté for 3 to 4 minutes. Add flour and incorporate into vegetables. Add stock and stir well to avoid lumps, turn heat down to medium. Drain oysters, reserve stock and 8 oysters. Add stock and remaining oysters to the soup. Rough chop the artichoke and add to soup. Bring soup to a simmer and cook for 15 minutes. Be careful not to allow flour to build up on the bottom of the pan while soup is coming to a simmer, stir with a whisk to avoid this, using a hand held good blender to purée soup. Add heavy cream, Cajun seasoning, salt and pepper. Garnish soup with 1 whole oyster, oyster crackers and a purée of the reserved artichoke bottoms and fresh basil. Serves 8.

## LOUISIANA CRAB & CRAWFISH CAKES WITH LEMON FENNEL REMOULADE

| | | | |
|---|---|---|---|
| 1 | pound fresh crawfish tail meat | 1 | tablespoon garlic, minced |
| 1 | pound lump crab meat (cleaned for shells) | 1 | teaspoon dry mustard |
| 1 | cup dry bread crumbs | 1 | tablespoon lemon juice |
| 1 | tablespoon olive oil | 1 | tablespoon Dijon mustard |
| ½ | cup onions, finely diced | 1 | tablespoon Worcestershire |
| ½ | cup celery, finely diced | 1 | teaspoon Tabasco sauce |
| ½ | cup green pepper, finely diced | 2 | tablespoons mayonnaise |
| 2 | tablespoons jalapeño pepper, finely diced (no seeds) | 3 | eggs |
| 1 | teaspoon thyme, fresh-chopped | | Pinch of Cajun seasoning |
| 1 | teaspoon basil, fresh-chopped | | Pinch of cayenne pepper |
| 1 | tablespoon parsley, fresh-chopped | 1 | teaspoon salt |
| | | 2 | cups fresh bread crumbs |

Sauté onions, celery and peppers lightly, allow to cool. Pick through crab meat to remove all shell pieces. Fold all ingredients together. Gently mix so as not to break up crab meat too much. **Preparation of Crab & Crawfish Cakes:** Portion mixture into 3-ounce cakes. Form into uniform medallions and dredge through fine bread crumbs. Preheat oven to 400 degrees. Sauté cakes in a medium to high heat skillet in vegetable oil. Place in oven to heat through, 5 minutes. Place 2 cakes on each plate with 2 ounces of remoulade and add a green salad garnished with thinly sliced fresh fennel and tomatoes. Serves 8.

### LEMON-FENNEL REMOULADE

| | | | |
|---|---|---|---|
| 1 | bulb of fresh fennel with greens (reserve 2 tablespoons of chopped greens) | 2 | tablespoons gherkins, chopped |
| 4 | shallots, sliced | 1 | teaspoon dry mustard |
| ¼ | cup Pernod | 2 | egg yolks |
| 2 | lemons, zest and juice | 1 | cup + 2 tablespoons vegetable oil |
| 2 | tablespoons capers, chopped | | Salt to taste |
| | | | Cayenne to taste |

In 2 tablespoons oil, sauté fennel and shallots until transparent. Deglaze with Pernod. Continue to cook for 30 seconds, remove and cool. Remove this mixture to food processor. Add all other ingredient except oil, salt and cayenne. Begin to purée ingredients while slowly drizzling oil into processor. This should form an emulsion to build a mayonnaise. Add all of the oil. Remove to an appropriate container. Add chopped fennel greens and season to taste. Serves 8.

## LOW COUNTRY SHRIMP & GRITS

| | | | |
|---|---|---|---|
| 2 | pounds shrimp-peeled, 16 to 20 count per pound | 4 | ounces dry white wine |
| 4 | teaspoons Cajun seasoning | 8 | ounces shrimp stock |
| 4 | tablespoons vegetable oil | 4 | tablespoons whole butter |
| 4 | tablespoons minced garlic | 4 | tablespoons chopped scallions |
| 4 | ounces diced tasso ham | | Salt to taste |
| 4 | tablespoons chopped fresh herbs (parsley, thyme, rosemary and basil) | 1 | recipe speckle heart grits (recipe follows) |

Pre-heat a large skillet to medium-high heat. Toss shrimp in Cajun spice. Add oil to skillet, add garlic, tasso and shrimp to pan. Sauté for 2 to 3 minutes, add herbs and wine. Cook for an additional 1 to 2 minutes. Add shrimp stock and bring to a boil. Portion grits into 4 to 6 large bowls and place equal portions of shrimp in each bowl, on top of grits. Return pan to heat and bring to a simmer. Reduce by up to ½ volume, remove from heat and whisk in whole butter. Pour sauce evenly over the top of each bowl of shrimp and grits. Garnish with chopped scallions. Serves 8.

## SPECKLE HEART GRITS

| | | | |
|---|---|---|---|
| 3 | cups chicken stock | | Salt to taste |
| 2 | cups milk | | Tabasco sauce to taste |
| ¼ | cup whole butter | | |
| 1 | cup stone ground grits | | |

Combine 2 cups stock (reserve 1 cup stock), milk and butter in a double boiler and bring to a simmer. Add grits while stirring constantly for 5 minutes. Place in a double boiler and cook for 1 to 2 hours, stirring occasionally. Add additional stock while cooking to adjust to desired consistency. Season with salt and Tabasco sauce to taste (take care not to oversalt). Serves 4 to 6.

## JARRETT'S
### 5687 Quince Avenue
### Memphis, TN 38119

**Rick & Barbara Farmer, Owners**
*Chef Richard Farmer has been voted one of the city's top chefs (**Memphis Magazine** and **The Memphis Flyer**). Perhaps the finest flattery to be bestowed on Jarrett's was the invitation to cook at The James Beard Foundation in New York City in 1999. Chef Rick took his cooking team and received rave reviews for their imaginative cuisine.*

## LOBSTER GAZPACHO

| | | | |
|---|---|---|---|
| | Lobster meat from 2 whole lobsters | 5 | cucumbers (diced ½ inch) |
| 2 | red peppers (seeded and chopped -inch) | ⅔ | cup lemon juice |
| 2 | green peppers (seeded and chopped 1 inch) | 2 | tablespoons Tabasco brand hot sauce |
| 4 | cloves garlic (chopped) | 2 | tablespoons sugar |
| 2 | red onions (chopped 1 inch) | 2 | tablespoons salt |
| 1 | quart canned chopped tomatoes | 1 | tablespoon pepper |
| 4 | carrots (peeled chopped ½ inch) | 2 | 48-ounce cans V-8 juice |
| | | 1 | cup extra virgin olive oil |
| | | 1 | bunch fresh cilantro (chopped) |
| | | 1 | quart lobster stock |

Using the pulsing action of a food processor, blend 2 cups of the vegetable mixture with 1 cup V-8 juice at a time until all vegetables are used up. Add lobster stock and all seasonings, lemon juice and olive oil (using a wire whisk). Chill overnight and serve in frozen goblets and garnish with cucumber slices, fresh chopped cilantro and lobster meat.
Serves 8.

## JARRETT'S HERB BREAD

| | | | |
|---|---|---|---|
| 1 | quart water | 4 | pounds bread flour |
| ½ | cup sugar | 4 | tablespoons herbs, chopped (rosemary, thyme, parsley, etc.) |
| 2 | ounce yeast (instant) | | |
| 4 | ounces olive oil | | |
| 1 | ounce salt | | |

Dissolve sugar, water and yeast in mixer on low speed until thoroughly blended. In about 5 minutes, add flour, olive oil, herbs and salt and knead until dough is smooth and elastic. This should take about 15 minutes. Leave dough in bowl, covered in plastic wrap and allow to rise until double in volume. Punch down dough and place on floured working surface. Cut dough into 5-ounce pieces and form into balls. Flatten out balls and place on papered sheet pans. Decorate with whatever you want – fresh tomatoes, more herbs, olives, etc. Drizzle a little more olive oil on the dough and allow to rise until double in volume again. Bake in preheated 350 degree oven until a nice thick brown crust forms (about 12 minutes). Bread will stay good for 2 or 3 days. Makes about 12 boules.

## HERB GLAZED & ROASTED SALMON

### FOR THE HERB BUTTER

| | | | |
|---|---|---|---|
| ¼ | pound butter | 2 | cloves garlic (chopped) |
| 1 | tablespoon freshly chopped tarragon | 1 | ounce cognac |
| 1 | tablespoon chopped parsley | 2 | ounces port wine |
| 1 | teaspoon fresh thyme | | Salt and freshly ground pepper to taste |
| 1 | large shallot (chopped) | | |

Place all ingredients in food processor and pulse until smooth.

### FOR THE MUSTARD GLAZE

| | | | |
|---|---|---|---|
| 2 | ounces Creole mustard | 2 | ounces honey |

Place four 6-ounce portions salmon in sauté pan with 4 ounces white wine. Brush fish with honey mustard mixture. Then with a large dollop of the herb butter, place in broiler on top rack and cook until golden brown. Remove fish from pan and place wine mixture back on heat and reduce liquid to ⅓ the original amount. Whisk in about 2 tablespoons more of the herb butter. This is your sauce . . . enjoy.
Serves 4.

## HORSERADISH ENCRUSTED GROUPER WITH COLCANNON POTATOES & FRESH ASPARAGUS

| | | | |
|---|---|---|---|
| 8 | (4 ounce) portions fresh grouper fillets | 1 | can plain bread crumbs |
| 1 | (4 ounce) jar fresh prepared horseradish | | Salt and pepper to taste |
| 6 | eggs | 24 | spears fresh asparagus blanched in salted water for one minute |

In a mixing bowl, whisk eggs, horseradish, salt and pepper together. Dredge fish first in the horseradish mixture then in bread crumbs. Sauté the fish in vegetable oil until golden brown on both sides. Don't overcook! Serve over colcannon potatoes and fresh asparagus spears.

### COLCANNON POTATOES

| | | | |
|---|---|---|---|
| 8 | Idaho potatoes (peeled and quartered) | ½ | cup extra virgin olive oil |
| 1 | cup white cabbage and garlic purée (explanation below) | 1 | bunch scallions (chopped) Salt and coarse ground pepper to taste |

Boil potatoes in salted water until tender. Drain in colander and place in large mixing bowl. While still hot, work potatoes with masher until somewhat smooth. Add cabbage purée, olive oil, scallions, salt and pepper and whisk until smooth. Hold in a warm place until ready to serve.

Serves 6 to 8.

## HEART OF ROMAINE SALAD WITH ROQUEFORT CRUMBLES, TOASTED WALNUTS & TARRAGON VINAIGRETTE

| | | | |
|---|---|---|---|
| 4 | heads fresh Romaine lettuce (outer leaves removed, exposing the lighter, more tender heart) | 1 | cup Roquefort cheese (crumbled) |
| | | 1 | cup walnut halves and pieces (toasted) |
| | | 1 | cup tarragon vinaigrette |

Slice Romaine hearts lengthwise into 1-inch ribbons. Arrange decoratively into bowls and top with Roquefort and walnuts. Ladle 1-ounce vinaigrette onto salads and garnish with fresh tomato wedges. Serve immediately.

### FRESH TARRAGON VINAIGRETTE

| | | | |
|---|---|---|---|
| 1 | cup red wine vinegar | 1 | tablespoon black pepper (coarse grind) |
| 1 | cup extra virgin olive oil | | |
| 3 | fresh shallots (finely chopped) | 2 | tablespoons fresh tarragon (chopped) |
| 2 | tablespoons honey | | Salt to taste |

Whisk together all ingredients in a stainless steel bowl and chill until ready to use. This vinaigrette will keep for at least a week in the refrigerator.

## MOUSSE AU CHOCOLAT WITH GRAND MARNIER

| | | | |
|---|---|---|---|
| 16 | ounces chocolate | 1 | cup granulated sugar |
| 8 | ounces unsalted butter | 10 | egg whites |
| 10 | egg yolks | 3 | cups heavy cream |
| 3 | ounces Grand Marnier | ½ | teaspoon salt |

Melt chocolate and butter over simmering water. Hold. Whisk egg yolks, sugar and Grand Marnier until a ribbon forms and has a light lemon color. Put salt in the chocolate mixture and allow to cool to room temperature. Add egg mixture to the chocolate. Beat egg whites until stiff peaks form and fold into the chocolate mixture ⅓ at a time. At this point you can simply pipe the mousse into serving glasses and decorate as you wish or you can put it into moulds of various shapes and refrigerate until set.

## JIM'S PLACE EAST

### 5560 Shelby Oaks
### Memphis, TN 38134

**Costa Taras, Dimitri Taras & Angelo Liollio, Owners**

*Jim's Place, celebrating it's 79th year in business, is honored to be featured in the March 2000 edition of Food & Wine Magazine as one of the "Best Restaurants of Tennessee." Located in wooded surroundings off Summer Avenue, Jim's Place features American, Greek and Continental cuisine with such specialties as souflima (pork tenderloin), Mediterranean red snapper and hand-cut grilled steaks.*

## BREEZOLES TIS SKARAS

*(Greek for Charcoal Broiled Lamb Chops)*

| | | | |
|---|---|---|---|
| 8 | lamb chops | 2 | cloves garlic, |
| | Salt and pepper to | | minced |
| | taste | | Juice of 1 lemon |
| ¼ | cup vegetable oil | ½ | teaspoon oregano |

Prepare charcoal for grilling. Salt and pepper lamb chops. Mix remaining ingredients and brush chops with some of this mixture, reserving ½ for basting. When coals have turned white, place chops on grill. Cook to desired doneness on each side, basting often. Remove to warm platter and serve.

Serves 4.

## *Jim's Place*

### *Since 1921*

## ASPARAGUS MOUSSE

| | | | |
|---|---|---|---|
| 6 | ounces cream cheese | 1 | (8-ounce) can asparagus (save asparagus juice) |
| 7 | ounces lemon gelatin | 1 | cup asparagus juice |
| 2 | cups boiling water | 2 | teaspoons almond extract (not any more) |
| 1⅓ | cups mayonnaise | | |
| 1 | cup sliced almonds | | |

Whip asparagus juice in cream cheese. Add mayonnaise and well-mashed asparagus. Set aside. Dissolve gelatin in boiling water and cool. When cool, combine ingredients and add extract and sliced almonds. Refrigerate until firm.

Serves 20.

## CREMA CARAMELLA

| | | | |
|---|---|---|---|
| 8 | eggs | 1 | tablespoon vanilla extract |
| 1 | cup sugar | ⅛ | cup brandy |

Beat eggs, sugar, vanilla, and brandy.

| | | | |
|---|---|---|---|
| 1 | cup sugar caramelized in skillet | 1 | pint whipping cream |
| | | 1 | pint half-and-half |

Heat whipping cream and half-and-half till warm. Mix eggs and half-and-half and whipping cream together gently. Pour caramelized sugar into 10 ounce Pyrex cups. Then pour half-and-half whipping cream into cups. Cook at 300 degrees for 45 minutes.

Serves 9.

## BRUSCHETTA
*(Appetizer)*

| | | | |
|---|---|---|---|
| 1 | loaf French bread | 1 | tablespoon |
| 3 | small tomatoes, | | chopped garlic |
| | chopped small dice | 4 | tablespoons grated |
| ¼ | cup aged balsamic | | Asiago cheese |
| | vinegar | | Salt and pepper to |
| ½ | cup virgin olive oil | | taste |

Cut French bread on angle ¼-inch in thickness and bake at 350 degrees until light brown. Mix all other ingredients together and let marinate for 30 minutes. Spoon on top of each slice of toast and sprinkle Asiago cheese on each piece.

Serves 4.

## BAKED OYSTER MAX
*(Appetizer or Entrée)*

| | | | |
|---|---|---|---|
| 2 | pints mayonnaise | 1 | cup Asiago cheese, |
| | (Hellmann's brand) | | grated |
| 2 | tablespoons | 3 | egg yolks |
| | Worcestershire | 1 | teaspoon salt |
| | sauce | ¼ | teaspoon white |
| 3 | tablespoons sugar | | pepper |
| 3 | lemons (juice only) | 36 | oysters |

Wash oysters and shuck on half shell, lay out on baking pan. Mix all of the ingredients together well and top each oyster (covering completely). Bake at 425 degrees for 5 minutes or until lightly brown. Serve with lemon wedge.

Serves 4.

# LULU GRILLE

## 565 Erin Drive at Poplar
## Memphis, TN 38117

**Don & Leigh McLean, Owners**
*This popular East Memphis bistro has delightful salads, delicious pastas, and tasty sandwiches. Entrées include grilled seafood, pasta, meats, wild game, chicken and lamb. The homemade desserts are made from scratch and served in large portions. The bistro has an award-winning patio for your warm weather enjoyment. The full bar includes an extensive wine list.*

*Scott De Larme, the Executive Chef, is a graduate of Johnson & Wales in Charleston, South Carolina.*

## GRILLED PORTABELLO MUSHROOM WITH SMOKED SALMON, CARAMELIZED ONION & DILL HAVARTI

| | | | |
|---|---|---|---|
| 4 | each Portabello mushrooms | 8 | ounces dill havarti cheese |
| 8 | ounces smoked salmon | 2 | ounces butter |
| 1 | each red onion | | Salt and pepper |

Brush mushrooms with melted butter, season with salt and pepper and grill for two minutes on each side. Slice onion very thin and cook in a large sauté pan until caramelized, set aside to cool. Layer mushroom, salmon, onion and cheese. Bake in a 450 degree oven for 4 to 5 minutes or until hot. Serve with marinara sauce (smoked tomato sauce). Garnish with thyme or other herbs. If dill havarti cheese is unavailable, substitute other cheeses. Serves 4.

## CITRUS MARINATED & GRILLED JUMBO SHRIMP

| | | | |
|---|---|---|---|
| 16 | 16 to 20 count shrimp (*4 to 6 per person for entrée or 2 per person for appetizer). | 8 | ounces of orange juice |
| | Onion | 2 | fresh lemons |
| 3 | cloves garlic | 2 | fresh limes |
| 1 | tablespoon of Jerk sauce | 2 | fresh oranges |
| | | ½ | cup olive oil |
| | | | Parsley, cilantro |
| 2 | tablespoons of soy sauce | | Pinch crushed red pepper |
| | | | Pinch cumin |

Peel and remove vein from shrimp. Slice onion and peel and chop garlic. Zest and juice fruits and combine in a large bowl with remainder of ingredients. Add shrimp and marinate for 2 to 4 hours. (Zip lock bags are good for marinade). Grill over high heat for 2 to 3 minutes per side. Serve with Pineapple Relish (see below).

*Serves 4 to 6.

## PINEAPPLE RELISH

| | | | |
|---|---|---|---|
| 1 | Diced fresh pineapple red bell pepper (medium to fine dice) | | Chopped garlic Crushed red pepper |
| | Diced red onion Scallion (for green color) | 2 | tablespoons sherry vinegar |
| | | 2 | tablespoons melted brown sugar |
| | | | Black sesame seeds |

Mix all of the relish ingredients. It will be ready in as little as 10 minutes.

**Presentation:** Put the relish in center of plate. Surround with shrimp. Garnish with cilantro.

## SAUTÉED ELK MEDALLIONS WITH A SUNDRIED CRANBERRY & WALNUT SAUCE

| 2 | pounds of elk tenderloin (venison, pork loin or beef tenderloin may be substituted) | 2 | shallots |
| 1 | cup sundried cranberries | 3 | cloves garlic |
| 1 | cup walnuts | 1 | cup port wine |
| 4 | cups elk of venison glacé (beef or veal stock may be substituted and reduced) | 2 | tablespoons whole butter |
| | | 2 | tablespoons clarified butter |
| | | 2 | cups flour |
| | | | Salt and pepper to taste |
| | | 2 | teaspoons thyme |

Slice shallots thinly, peel and fine dice garlic. Set aside. Slice the elk into medallions approximately ¼-inch thick. Pound the medallions with a mallet if necessary (depends on the cut of meat used). Place a small amount of clarified butter in a large sauté pan and heat well. Dust the elk medallions in the seasoned flour and sauté quickly on both sides (do several batches if necessary). Set aside – keep warm. Add a little more butter to the same pan if needed and sauté the shallots and garlic together until soft. Add sundried cranberries, walnuts and thyme and sauté 1 minute longer. Add the port wine to sauté mixture and reduce by ⅔. Add game stock and reduce by ½ again. Add whole butter slowly, piece by piece, stirring constantly. Place medallions on a warm serving platter or plates. Top with the sauce and serve immediately.

*Note: Most cuts of elk or venison will work for this recipe as long as the meat is cut right and pounded if necessary.*

Serves 4 to 5.

Lulu grille
A Neighborhood Restaurant

## RINALDO GRISANTI AND SONS

### 2855 Poplar Avenue Memphis, TN 38111

**Judd Grisanti, Chef**
**Alex Grisanti, Chef**
**Ryan Luttrell, Pastry Chef**
*Rinaldo Grisanti and Sons restaurant was voted the No. 1 Italian restaurant seven years in a row by the Reader's Poll in* **Memphis Magazine**. *This restaurant has been featured in* **Southern Living** *magazine.*

## CHEESECAKE

| 40 | ounces cream cheese | 2 | teaspoons vanilla extract |
| 1½ | cups sugar | | |
| 2 | ounces cornstarch | ½ | cup heavy cream |
| 5 | eggs | 2 | (9½ inch) springform pans |
| 2 | egg yolks | | |

### FOR CRUST

| 28 | ounces graham cracker crumbs | 6 | ounces butter |

Mix crumbs with the butter and form in the 2 springform pans.

Whip cream cheese until very soft. Add eggs and yolks gradually, scrape occasionally. Add sugar and cornstarch, then scrape. Add heavy cream and vanilla and then pour into pans. Bake at 325 degrees F for 42 minutes.

Makes 2 pans.

## KEY LIME PIE

| 24 | ounces cream cheese | 3 | (14 ounce) cans sweetened condensed milk |
| 3 | egg yolks | | |
| | | 1¼ | cup key lime juice |

### FOR CRUST

| 16 | ounces chocolate wafers, crushed | 3 | ounces butter |

Mix the wafers with the butter to make crust. Form and place in freezer.

Whip cream cheese until soft. Add yolks, milk and key lime juice. Mix well, pour into 9½" springform pan and freeze for 24 hours.

# MANTIA'S

## 4856 Poplar Avenue
## Memphis, TN 38117

**Alyce Mantia, Chef/Owner**
*Mantia's is a Mediterranean café, deli and market with a variety of soups, salads, pasta and sandwiches at lunch and a changing menu of special entrées at dinner.*

*A mostly do-ahead Italian dinner for eight:*

## CROSTINI DI POLENTA AL PEPERONI ROSSI

*(Antipasto)*

| | | | |
|---|---|---|---|
| 1 | recipe "polenta aglio odon" (recipe follows) | 1 | tablespoon heavy cream |
| 2 | tablespoons extra-virgin olive oil | 1 | (7 ounce) jar roasted peppers |
| 2 | cloves garlic, minced | 3 | anchovy filets, patted dry |
| 1 | small onion, chopped | | Minced fresh parsley |
| | | | Black olives |

Make polenta according to the recipe. Heat olive oil in a small skillet. Add garlic and stir a couple of times. Add onion and cook until onion is golden and very soft. Place roasted peppers with their juice in a blender or food processor. Add onion mixture and purée until smooth. Add cream and anchovy filets and pulse just to blend. Season with salt and white pepper to taste. Pour into a small pan and heat until just barely hot. DON'T BOIL. (Sauce may be made ahead and refrigerated covered, and reheated at serving time.)

Oil or butter a baking sheet or broiler pan. Cut polenta ½-inch thick and arrange in a single layer on prepared pan. Broil 3 to 4 inches from heat until a golden crust is formed, 4 to 5 minutes. Turn and broil on second side until golden, another 4 minutes or so.

Put a couple of tablespoonfuls of red pepper sauce on an individual serving plate and place polenta on top. Sprinkle generously with minced parsley and garnish with a couple of black olives. Serve at once. Makes about 12 antipasto servings.

# POLENTA AGLIO ODORI

*(Polenta With Herbs)*

| | | | |
|---|---|---|---|
| 8 | cups water | ½ | cup freshly grated Parmesan |
| 2 | teaspoons salt | | |
| 2 | cups polenta (Italian coarse-ground corn) | 1 | teaspoon minced fresh sage |
| | | 1 | teaspoon minced fresh rosemary |
| 4 | tablespoons butter | 1 | teaspoon pepper |

Oil or butter a large loaf pan and set aside. In a large saucepan, bring water and salt to boil. Add polenta in a slow stream, stirring constantly. Reduce heat and cook, stirring constantly for 15 minutes. Reduce heat to low and cook, stirring, until polenta starts to pull from the sides and is the consistency of thick cereal. Remove from heat and stir in remaining ingredients. Pour into prepared loaf pan (if you don't have one big enough, use two smaller ones). Smooth top and cover with plastic wrap. Chill until firm, 6 hours or overnight.

Preheat broiler. Oil or butter a baking sheet or broiler pan. Unmold polenta. Cut into ½-inch to ¾-inch slices (sawing into slices with dental floss works well for this) and arrange in a single layer on prepared pan. Broil 3 to 4 inches from heat until a golden crust is formed, about 5 minutes. Turn and broil on second side until golden, another 4 to 5 minutes.

This makes a good base for almost any substantial sauce that you might put on pasta, and served as a first course. You can also use it as a base for broiled meats, with some of the meat juices dribbled over. A couple of tiny grilled quail (or 1 larger one) will just fit on a slice for a good-looking presentation with complementary flavors.

To serve as an antipasto, cut into thinner slices (about ¼-inch), cut each slice diagonally into 2 triangles, and broil as above. Serve plain, or with a marinara sauce for dipping. A taste variation is to either add to the above recipe, or use instead of the herbs, ½-pound Italian sausage (mild or hot, according to your taste). Remove it from the casings (or buy bulk) and cook, crumbling finely, until just no longer pink. Drain well before adding to the polenta. This makes a great antipasto or appetizer. Cut thin, arrange on a plate and dust with finely minced fresh parsley.

## ZUPPA DI RUCOLA

*(Arugula Soup)*

| | | | |
|---|---|---|---|
| 1 | large onion, chopped | 3 | cups chicken broth, vegetable stock or water |
| 1 | large leek, chopped, with some of the green part | 8 | ounces arugula, de-stemmed, chopped |
| 2 | large potatoes; peeled, chopped | 1 | cup half-and-half or milk* |
| 3 | tablespoons unsalted butter | | Freshly grated Parmesan White truffle oil; optional |

Sauté onion and leek (be sure to clean it well!) in butter until just barely soft. Add potatoes and cook, stirring occasionally 2 to 3 minutes. Add broth (vegetables should be covered; if not, add a bit more broth) and simmer, covered until potato is very tender, 15 to 20 minutes. Add arugula and stir a couple of times, just until it wilts.

Remove from heat and purée in a blender or food processor. Return to pan and add cream or milk. When ready to serve, reheat gently but do not boil. Salt and pepper to taste. Serve immediately, passing Parmesan at the table. This recipe works extremely well with watercress or spinach.

*For a lighter soup, leave out the cream or milk, and add more broth.

## MELONE CON GRAPPA

*(Melon with Grappa)*

| | | | |
|---|---|---|---|
| ⅔ | cup sugar | ½ | cup grappa (Italian liqueur) |
| ½ | cup water | | |
| 1 | teaspoon grated lime zest | 8 | cups mixed melon balls |
| ¼ | cup + 2 tablespoons fresh lime juice | | Fresh mint (for garnish) |

Combine sugar and water in a small pan. Heat until the sugar dissolves then let simmer 5 minutes. Add grated lime zest and remove from the heat. Let cool about 5 minutes, then add lime juice and grappa. Pour over melon balls and refrigerate at least 3 hours and up to 6 hours, tossing occasionally. To serve, place in dessert dishes, divide the syrup among the dishes and garnish with fresh mint sprigs. Serves 8.

## QUAGLIE IN TEGAME

*(Quail Italian Style)*

| | | | |
|---|---|---|---|
| 16 | small quail, cleaned and ready to cook | 3 | tablespoons extra-virgin olive oil |
| 16 | very thin slices pancetta | | Salt and pepper |
| 16 | large fresh sage leaves | 3 | cloves garlic, finely minced |
| 4 | tablespoons butter | 1½ | cups dry white wine |

Rinse the quail in cold running water inside and out. Let drain thoroughly. Pat dry. Stuff the cavity of each with one slice pancetta and one sage leaf and tie their little legs together. In a large lidded sauté pan heat butter and oil on high. When hot, slip in the quail and brown on all sides. Sprinkle with salt and fresh ground pepper. Add garlic to fat in pan and stir a bit. Add wine, bring to a slow boil. Lower heat, cover and simmer until birds are tender-done, about 20 minutes. Let cool and place quail in a large baking pan. When ready to serve, place in 450 degree oven and bake uncovered just until browned. Serve with pan juices. Serves 8.

## ZUCCHINI GRATINATI

| | | | |
|---|---|---|---|
| 3 | pounds zucchini; small, scrubbed | 4 | tablespoons freshly grated Parmesan |
| 4 | 1 inch slices crusty Italian bread | 1 | pinch nutmeg, freshly grated |
| 2 | ounces prosciutto (Italian ham) | 2 | large eggs, beaten lightly |
| 1 | small onion, minced | 2 | tablespoons good quality olive oil |
| 1 | clove garlic, finely minced | | |

Preheat oven to 350 degrees. Slice zucchini into ¼-inch slices. In a food processor, mince bread and ham together into fine crumbs. Heat oil in a wide skillet and add onion and garlic. Cook, stirring, until onion is soft. Take off heat and stir in crumbs, Parmesan and nutmeg. Mix in egg. Layer zucchini and crumb mixture in a baking dish, reserving enough of the crumb mixture to cover the top well. Drizzle with a little more olive oil and bake 30 minutes, until zucchini is tender but not soggy. This can be made up a couple of hours ahead; let set at room temperature until ready to bake. Serves 8.

## NAPA CAFÉ

### 5101 Sanderlin Avenue
### Memphis, TN 38117

*This new restaurant won the prestigious 1999 "Award of Excellence" from the **Wine Spectator**. In a cozy, cordial ambience, wines of the Napa Valley are featured. "Good food, exemplary service" — Fred Koeppel, **The Commercial Appeal**.*

## ROCK SHRIMP CAKES

| | | | |
|---|---|---|---|
| 1 | pound rock shrimp | 2 | teaspoons Worcestershire sauce |
| ¼ | cup white wine, dry | | |
| 1 | large egg, beaten | | |
| 1 | cup + bread crumbs | 10 | drops Tabasco sauce |
| 5 | tablespoons mayonnaise | ¼ | cup sun-dried tomatoes, julienne |
| ½ | teaspoon dry mustard | | Salt and pepper to taste |
| 2 | tablespoons parsley, minced | | Cajun seasoning to taste |
| 2 | tablespoons scallion, white part only | | |

Poach shrimp in wine for 1 minute. The shrimp will not be completely cooked. Drain the shrimp reserving the liquid. Cool and chop finely. Return the shrimp liquid to pan and reduce until a syrup. In a pan, add the remaining ingredients. Fold in the rock shrimp and reduced wine. Season with salt and pepper. Form into 8 cakes. Sauté the cakes in clarified butter. Serve with red pepper aioli (recipe follows), chive oil and 1 serving of corn sauté.

Serves 4.

## ROASTED RED PEPPER AIOLI

| | | | |
|---|---|---|---|
| 2 | cups mayonnaise | 2 | tablespoons garlic |
| 1 | cup red roasted peppers | | Salt and pepper to taste |

Drain peppers well. Purée in blender (not robocoup). Store in squeeze bottle in cooler.

## DEEP DISH BUTTERMILK PIE

| | | | |
|---|---|---|---|
| 8 | large eggs | 2 | cups sugar |
| 1 | pound cream cheese, softened | 1 | cup heavy cream |
| | | 1 | cup sour cream |
| 2 | cups buttermilk | 1 | teaspoon vanilla |

### CRUST

| | | | |
|---|---|---|---|
| 4 | cups graham cracker crumbs | ½ | cup butter, melted |
| | | ¼ | cup sugar |

**Crust Preparation Method:** Mix graham cracker crumbs and sugar. Slowly add butter until it holds together. Place in pans and bake for 10 minutes at 350 degrees.

**Pie Preparation Method:** In mixer fitted with whisk, combine all ingredients except eggs until smooth. Add eggs 1 at a time and blend after each addition until smooth. Pour into 10" springform pan with graham cracker crust. Wrap springform pan in aluminum foil around side only. Bake in hot water bath at 300 degrees for 70 minutes. Cool completely before removing springform sides. Chill overnight.

Yield: 1 pie

*Note: Serve with Brown Sugar Sauce (recipe follows).*

## BROWN SUGAR SAUCE

| | | | |
|---|---|---|---|
| 2 | cups sour cream | 1 | quart heavy cream |
| 1 | pound dark brown sugar | 1 | cup milk |

Heat in heavy saucepan. Reduce by ⅓. Remove and chill before serving.

Yield: 1½ quarts

*Note: Use with buttermilk pie.*

# OWEN BRENNAN'S

## 6150 Poplar Avenue
## Memphis, TN 38119

**Mark Schielke, General Manager**
**Steve Hornecker, Executive Chef**
*You don't have to go to New Orleans to enjoy French Quarter cuisine. It's right here at Owen Brennan's. Whether your tastes run spicy or mild you'll find something wonderful. Like tender steaks, hand-cut to your specification. Owen Brennan's was voted " Best Sunday Brunch" by* **Memphis Magazine's** *Reader's Poll.*

## OYSTER ROCKEFELLER SOUP

| | | | |
|---|---|---|---|
| 2 | cups fresh shucked oysters | ¼ | cup fresh parsley, finely chopped |
| 2 | quarts cold water | 2 | cups heavy cream |
| ¾ | cup butter | | Salt and pepper to taste |
| ¾ | cup chopped celery | | |
| ½ | cup flour | | |
| ⅓ | cup Pernod | | |
| 8 | ounces fresh spinach leaves, washed, stemmed and coarsely chopped | | |

Melt the butter in a large pot and sauté the celery until tender. Stir in the flour, then add oysters and oyster stock. Reduce the heat to simmer for 10 minutes until thickened. Add the Pernod, spinach and parsley and season to taste with salt and pepper. Pour in cream and simmer several minutes until the soup is hot, then serve.

Serves 6 to 8.

## OWEN BRENNAN'S BREAD PUDDING

| | | | |
|---|---|---|---|
| 1 | quart milk | 1 | teaspoon vanilla extract |
| 1 | cup sugar | 2 | teaspoons lemon zest |
| 10 | ounces stale French bread cut into 1-inch cubes | 2 | teaspoons cinnamon |
| 4 | eggs | 1 | pinch nutmeg |

In a 2-quart saucepan dissolve the sugar in the milk over medium heat. After the sugar has dissolved, remove from heat and allow mixture to come to room temperature. In a large mixing bowl, whip the eggs thoroughly. Add the milk and sugar mixture to the eggs. Add the remaining ingredients (except the bread) to the mixture and blend well. Add the bread to the mixture and allow it to absorb most of the liquid. Pour the bread mixture into a 12x8x2-inch buttered baking dish. Bake in a preheated 325 degree oven for 40 minutes or until firm. Allow the bread pudding to cool for 15 minutes after it is done. Serve with rum sauce (see accompanying recipe) and whipped cream.

Serves 8 to 10.

## RUM SAUCE

| | | | |
|---|---|---|---|
| ½ | pound butter | 5 | tempered eggs (see note) |
| 1 | pound sugar | | |
| 3 | ounces rum | | |

Melt butter in a 2-quart saucepan over medium heat. Add sugar, stirring constantly until sugar melts into the butter. Add rum carefully: It might ignite. Slowly add tempered eggs; stirring constantly. Cook for an additional 30 minutes and then remove from heat. Strain through a sieve.

*Note: To temper eggs; Place eggs, in their shells, in hot tap water (approximately 120 degrees) for 2 minutes. Remove the eggs from water and crack them into a separate mixing bowl. Whisk the eggs.*

## SALSA MEXICAN RESTAURANT

### 6150 Poplar Avenue, Ste. 129
### Memphis, TN 38119

**Cesar N. Perra, Chef/Owner**

*Real Mexican food aficionados choose Salsa Cocina Mexicana. This popular upscale California-style East Memphis restaurant offers a variety of traditional entrées and new Southwestern seafood specials, plus the best salsa in the Mid-South! At Salsa, everything is made from scratch. Although Salsa offers the full range of Mexican specialties such as enchiladas, chimichangas, and fajitas, it also serves up several shrimp and red snapper entrées.*

## CARNE ASADA A LA TAMPIQUENA

| | | | |
|---|---|---|---|
| 4 | strips of tender steak (8 inches long, 2 inches wide and between ¼ and ½ inch thick) | 4 | ounces guacamole |
| 4 | enchilada sencillas (cheese enchiladas topped with enchilada sauce or salsa roja) | 8 | ounces refried beans |
| | | 4 | ounces lettuce garnish |

**To prepare the meat:** Open a 4-inch slice of filet to make a flat strip. Cut through the slice along the grain to within ½ inch of the underside. With a sharp knife open up each side, cutting the meat as if you were unrolling a jelly roll. Cut the meat in four 2-inch wide lengths. Flatten the meat a little with the side of a heavy cleaver. Season the meat well on both sides with salt, pepper and a splash of lime juice.

Sear the meat quickly on both sides on a very hot, well-greased iron griddle.

Cook to taste and serve immediately surrounded by enchiladas, guacamole, refried beans and enchiladas.

Serves 2.

## SOPA DE TORTILLA

This Mexican version of a tomato soup can be used as a first course or as a main course for a light meal. Serve the fried tortilla strips in a basket, the broth in a tureen and the cheese in a bowl. Allow guests to assemble their own soup.

| | | | |
|---|---|---|---|
| 6 | to 8 corn tortillas cut into ¼ inch strips | | Oil ¼ inch deep for frying |
| 3 | tablespoons oil | 8 | cups lightly seasoned chicken broth |
| ½ | onion, chopped | | |
| 2 | cloves of garlic, finely minced | ⅓ | cup fresh chopped cilantro |
| 1 | (28 ounce) can chopped tomatoes in juice | | Salt to taste |
| | | ½ | pound mild jack cheese, shredded |

Fry tortilla strips in hot oil (400 degrees F) until hardened but not brown. Drain on paper towel.

In a stockpot, heat 3 tablespoons oil, add onion and garlic. Cook onions until soft. Add puréed tomatoes and chicken stock and bring to boil. Reduce heat and simmer for 15 minutes. Add cilantro and salt to taste.

**To serve:** In bottom of each bowl, place a handful of prepared tortilla strips. Ladle the soup over strips and top with grated cheese.

*Note: Chopped avocado may be added for extra flavor.*

Serves 4 or more.

## BLUE MOON RESTAURANT & TROPICAL BAR

### 3092 Poplar Avenue
### Memphis, TN 38111

**John Pearson, Executive Chef**
*Chef Pearson started his culinary career with Ruby Tuesdays in 1982. After a stint as a caterer, he returned to the restaurant business and has worked for Squash Blossom, In Limbo, Café Society and recently for McEwen's as executive chef.*

## PAN-SEARED GROUPER WITH GEORGE DICKEL PEACH BEURRE BLANC, ARROZ ROJO & CREOLE RATATOUILLE

### GEORGE DICKEL PEACH BEURRE BLANC

| | | | |
|---|---|---|---|
| 4 | minced shallots | ½ | cup George Dickel |
| 2 | habaneros, minced | | whiskey |
| 15 | peaches, diced | 1 | quart cream |
| 2 | tablespoons peach preserves | | Butter |

**To make sauce:** In a saucepan, heat butter and sauté shallots and habaneros for about 60 seconds. Add peaches, toss for about 30 seconds, deglaze with most of the bourbon. Incorporate preserves and cream and reduce. Finish the sauce with remaining bourbon, softened butter and add salt and pepper.

### ARROZ ROJO

| | | | |
|---|---|---|---|
| 5 | hickory smoked Roma tomatoes | ½ | onion, chopped |
| | | | Minced garlic |
| 3 | roasted red bell peppers | 6 | cups basmati rice |
| | | 8 | cups chicken stock |
| 4 | ribs of celery, chopped | | Butter |

**To make rice:** In a rice pot, heat butter and sauté onions, celery and garlic for about 2 minutes. Add smoked tomatoes and roasted red peppers (which have been puréed). Add basmati rice, salt and pepper and stir for about 45 seconds. Add stock, bring to a simmer, cover and cook for 15 minutes.

### CREOLE RATATOUILLE

| | | | |
|---|---|---|---|
| 6 | zucchini, diced | 10 | Roma tomatoes, chopped |
| 1 | onion, chopped | | |
| 4 | ribs celery, chopped | | White wine |
| | | 3 | tablespoons parsley |
| | Garlic, minced | | Salt and pepper |
| 3 | jalapeños, minced | | Olive oil |

**To make ratatouille:** In a large sauté pan, heat olive oil, add onions, celery and bell pepper and cook for about 2 to 3 minutes. Add garlic, tomatoes and zucchini. Deglaze with wine and simmer for about 2 minutes. Garnish with parsley and salt and pepper.

| | |
|---|---|
| 6 | (8 ounce) fillets grouper with salt and pepper |

**To pan-sear grouper:** In a large sauté pan, heat butter until brown. Sear fish until brown crust is formed. Flip and deglaze with wine. Finish in oven – bake for 8 to 10 minutes. Serve grouper alongside the side of rice and ratatouille and nappe sauce over fish.

Serves 6.

## SAUTÉED SHRIMP IN HABANERO VANILLA CREAM

| | | | |
|---|---|---|---|
| 2 | minced shallots | 1 | pint heavy cream |
| 3 | habanero peppers, minced | 1 | pinch flour |
| 5 | vanilla beans | 4 | shrimp per person (peeled and deveined) |
| 1 | tablespoon honey | | |

**To make sauce:** Heat ½ tablespoon butter in a saucepan. Add shallots and habaneros for about 60 seconds. Add ½ tablespoon flour, stir and deglaze with wine. Add vanilla beans, cream and reduce to nappe (until it coats the back of a spoon). Remove beans and finish with the honey and a tiny pinch of salt and pepper.

**To sauté the shrimp:** In large sauté pan, heat butter, add shrimp and sauté until just done. Deglaze with wine and sauce and finish the sauce. Serve and nappe with sauce.

Serves 6.

## WILTED SALAD OF ARUGULA, SPINACH & MESCLUN GREENS WITH RED ONION, MUSHROOMS & CANDIED PECANS IN BETT'S VINAIGRETTE

Equal parts arugula, spinach and mesclun greens
1 red onion, thinly sliced
3 cups candied pecans

### CANDIED PECANS

In a large sauté pan, add ½ tablespoon of butter, turn on medium heat. Shake or stir to prevent burning. When the pecans turn slightly golden, add a tablespoon of sugar and incorporate to ensure even coating, toast, shake or stir for 60 seconds and then transfer to another bowl.

### BETT'S VINAIGRETTE

3 tablespoons chopped green onions
2 tablespoons chopped parsley
2 tablespoons chopped cilantro
4 cloves minced garlic
1 cup rice wine vinegar
12 juiced lemons
3 tablespoons Dijon mustard
Honey
Pinch salt and pepper
Olive oil

Add all ingredients into a food processor except for the olive oil. Emulsify all ingredients and drizzle oil while the machine is turning to the proper consistency.

**To make salad:** Place spinach, arugula and mesclun in a large bowl. In a large pan, sauté mushrooms in olive oil, add salt and pepper, red onion, pecans and vinaigrette. Pour mixture over greens, toss and serve immediately.

## CAFÉ SOCIETY
### 212 North Evergreen Memphis, TN 38112

**Michel Leny, Chef/Owner**
**Harvey Ingram, Chef**
**Tony Gault, Chef**
*Known for being one of Memphis' best-kept secrets, this upscale midtown neighborhood restaurant offers a new continental menu plus weekly specials. It features a full bar which offers 36 wines by the glass.*

## PORK & ONION CONFIT STUFFED MUSHROOMS

8 to 12 button mushrooms with stems removed and brush cleaned with cloth
½ pound ground pork
1 medium yellow onion, sliced
1 teaspoon cumin
1 teaspoon paprika
Pinch cayenne
Salt and pepper to taste
1 teaspoon fresh chopped rosemary
1 teaspoon fresh chopped thyme
1 teaspoon fresh chopped basil
2 tomatoes, chopped fine

Season pork with salt and pepper and brown. Drain some of the fat. Add sliced onions. Cook until tender over medium heat. Add tomatoes and the rest of the ingredients except the basil. Finish cooking for 10 to 15 minutes on low heat. Cool mixture completely. Pre-heat oven to 425 degrees. Stuff mushrooms with pork mixture. Place in oven for 15 to 20 minutes or until hot. Place on serving tray. Garnish with chopped basil.

Yield: 8 to 12 mushrooms

## ALMOND CRUSTED TUNA WITH HERB YOGURT SAUCE

| | | | |
|---|---|---|---|
| 4 | tuna steaks | 1 | teaspoon honey |
| 1 | (8 ounce) container plain yogurt | 2 | tablespoons of fresh chopped cilantro and basil |
| 1 | tablespoon red wine vinegar | 2 | cups peeled sliced almonds |
| 1 | tablespoon milk | | |

Preheat oven to 400 degrees. Season tuna on both sides with salt and pepper. Press almonds firmly into tuna. Sear in pan over medium-high with a little oil. When the almonds begin to brown, place in oven and continue cooking to desired doneness. Mix yogurt, red wine vinegar, salt and pepper to taste, and milk. Whisk together. Add fresh herbs. Place tuna on plate pouring yogurt sauce over ½ of tuna. Garnish with diced tomatoes.

Serves 4.

## CRÊPES WITH BANANAS & ICE CREAM

| | | | |
|---|---|---|---|
| 1 | teaspoon butter | 2 | bananas, sliced |
| 1 | tablespoon brown sugar | | Vanilla ice cream |

Melt butter over medium heat. Add bananas and brown sugar. Cook for 5 minutes or until sugar is dissolved. Fold crepe in half, spoon banana mixture over 1 side of folded crepe. Fold over and add a scoop of ice cream.

Serves 1.

## THE DELIBERATE LITERATE BOOKSTORE & CAFÉ

### *1997 Union Avenue Memphis, TN 38104*

**Sarah Hull, Chef/Owner**

*The Deliberate Literate offers a variety of gourmet foods including their famous grilled panini sandwich, soups and salads. They also offer a great selection of baked goods and coffee drinks.*

## CORN & POTATO CHOWDER

| | | | |
|---|---|---|---|
| 1 | cup chopped onion | 1 | (12 ounce) can evaporated milk |
| 2 | tablespoons butter | ¼ | cup cornstarch |
| 2 | cups chopped potatoes | ½ | cup water |
| 2 | cups chicken broth | 2 | tablespoons chopped parsley, for garnish |
| ½ | teaspoon salt | | |
| ¼ | teaspoon pepper | | |
| 2 | cups fresh corn kernels | | |

Sauté onion in butter in 4-quart stockpot until tender. Add potatoes, broth, salt and pepper and mix well. Simmer, covered, for 15 minutes or until potatoes are tender; remove from heat. Add corn and evaporated milk. Stir in mixture of cornstarch and water. Cook over medium heat until soup is thickened and corn is tender, stirring constantly. Garnish with parsley.

Serves 6.

## CHEESY ARTICHOKE & CHILI DIP

1 (14 ounce) can artichoke hearts
1 (4 ounce) can chopped green chilies
1 (4 ounce) can chopped black olives
1 cup mayonnaise
1 cup grated Parmesan cheese
1 cup shredded cheddar cheese

Drain and chop artichoke hearts. Mix with remaining ingredients except cheddar cheese in bowl. Spoon into a 10-inch quiche pan; sprinkle with cheddar cheese.

Bake at 350 degrees F for 20 minutes. Serve with tortilla chips or wheat thins.

Yield: 12 servings

## CRANBERRY ORANGE SCONES

2 cups plain flour
2 tablespoons sugar
2 teaspoons baking powder
½ teaspoon salt
¾ cup butter (no substitutes)
1½ cups dried cranberries
1 teaspoon fresh orange zest
½ to ¾ cup milk

Cut flour, sugar, baking powder, salt and butter with a pastry cutter until mixture resembles coarse meal. Stir in cranberries and orange zest. Add milk and stir just until moistened. Turn out onto floured board and knead 4 or 5 times. Roll out to ½-inch thickness and cut with 2-inch biscuit cutter. Bake on greased cookie sheet at 450 degrees F for 8 to 10 minutes or until lightly browned.

Yield: 2 dozen

## BOURBON-PECAN POUND CAKE

2 cups butter
3 cups sugar
8 large eggs, separated
2 teaspoons vanilla extract
2 teaspoons almond extract
¼ cup bourbon
3 cups all-purpose flour
2 cups chopped pecans

Preheat the oven to 300 degrees F. Line the bottom of a 10-inch tube pan with wax paper. Grease sides well. Cream the butter and sugar together. Add the egg yolks, 1 at a time, beating well after each addition. Mix extracts and bourbon. Alternately add the flour and the liquids. In another bowl, beat the egg whites until stiff, then fold into the batter. Sprinkle the bottom of the cake pan with ½ the pecans, then pour in the batter. Sprinkle the top of the batter with the remaining pecans. Bake for 1½ hours. Allow the cake to cool, then remove from pan. You may let it set for a day or two before serving.

*Note: This cake does not have a chemical leavening agent (baking powder or baking soda), therefore ingredients must be creamed well during preparation.*

Yield: One 10-inch pound cake (or 20 slices)

# KOTO

## 22 South Cooper
## Memphis, TN 38104

**Trey Allison, Executive Chef**
*Koto is the brainchild of Jimmy Ishii and Erling Jensen. It has been named "Best New Restaurant" by* **The Commercial Appeal** *and* **Memphis Magazine.** *It is known for its sophisticated East/West fusion cuisine. Koto blends European-style cooking techniques and presentations with traditional Japanese ingredients and flavorings.* **The Commercial Appeal** *awarded Koto its coveted 4-star rating in 1999.*

## RED PEPPER PAINTED SEA BASS WITH STIR-FRIED FENNEL, SHIITAKES & TRUFFLES

| | | | |
|---|---|---|---|
| 4 | (7 ounce) portions sea bass | 2 | cups julienne fresh fennel |
| 1 | tablespoon minced fresh garlic | 1 | cup sliced shiitake mushrooms |
| 1 | tablespoon minced fresh thyme and rosemary | 1 | ounce sliced truffles |
| | Salt and white pepper to taste | 3 | ounces truffle oil |
| | | 2 | tablespoons butter |
| | | 1½ | cups stock |

Season sea bass thoroughly with garlic, herbs and salt and pepper to taste. Using a ladle or squeeze bottle, carefully cover top of sea bass portions with red pepper coulis. Daub each top with small amount of butter. Add 1½ inches stock to pan – do not cover fish. Cook in 475 degree oven for 10 minutes. Bass should be cooked through and beginning to brown – additional time may be needed. Remove and keep warm when fully cooked. Heat truffle oil in sauté pan, add butter, fennel, shiitakes and sliced truffles. Sauté until fork tender and slightly browned. Season to taste with salt and pepper and serve immediately. Serves 4.

## RARE FENNEL GRILLED TUNA WITH CARROT-GINGER PATÉ & SAUTÉED SNOW PEAS

| | | | |
|---|---|---|---|
| | Sushi grade tuna in (4 ounce) portions, ⅕-2-inch thick | 5 | carrots, peeled and roughly chopped |
| | Fresh minced garlic | 1 | inch gingerroot, peeled and roughly chopped |
| | Fresh minced thyme | ½ | cup honey |
| | Ground fennel | 2 | cups olive oil or blended oil |
| ½ | cup olive oil or blended oil | 2 | cups trimmed snow peas, blanched |
| | Salt and pepper to taste | 1 | teaspoon butter |

Boil carrots, ginger and honey in 4 cups of water until fork tender. Strain and place carrot mixture in food processor with 2 cups oil. Purée for approximately five minutes, until very smooth. Strain mixture through very fine mesh sieve. Reserve paté mixture, and also oil, which should be bright orange. Drizzle tuna pieces with oil, season with salt and pepper, garlic, chopped thyme and ground fennel. Place on very hot grill for approximately two minutes on each side, until rare. On your plates, spoon carrot paté into small ramekin to mold and overturn onto each plate. Sauté the snowpeas in butter and season with salt and pepper, and then arrange around the paté. Place the tuna on the plate and drizzle around the plate with the carrot-ginger oil for color and taste.

## HEART OF ROMAINE SALAD WITH PLUM WINE VINAIGRETTE & GORGONZOLA

| | |
|---|---|
| Chopped romaine hearts | Pickled ginger (optional) |
| Gorgonzola, crumbled | Plum wine vinaigrette |

**For Vinaigrette:** Reduce 1 bottle plum wine to ⅓. Should equal approximately 1½ cups of wine reduction. Purée in blender or food processor with ¾ cup rice wine vinegar. Slowly and in a steady stream, add 2½ cups blended olive oil to mixture.

Toss romaine hearts with vinaigrette in a large bowl until thoroughly coated. Place on individual salad plates and dress with crumbled Gorgonzola. Garnish with pickled ginger and edible flowers if desired.

# LA TOURELLE

## 2146 Monroe Avenue
## Memphis, TN 38104

**Glenn & Martha Hays, owners**
*La Tourelle serves French cuisine with an emphasis on fresh seafood. The menu changes seasonally. La Tourelle has received DiRoNa awards since 1993. It was awarded a 3-star rating in the **Mobil Guide** and was recognized for its "Outstanding Wine List" in **The Wine Spectator**. It was rated the "Best French/ Continental" by **Memphis Magazine**'s reader's poll in 1997 & 1999.*

**Ralph McCormick, Executive Chef**
*Chef Ralph is a graduate of LeMaison Meridian Culinary School. He has worked for 3½ years at La Tourelle and trained under Lynn Kennedy-Tilyou C.C.S. for 2½ years.*

## BEER BATTERED FRIED OYSTERS WITH ARUGULA & HORSERADISH AIOLI

*(Appetizer)*

### BEER EGGWASH:

| | | | |
|---|---|---|---|
| 1 | (12 ounce) beer | 6 | eggs |

Combine and mix well.

### CORNMEAL MIXTURE

| | | | |
|---|---|---|---|
| 1 | cup cornmeal | 1 | tablespoon |
| 3 | cups all-purpose flour | | paprika |
| 2 | tablespoons ancho powder | 2 | tablespoons salt |

Combine and mix well.

### HORSERADISH AIOLI

| | | | |
|---|---|---|---|
| 1 | cup mayonnaise | 2 | tablespoons |
| ½ | tablespoon finely chopped garlic | | lemon juice |
| ¼ | cup prepared horseradish | | Salt and pepper to taste |

Combine all ingredients and mix well.

| | |
|---|---|
| 20 | oysters (5 per person) |

Once you have combined the beer egg wash, add oysters to this mix and soak oysters for 1 hour. Then add the oysters to the cornmeal mix and coat liberally. Remove from cornmeal and let sit for 2 minutes. Deep fry at 350 degrees until oysters float.

**To assemble plate:** Take a small handful of arugula and place it in the center of the plate. Arrange oysters around arugula. Drizzle horseradish aioli over all and serve.

Serves 4.

*Note: Store-bought pre-shucked oysters work fine for this dish.*

## CHOCOLATE CRUSTED MASCARPONE CHEESECAKE

### FOR THE CRUST

15 Oreo cookies – finely ground in food processor. Add ¼ cup melted butter to ground cookies to the point that when grasped in hand, the crust holds together. Press this mix into bottom of 9-inch spring-form pan and bake at 350 degrees for 10 minutes. Set aside to cool.

### FOR THE FILLING

| | | | |
|---|---|---|---|
| 2 | pounds cream cheese | 1¼ | cups sugar |
| ½ | pound mascarpone | 2 | large eggs |

Take the cream cheese and the mascarpone and put in bowl of electric mixer with the paddle attachment. On medium speed beat until smooth and slowly add sugar until cheese and sugar mixture is smooth and not grainy. Add eggs 1 at a time and continue to mix 3 to 4 minutes. Pour batter on cooled crust and bake at 300 degrees with a pan of hot water in bottom of oven. This will stop the cheesecake from cracking and a crust forming on top. Bake for approximately 60 minutes. Center of cake will be slightly loose. This is okay. Pull out of oven and cool 30 minutes then refrigerate for several hours until cold. Do not try and slice while still warm.

Serves 10 to 12.

## OVEN ROASTED SEA BASS ON ASPARAGUS RISOTTO WITH CITRUS DIJON CREAM SAUCE

### SEABASS

| | | |
|---|---|---|
| 4 | (6 ounce) fillets coated with garlic, chopped fine | Olive oil Salt and pepper |

Roast for 8 to 10 minutes at 475 degrees.

### CITRUS DIJON CREAM SAUCE

| | | | |
|---|---|---|---|
| 2 | shallots, chopped fine | 1 | tablespoon Dijon mustard |
| 1 | tablespoon chopped garlic | 1 | cup fresh orange juice |

Combine all ingredients and simmer till almost all the liquid is evaporated. Add 2 cups of heavy cream and simmer till it is reduced by half, strain liquid and reserve in warm place.

### ASPARAGUS RISOTTO

| | | | |
|---|---|---|---|
| 1 | cup arborio rice | 1 | tablespoon olive oil |
| ½ | sweet yellow onion | | |
| 6 | asparagus spears, sliced thin | 2 | cans store-bought chicken broth |

In a 2-quart pan, add oil and heat on medium till hot. Add onion and cook until tender but not browned. Add rice and stir to coat grains with oil and cook for 3 to 4 minutes. Add approximately ½ cup chicken broth and simmer until all liquid is absorbed and repeat this process about 3 to 4 times stirring frequently till rice is cooked to desired doneness. Add salt and pepper (to taste), chopped asparagus and 3 ounces of heavy cream. Cook until hot and creamy.

**To assemble:** Place asparagus risotto on center of plate and arrange sea bass on top, pour citrus Dijon cream around plate and garnish with chopped chives.

Serves 4.

---

## MARENA'S
### *1545 Overton Park Avenue Memphis, TN 38112*

**Rena & Jack Franklin, Chef/Owners**
*Award-winning restaurant features authentic foods of the Mediterranean with a changing menu monthly to spotlight two different countries – one from each side of the Mediterranean shores. All four of the recipes listed below are from the Morgan Keegan Executive Dining Room Cookbook by Rena Franklin.*

## CRABMEAT CHOWDER

| | | | |
|---|---|---|---|
| 1 | cup leeks, chopped and washed | 2 | teaspoons dried basil |
| ⅓ | cup olive oil | 1 | teaspoon dried thyme |
| 1 | cup chopped onions | 10 | ounces peas |
| 1 | cup chopped celery | | Salt and pepper to taste |
| 4 | cups chicken stock or broth | ½ | pound crab meat |
| 1 | (28 ounce) can Italian tomatoes with liquid | ⅓ | cup Amontillado sherry |
| 2 | cups white fish stock or bottled clam juice | | |

Heat ⅓ cup of olive oil. Add leeks, onions and celery. Cook over low heat for 30 minutes. Add chicken stock, Italian tomatoes with liquid, fish stock, basil and thyme. Simmer for 1 hour and 15 minutes. Add peas and salt and pepper. Simmer until peas are just tender. Stir in crab meat and sherry. Simmer 5 minutes or until desired serving temperature.

Serves 8.

## ITALIAN STYLE DRESSING
*(New York Style)*

| | |
|---|---|
| 1 cup olive oil | 1½ teaspoons Worcestershire sauce |
| ½ cup red wine vinegar | |
| 2 tablespoons lemon juice | 2 tablespoons grated Parmesan |
| 1½ teaspoons salt | ½ teaspoon dried oregano |
| ¼ to ½ teaspoon pepper | ½ to 1 teaspoon dried sweet basil |
| 1½ teaspoons dry mustard | |

Blend all of the above ingredients together in a blender jar for 1 minute. Use on any lettuce you like, but it is especially good on romaine.

## CHOCOLATE MERINGUE

| | |
|---|---|
| ¾ cup confectioner's sugar | 1 tablespoon butter |
| ⅔ cup cocoa | 3½ tablespoons sugar |
| 1½ teaspoons ground cinnamon | 1½ cup heavy cream |
| 6 egg whites | 2 tablespoons Oloroso sherry |
| 4 to 6 ounces of semi-sweet chocolate | |

**For the meringue:** Stir together confectioner's sugar, cocoa and ground cinnamon. Beat until stiff the egg whites. Fold 2 mixtures together gently but thoroughly. Spoon into a 3-cup buttered ring mold. Place mold in a pan of hot water that comes ½-way up the sides of the mold. Bake in 325 degree F oven for 45 minutes. Remove pan from water and cool to room temperature. Unmold and cut into 6 portions.

Put on a serving plate the chocolate sauce (recipe below). Lay a serving of the meringue on the sauce. Pipe on the meringue in a ribbon, a portion of sherry flavored whipped cream (recipe below).

**For the chocolate sauce:** Melt and cook together very gently semi-sweet chocolate, butter and 1 cup of heavy cream. It should not be too thick. Add more heavy cream to thin.

**Sherry flavored whipped cream:** In a chilled mixing bowl beat until stiff 1½ cups heavy cream, 1½ tablespoons sugar and sherry.

Serves 6.

## STUFFED PORK TENDERLOIN WITH SCALLION SAUCE

| | |
|---|---|
| 2 cups chopped scallions | 3 to 4 eggs |
| 1¼ to 1½ cups chicken broth | 6 tablespoons grated Parmesan cheese |
| 2 teaspoons pepper | 3 cloves garlic, crushed |
| 2 teaspoons cornstarch | 4 tablespoons minced parsley |
| 2 tablespoons butter | 1 teaspoon salt |
| 6 thin slices stale bread | ¼ to ½ teaspoon pepper |
| ½ to ¾ cup milk | 2 ¾ to 1 pound pork tenderloins |
| 1½ pounds chopped or ground veal | Whole green beans |

**For the sauce:** In blender mix scallions, chicken broth, 2 teaspoons pepper and cornstarch. Put in a pot and bring to a boil. Simmer for 10 to 15 minutes. Strain, using the bottom of a soup ladle to press out all the liquid through the mesh. Return to pot and add butter. Set aside.

**For the stuffing:** Soak for 5 minutes bread and milk. Squeeze and discard any hard pieces.

**Combine in a bowl:** Chopped veal, eggs, Parmesan cheese, garlic, parsley, 1 teaspoon salt and ¼ to ½ teaspoon pepper and soaked bread. Knead with your hands to mix and stiffen the mixture.

Trim, cutting away any fat, 2 to 3 inches of the flat tail, and the shiny "skin" of the top side of the meat from the pork tenderloins. Cut each one open lengthwise, leaving the 2 pieces attached. Cover with waxed paper and pound each side to flatten as much as possible without tearing the meat. Place on each tenderloin, down the middle an equal amount of stuffing. Roll the sides of the meat around the filling to enclose it. Lay on a buttered foil-lined 10 by 15-inch shallow pan in two places 2 to 3 slices of bacon. Set the stuffed tenderloins cut-side down on the bacon. Cover each tenderloin lengthwise with 2 to 3 slices of bacon.

Roast at 400 degree F for 30 minutes; bacon should be crisping at edges. Remove and discard bacon. Cut each tenderloin into ½-inch slices. Put on each plate a pool of sauce. Lay on the sauce portioned slices of the meat. Serve garnished with buttered whole green beans and sprinkle with minced parsley.

Serves 8.

# MELANGE

## 948 South Cooper
## Memphis, TN 38104

**Scott Lenhart, Chef/Owner**
**David Nestler, Operating Manager/Owner**
*Jimmy Ishii, Scott Lenhart and David Nestler joined forces to open the restaurant. They chose the name Melange to reflect their dual plans for the facility. On the restaurant side, they provide their patrons with fine dining – American-French fusion cuisine, while an upscale bar serves tapas (little plates of food but not in the Spanish tradition).*

## CHILLED PURÉE OF CUCUMBER SOUP WITH SEARED SCALLOPS

| | | | |
|---|---|---|---|
| 3 | European cucumbers, ½ peeled | | Pinch nutmeg |
| ¼ | cup dry vermouth | 1 | tablespoon fresh chopped dill |
| 2 | cloves garlic, minced | 1 | tablespoon fresh chopped fennel tops |
| 1 | medium Vidalia onion, diced | ½ | yellow bell pepper, diced |
| 2 | cups light white fish broth | ½ | red bell pepper, diced |
| 6 | medium-large scallops | | Salt to taste |
| ¼ | teaspoon white pepper | ½ | cup olive oil |

Sauté onion, garlic and ½ of the cucumber in a bit of olive oil. When translucent, add vermouth, fish broth and simmer for about 10 minutes. Chill. Add the rest of the cucumber, white pepper, salt and nutmeg and purée thoroughly. Strain and drizzle in olive oil. Add herbs and peppers and allow to chill overnight. Season sea scallops with salt and pepper and sear. Serve sea scallops at room temperature atop the soup.
Serves 6.

# ROASTED PORK TENDERLOIN

| | | | |
|---|---|---|---|
| 3 | trimmed pork tenderloins | 1 | fresh serrano pepper, puréed |
| 1 | cup fond de veau (veal stock) | ½ | cup dry white wine |
| 1 | tablespoon fresh thyme, chopped | 1 | teaspoon turmeric |
| ½ | stick fresh lemongrass, chopped | ¼ | teaspoon white pepper |
| | | | Salt to taste |
| | | 2 | tablespoons butter |

Marinate pork in soy, honey and chopped serrano pepper for at least 8 hours, but no more than 18 hours. Sear pork in a small amount of oil until all sides are lightly caramelized. Remove from pan and roast in the oven at about 350 F. Deglaze sauté pan with white wine, fond de veau and ⅓ of the marinade and reduce to about 1½ cups. Add spices, lemongrass and thyme and allow to steep for 5 minutes like a tea. Strain sauce, reheat and mount with butter. Season to taste. Remove pork from oven when about medium and slice thin. Use small amounts of the sauce to complement the pork. This dish serves well with sweet potatoes, rice and most vegetables from the cabbage family like kohlrabi, broccoli, rapini and cauliflower.
Serves 6.

*The Fontaine House*

## FROZEN ORANGE SOUFFLÉS WITH BERRY BROTH

### SOUFFLÉS

| | | | |
|---|---|---|---|
| 3 | cups heavy cream | ½ | cup finely chopped quality chocolate |
| 4 | eggs, separated Zest of 3 oranges and juiced | 4 | tablespoons butter at room temperature |
| ¼ | cup Grand Marnier | | |
| ¾ | cup sugar | | |

Line soufflé dish with a round 5-inch tall parchment or wax paper, buttered very well. Whip cream to a medium peak and set aside. In a double boiler, whip egg yolks, sugar, Grand Marnier and orange juice until frothy and lemony looking and continue whipping off the heat until cool. Add orange zest. Whip egg whites to a medium peak and set aside. Add whipped cream to yolk mixture. Fold in chocolate and egg whites and pour into soufflé dishes. Freeze.

### BERRY BROTH

| | | | |
|---|---|---|---|
| 2 | cups water | ½ | pint raspberries |
| 1 | cup sugar | ½ | pint blueberries |
| ½ | cup Cointreau | 1 | green apple unpeeled, sliced thinly |
| ¼ | cup Kirsch (cherry) | | |

Bring water and sugar to a boil and chill thoroughly. Add the rest of the ingredients and allow to sit refrigerated overnight. Remove soufflé from the dishes and serve over broth.

Serves 6.

## PAULETTE'S
### *2110 Madison Avenue Memphis, TN 38104*

*1999 Memphis Magazine poll honored Paulette's as the silver award winner in the "Best Restaurant in Memphis" category. Paulette's also ranked among the top 3 in five other categories. Trailed only Corky's and Rendezvous as the "Best Place to Take Out-of-Towners."*

## FILET PAULETTE

| | | | |
|---|---|---|---|
| 2 | (4 ounce) filets | 2 | teaspoons black pepper, course ground |
| 6 | ounces onions, julienne cut | ½ | cup heavy cream (36%) |
| 6 | ounces bell peppers, julienne cut | ½ | ounce Worcestershire sauce |
| 4 | ounces tomatoes, julienne cut | 1 | ounce white wine |

Coat both sides of filets with black pepper. Sauté in a skillet in hot butter until cooked to desired temperature, then remove. In the same pan, sauté onion and bell pepper until tender (add more butter if necessary. Add white wine, Worcestershire sauce and heavy cream. Reduce sauce until slightly thickened. Return filets to sauce. Cook for 1 more minute. Remove filets and top with vegetables. Pour cream sauce over all. Top with julienne tomatoes.

Serves 1.

*Rhodes College*

## KAHLUA MOCHA PARFAIT PIE (K-PIE)

### COCONUT PECAN CRUST

| 2 | pounds, 3 ounces coconut flakes | 10 | tablespoons all-purpose flour |
| 2½ | cups salted butter | 1 | pound, 4 ounces pecans, grated |

Melt butter completely in separate pan on stove. Combine coconut, flour and pecans in large bowl. Add melted butter and mix well until all dry ingredients are wet. Press out coconut mixture into 10-inch metal pie shell. Pack crust into sides and bottom corners of pie tin. Be sure crust is level with pie tin at sides to prevent burning when cooked. Crust mixture should be evenly distributed over pie tin. Bake in 325 degree (F) oven until golden brown color results. Cool baked crust completely prior to filling. Crust may be frozen until needed.

**Filling:** Pack crust with 6 pounds of Angel Food Coffee Chip ice cream, forming a large, rounded pie. Refreeze.

**Point of Sale:** Cut K-Pie into 8 equal parts. Place 1 slice of K-Pie upright on a 9-inch clear thumbprint plate. Top with 1 heaping tablespoon of whipped cream and 1 tablespoon of chocolate shavings. Serve with 1 ounce of Kahlua in cordial glass on side. Serves 8.

## THE UNIVERSITY CLUB
### 1346 Central Avenue Memphis, TN 38104

**Stan Gibson, Chef**
*Stan Gibson has worked for 10 years as the chef of the University Club. Chef Gibson has worked with the likes of Jammie Shannon, Charlie Trotter and a collection of local chefs.*
*A member of the James Beard Foundation, he has organized events for the Foundation in Memphis and in New York City. His list of supported charities include Share Our Strength, United Cerebral Palsy, March of Dimes and Youth Villages. He also travels the nation competing in ice carving competitions as a hobby.*

## UNIVERSITY CLUB FRIED CHICKEN

| 2 | chickens (cut up), about 16 pieces | 3 | eggs |
| | | 3 | quarts of ice water |

### FLOUR MIXTURE

| 2 | quarts all-purpose flour | 2 | tablespoons white pepper |
| 3 | tablespoons kosher salt | 1 | tablespoon poultry seasoning |

Wash cut-up chicken and let soak in ice water with the eggs. Sift all the dry ingredients together. Heat deep fryer with vegetable oil to exactly 350 degrees. Dredge chicken in flour mixture, shaking off all excess flour and deep fry for 12 minutes or till chicken begins to float in the deep fryer. Let rest for 5 minutes and serve.

Yield: 16 pieces

## KENNY'S CORNBREAD

| | | | |
|---|---|---|---|
| 3½ | cups self-rising white cornmeal | 1 | tablespoon baking powder |
| ½ | cup flour | 6 | eggs |
| ½ | cup sugar | 4 | cups buttermilk |
| | | ½ | cup melted butter |

Combine all ingredients and portion into heated muffin cups that have been oiled with a little butter or bacon drippings. Bake for 12 to 15 minutes at 375 degrees.

Yield: 24 muffins

## STONE GROUND CORNMEAL CRUSTED CATFISH WITH CRAWFISH HOPPIN' JOHN & CRAWFISH BUTTER

| | | | |
|---|---|---|---|
| 6 | (6 ounce) filets of catfish | 2 | cups ice water |
| 2 | eggs | | |

### CORNMEAL BREADING

| | | | |
|---|---|---|---|
| 2 | cups stone ground cornmeal | 1 | tablespoon Creole seasoning |
| 2 | cups cracker meal | | |

### HOPPIN' JOHN INGREDIENTS

| | | | |
|---|---|---|---|
| 12 | ounces fresh or frozen purple hull peas | 3 | ounces butter or bacon drippings |
| 1 | bell pepper, diced | 6 | cups chicken stock |
| 1 | medium onion, diced | 2 | tablespoons Creole seasoning |
| 1 | crushed clove garlic | 1 | cup rice |
| | | ½ | pound crawfish tail meat |

### CRAWFISH BUTTER

| | | | |
|---|---|---|---|
| ¾ | stick butter | 3 | tablespoons chopped tomato |
| ½ | pound crawfish tail meat | 2 | tablespoons chopped parsley |
| | Dash of Creole seasoning | | |

**To prepare the catfish cakes:** Bread by putting the catfish in a eggwash made with the eggs and the ice water. Mix the cornmeal ingredients together and dredge the catfish filets in the mixture. Pan sear in hot vegetable oil or olive oil on both sides till golden brown and reserve on a sheet pan.

**To prepare the Hoppin' John:** Sauté with onion, bell pepper and garlic in the butter or bacon drippings until tender and add the chicken stock, Creole seasoning and the purple hull peas. Simmer for 30 minutes or till the peas start to get tender. Adjust seasoning with salt and pepper if necessary. Add rice and crawfish tail meat and simmer till the rice has bloomed and is tender about 15 minutes. Add a little water if necessary.

**To prepare the crawfish butter:** Add all the ingredients in a food processor and pulse till roughly incorporated.

**To assemble:** Bake the catfish at 350 degrees for about 12 minutes till crispy and the filets are tender. Place a generous amount of the Hoppin' John on a warm plate or platter. Top with the catfish and garnish with the crawfish butter on top. Serves 6.

## BANANA BREAD PUDDING WITH BANANA CARAMEL SAUCE

| | | | |
|---|---|---|---|
| 1½ | cups baguette bread (day old and cut into cubes) | 4 | egg yolks |
| | | ½ | cup sugar |
| 2 | chopped fresh banana | 1 | tablespoon vanilla |
| | | 1 | tablespoon banana liqueur |
| ½ | cup chopped walnuts | 1 | tablespoon dark rum |
| 2 | cups heavy cream | | |

### BANANA CARAMEL SAUCE

| | | | |
|---|---|---|---|
| ¼ | pound brown sugar | 3 | tablespoons dark rum |
| ½ | stick butter | 3 | tablespoons heavy cream |
| 1 | chopped banana | | |
| 1 | tablespoon banana liqueur | | |

In a large bowl, mix the bread cubes, banana and walnuts. In another bowl, combine the egg yolks, sugar, vanilla, banana liqueur and the rum. Heat the cream to a simmer and pour while whisking into the yolk mixture. Divide into 6 large individual soufflé cups and bake for 35 minutes at 325 degrees till golden and well set.

**To prepare the banana caramel sauce:** Melt the butter in a saucepot and combine with the brown sugar and the chopped banana. Heat till well combined and the sugar starts to caramelize. Flambé with the banana liqueur and the rum and then add the heavy cream to fatten and smooth the sauce.

Serve the bread pudding hot from the oven and serve with a generous amount of caramel sauce on the side. Serves 6.

# TSUNAMI

## 928 South Cooper Street
## Memphis, TN 38104

**Ben Smith, Chef/Owner**
**Colleen Smith, General Manager**
*Tsunami is a Pacific Rim restaurant specializing in seafood with a strong Asian influence. It is one of the most innovative restaurants in the area. In **Memphis Magazine**'s readers survey for 1999 Tsunami was voted the Best New Restaurant for 1999. This year, in **Memphis Magazine** it garnered one of the top two awards for "Best Seafood" in the reader's poll! Tsunami has a full bar and a well-rounded wine list that complements the cuisine.*

## TUNA TARTARE WITH WASABI VINAIGRETTE

| | | | |
|---|---|---|---|
| 1 | pound very fresh, sushi grade tuna | ½ | teaspoon crushed red pepper |
| 2 | cucumbers, peeled, scooped of seeds and diced (about 1 cup) | | Juice of one lemon Thinly sliced cucumber rounds for garnish |
| ½ | cup diced red onion | | Toasted sesame seeds for garnish |
| 3 | tablespoons soy sauce | | Wasabi vinaigrette (recipe below) |
| 1 | teaspoon sesame oil | | |

Trim any skin and/or nerves from the tuna (the nerves are white and stringy) Dice and set aside in the refrigerator. Put the diced cucumber, red onion, soy sauce, sesame oil, crushed red pepper, and lemon juice in a stainless steel bowl and mix well. Add tuna to mixture and mix well.

Serve immediately on chilled plates streaked with wasabi vinaigrette and garnished with cucumber slices and toasted sesame seeds.

### WASABI VINAIGRETTE

| | | | |
|---|---|---|---|
| 1 | teaspoon fresh garlic, chopped | ½ | cup wasabi paste |
| 1 | tablespoon fresh ginger, chopped | ¼ | cup soy sauce |
| ¼ | cup rice wine vinegar | 2 | tablespoons sesame oil |
| | | 1 | teaspoon salt |
| | | 2 | cups olive oil |

Mix together garlic, ginger, rice wine vinegar, wasabi paste, soy sauce, sesame oil and salt in a stainless steel bowl. Gradually whisk in olive oil in a thin, steady stream until all oil is incorporated.

Serves 8 as appetizer.

## SALMON WITH SOY BEURRE BLANC SAUCE

| | | |
|---|---|---|
| 8 | (8 ounce) portions of salmon fillets | Kosher salt Ground black pepper |
| 1 | ounce olive oil, plain | |

Season salmon fillets lightly with salt and pepper. Preheat a 12-inch skillet until a drop of water "dances" on surface. Add olive oil, then salmon fillets seasoned side down first. Cook until golden brown on top, turn over and cook to desired doneness. Serve on bed of rice with 2 ounces of soy beurre blanc (recipe follows).

### SOY BEURRE BLANC

| | | | |
|---|---|---|---|
| 1 | tablespoon fresh chopped ginger | | Mushroom soy sauce, to taste |
| ½ | cup sake | ½ | pound unsalted butter, chilled |
| ¼ | cup heavy whipping cream | | |

Place ginger and sake in medium saucepan. Bring to boil, reduce to a simmer and cook until sake is nearly evaporated. Add the heavy whipping cream and continue simmering until cream is reduced by ½. While cream is simmering, begin to whisk in pieces of butter 1 tablespoon at a time. Add mushroom soy sauce to taste and keep warm until ready to serve.

Serves 8.

## SAKE STEAMED MUSSELS IN THAI RED CURRY SAUCE

| | | | |
|---|---|---|---|
| 4 | pounds fresh black mussels | | Red Thai curry sauce |
| 1 | cup sake | | Fresh chopped chives for garnish |

Rinse mussels thoroughly with plenty of cold, running water. Remove any beards and discard any mussels that won't close with a little prodding. Place mussels and sake in a large saucepan with a tight fitting lid.

Place over high heat and allow to steam until mussels open. Discard any unopened mussels. Gently strain off liquid and place mussels on a pre-heated platter or in individual warm bowls. Top with Thai red curry sauce, garnish with chopped chives and serve immediately.

### FOR THE THAI RED CURRY SAUCE

| | | | |
|---|---|---|---|
| 1 | can coconut milk (13.5 ounces) | 2 | tablespoons fresh ginger, chopped fine |
| ½ | cup lemon grass, chopped fine | 2 | tablespoons Thai red curry paste |
| 3 | leaves fresh basil | | |
| ½ | cup brown sugar | | |
| 2 | teaspoons fish sauce | | |

Place coconut milk, lemon grass, basil, brown sugar, fish sauce and ginger in a tall, heavy saucepan. (Coconut milk will expand and boil over if you are not careful.) Bring to a boil, stirring until sugar dissolves. Reduce to simmer and cook until half of its original volume. Whisk in Thai curry paste and cook an additional 5 minutes.

Serves 8 as appetizer.

## WOMAN'S EXCHANGE OF MEMPHIS, INC.

### 88 Racine Street Memphis, TN 38111

*The Woman's Exchange of Memphis is a non-profit community service organization whose motto is "Helping Others to Help Themselves." Founded in 1885 as the Crafts Exchange, the name was changed to The Woman's Exchange in 1935 and it has continued to grow, offering unique handmade items from more than 400 consignors.*

*The present location at 88 Racine Street was constructed in the early 1960s and the Tea Room was opened there in 1962. Our chef, Rev. Emmanuel Bailey, is a native Memphian, who came to us in 1992. He formerly worked at the University Club and at Doe's in Memphis. He is the pastor of a church in Arkansas.*

*The Woman's Exchange has been featured in **Southern Living, Creative Needle** and **Memphis Magazines**. The Woman's Exchange is open Monday through Friday and serves lunch daily.*

## TOMATO DILL SOUP

| | | | |
|---|---|---|---|
| 1 | (46 ounce) can tomato juice | 1½ | sticks butter |
| ½ | cup (dry) non-dairy creamer | 2 | tablespoons dill |
| | | ½ | teaspoon salt |

Simmer for at least 1 hour.

Serves 6 to 8.

## SWISS CHEESE, BELL PEPPER & BACON SANDWICH

| | |
|---|---|
| ½ | pound block Swiss cheese, shredded |
| ¼ | pound block mild cheddar cheese, shredded |
| ½ | pound bacon, cooked crisp |
| ⅓ | bell pepper, minced |
| ½ | cup mayonnaise Dash Worcestershire sauce Dash Tabasco sauce |

Chop bacon. Combine all the ingredients. Serve on bread of choice. Also great grilled or as an open-faced sandwich on English muffins or bread and broiled until cheese melts and begins to brown.

Makes about 8 sandwiches.

## BEEF TENDERLOIN

| | | |
|---|---|---|
| 1 | whole beef tenderloin (5 pounds when trimmed), at room temperature | Seasoned salt Black pepper Raw bacon |

Preheat oven to 350 degrees. Season tenderloin liberally with seasoned salt and black pepper. Cover the top and sides with raw bacon. Bake in preheated oven for 45 minutes. It will be well done on the small end and rare at the large end. The bacon will not be crisp, and will need to be removed before serving. Slice thinly and serve with Horseradish Sauce (see recipe below).

*A five-pound tenderloin will serve 10 people, generously for dinner and more when it is thinly sliced and served for a cocktail buffet.*

## HORSERADISH SAUCE

| | | |
|---|---|---|
| ½ | cup sour cream | |
| ½ | cup mayonnaise | |
| 1 | teaspoon horseradish (or more, to taste) | 1 teaspoon Worcestershire sauce |

Combine and chill several hours. Serve with beef tenderloin. Great used as a sauce in tearoom rolls with a slice of tenderloin. Serves 8 or more.

## CARAMEL BROWNIES

| | | | |
|---|---|---|---|
| 1 | box light brown sugar | 1 | teaspoon baking powder |
| 1 | stick butter, softened | ½ | teaspoon salt |
| 3 | eggs | 1 | teaspoon vanilla |
| 1½ | cups all-purpose flour | 1½ | cups pecans or walnuts, chopped |

Blend butter and sugar. Add eggs and beat well. Add remainder of ingredients, mixing well. Pour into greased 9x13-inch pan. Bake at 325 degrees for 30 minutes. Top with Brown Sugar Icing (below).

Yield: 18 to 20 pieces.

## BROWN SUGAR ICING

| | | | |
|---|---|---|---|
| ¾ | cup light brown sugar | 2¼ | teaspoons dark corn syrup |
| ⅔ | cup white sugar, granulated | ½ | cup heavy cream |
| | | ¼ | cup butter |

Mix all ingredients together and bring to a boil. Cook for 15 to 20 minutes to a soft ball stage (230 degrees on a candy thermometer). Stir several times. Pour over cool caramel brownies. Allow to cool before cutting. Covers 1 pan of brownies.

*Woman's Exchange of Memphis*

## CHEZ PHILIPPE
### PEABODY HOTEL

### 149 Union Avenue
### Memphis, TN 38103

**Master Chef José Gutierrez**

*Chef Gutierrez is an internationally renowned chef, with accolades from **Esquire Magazine** praising him as "one of the best chefs in the South in every respect," AAA honoring his restaurant, Chez Philippe, with a Four-Diamond rating for 10 years and **Memphis Magazine's** Reader's Poll naming his restaurant the "Best Restaurant in Memphis" for nine years." At Chez Philippe, where he has been executive chef since 1983, Chef José has set a culinary precedent with his unique marriage of the best of Southern cuisine with that from the south of France. A highlight of his culinary experience was working under the direction of one of France's most famous chefs, Chef Paul Bocuse, creator of Nouvelle cuisine. Perhaps the single greatest achievement in his career so far was his designation as a Master Chef of France in 1995. In addition to being featured in newspapers and magazines across the country, he has appeared on CNN, the Television Food Network and was selected for the Great Chefs series on the Discovery Channel in 1995.*

## LENTIL SOUP

| | | | |
|---|---|---|---|
| 1 | cup black lentils | ¼ | cup onion |
| ¾ | cup diced carrots | 1 | teaspoon chopped garlic |
| 4 | slices bacon, cut julienne | 1 | bouquet garni |
| ¾ | cup diced celery | 2½ | cups vegetable stock or water |
| ¾ | cup diced red pepper | 8 | ounces grilled chorizo |
| ¾ | cup diced potato | | |

Sauté the bacon until crisp, add the onion and garlic. Cook for 3 minutes. Add the blanched lentils. Add the liquid then the carrot, bell pepper, potato, celery and the bouquet garni. Add the grilled Spanish chorizo. Cook for 10 to 15 minutes and serve hot. Serves 6 to 8.

## ROAST VEAL LOIN "GRANDMA STYLE"

| | | | |
|---|---|---|---|
| 1 | pound veal loin | 2 | tablespoons of mixed herbs mixed with ⅓ cup of bread crumbs (thyme, chives, parsley, rosemary) |
| 1 | tablespoon peanut oil | | |
| | Salt and pepper to taste | | |
| 1 | tablespoon whole grain mustard | | |

Roast the loin with the peanut oil, season with salt and pepper to taste and then cook in the oven until medium. Let it rest 10 minutes. Brush the veal with mustard and bread with the herb crumbs. Set aside.

### SAUCE

| | | | |
|---|---|---|---|
| ½ | cup sliced shallots | 1 | bay leaf |
| 1 | tablespoon chopped garlic | 1 | cup red wine |
| 2 | sprigs fresh thyme | ½ | cup veal stock |
| | | ⅓ | cup unsalted butter |

Reduce together by ½ the red wine, shallots, garlic, thyme and bay leaf. Add the veal stock and let it cook for 10 more minutes. Whisk in the butter and set aside.

### VEGETABLES

| | | | |
|---|---|---|---|
| ½ | sliced savoy cabbage | 3 | slices of bacon |
| ⅓ | cup butter | | Salt |

Sauté the bacon in butter until crisp. Add the cabbage and salt. Cook until soft. Set aside.

### MASHED POTATOES

| | | | |
|---|---|---|---|
| 2 | large potatoes | 3 | tablespoons roasted bell pepper purée |
| 1 | tablespoon butter | | |
| ⅓ | cup of boiling milk | | |

Boil the potatoes until tender. Drain and put back in the pot. Add the milk, butter, salt and the pepper purée. Mash and set aside.

### MUSHROOMS

| | | | |
|---|---|---|---|
| ¾ | cup of sliced mushrooms | 2 | tablespoons peanut oil |
| | | | Salt |

Sauté the mushrooms in hot butter, add salt and set aside.

**Presentation:** In the middle of the plate, place the mashed potatoes. Place the cabbage on top of the potatoes and then place the mushrooms and the sauce around. Cut the veal and place 1 slice on top. Serve hot. Serves 4.

## ORANGE CRÈME BRÛLÉE WITH TANGERINE & COINTREAU

| | | | |
|---|---|---|---|
| 2 | cups half-and-half | 5 | tablespoons sugar |
| ½ | orange zest | 2 | tablespoons cornstarch |
| ½ | cinnamon stick | | |
| 4 | egg yolks | 4 | 3x3-inch molds |

Whisk the egg yolks and sugar until pale yellow. Add the cornstarch and mix well. Bring the half-and-half, orange zest and the cinnamon stick to a boil. Pour a small amount of the milk into the yolks mixture. Bring to a boil, whisking constantly. Pour into the molds and chill.

### GARNISH

| | | | |
|---|---|---|---|
| 8 | seedless tangerines, cut into pieces | | Confectioners' sugar |
| | Cointreau (orange-flavored French liqueur) | | |

**Presentation:** In a soup plate, place the crème brûlée (out of the mold). Place the tangerine pieces around and sprinkle with cointreau. Sprinkle with confectioners' sugar.
Serves 4.

## RACK OF LAMB WITH ROQUEFORT SAUCE

| | | | |
|---|---|---|---|
| 1 | rack of lamb | 2 | teaspoons mustard |
| 1 | teaspoon chopped garlic | ⅓ | cup bread crumbs |
| 1 | teaspoon peanut oil | 1 | tablespoon chopped parsley |
| 1 | pinch of salt | 1 | tablespoon chopped olives |

Put the garlic, salt and oil on top of the rack of lamb, and cook it in the oven for approximately 15 minutes. Then, let it rest for 4 minutes. Baste the rack with the mustard and the mixture of bread, parsley and the olives. Set aside.

### THE SAUCE

| | | | |
|---|---|---|---|
| ½ | cup dry white wine | 1 | small bay leaf |
| 1 | chopped shallot | 2 | ounces Roquefort cheese |
| 1 | branch fresh thyme | ⅓ | cup heavy cream |

In a saucepan, reduce together the wine, shallot, thyme and bay leaf for 4 minutes, then add the cream. Let it cook for 5 minutes. Add the cheese, cook it for a few more minutes, then strain the sauce. In a plate serve some vegetables such as asparagus, mushrooms sautéed with olive oil and garlic, and some mashed potatoes. Pour the sauce and the sliced rack of lamb on top. Serves 8 to 10.

## A MOUSSE OF CRAB SERVED ON A BED OF SPINACH WITH A MUSTARD SEED SAUCE

### CRAB MOUSSE

| | | | |
|---|---|---|---|
| 8 | ounces jumbo crab | ½ | bunch chives |
| 1 | cup cream | 1 | tablespoon butter |
| 2 | eggs | | Salt and pepper |

Clean crab meat, taking care to remove all of the shell. Mix cream, eggs, finely sliced chives and seasonings together. Butter 4-ounce soufflé cups. Place crab meat in cups. Pour cream mixture over the crab. Cook in a water bath at 350 degrees for 35 minutes.

### MUSTARD SEED SAUCE

| | | | |
|---|---|---|---|
| ½ | cup white wine | 3 | tablespoons mustard seed |
| 2 | each shallots | | |
| ⅓ | cup tomato paste | | Salt and pepper |
| | | 2 | leaves fresh basil |

Place white wine and finely chopped shallots in sauté pan and reduce one half. Add cream. Reduce one half. Add tomato paste and continue to cook for 2 minutes more. Add coarse grain mustard seed. Let stand for a few minutes to develop the flavor. Strain. Adjust taste with salt and pepper. Add thinly sliced basil.

### PRESENTATION

| | | | |
|---|---|---|---|
| 5 | ounces fresh spinach, blanched | 2 | tablespoons Arkansas caviar |
| | Salt and pepper | ½ | each red bell pepper, julienne |
| 2 | tablespoons butter | | |
| 2 | tablespoons mustard seed sauce | | Dill/chervil |

Remove all water from spinach by squeezing with your hands. Season with salt and pepper. Sauté spinach in butter. Place spinach in center of 4 plates to cover an area slightly larger than the mousse. Cover with the sauce. Place ½ teaspoon caviar on each portion. Surround base of mousse with red pepper. Serves 4.

# UPSIDE DOWN SWEET POTATO PIE WITH SUGAR CANE ICE CREAM & JACK DANIEL VANILLA SAUCE

| 4 | cups half-and-half | 4 | ounces Jack |
| 2 | cups sugar | | Daniel's bourbon |
| 12 | egg yolks | | |
| 2 | vanilla beans or 3 tablespoons vanilla extract | | |

Boil the half-and-half with the vanilla. Mix together yolks and sugar. Pour the milk into the yolks. Cook to simmer until the sauce thickens. Check with the back of the spoon for the thickness. Cool the sauce down in an ice water bucket. Add Jack Daniel's bourbon when it is cooled.

### SUGAR CANE ICE CREAM

| ¾ | cup brown sugar (cane sugar) | 1 | quart milk |
| ¼ | cup light molasses | 1½ | tablespoons vanilla extract |

Mix the brown sugar with molasses and yolks. Bring the milk and vanilla to boil. Pour the milk to the sugar mixture. Simmer 5 to minutes. Cool it immediately. Ready to go to the ice cream maker.

### SUGAR DOUGH

| 9 | ounces cake flour | 1 | egg yolk |
| 4.5 | ounces sweet butter | 3 | tablespoons water |
| 2 | ounces sugar | 1 | dash salt |

Cut the butter into cubes on top of the flour. Mix well with tips of fingers. Make a well with the flour. Add in the middle the egg yolk, water, sugar and salt. Mix well. Roll the dough 25 inches with a rolling pin then cut 6 circles of 4½-inch diameter.

### YAMS

| 5 | yams (medium, 1½ inches) | 3 | tablespoons white sugar |
| 3 | tablespoons brown sugar | | |

In a 6x4-inch black metal sauté pan, put white and brown sugar. Arrange the sweet potato, cover with the dough and cook it in the oven for 14 to 18 minutes. Reverse the pie in a plate immediately after taking it out of the oven. Pour the sauce in the middle of the plate, the pie and scoop the ice cream on top and serve. Hot and cold.

Yield: 1 pie.

# LEMON CUSTARD GRATINE WITH FRESH BERRIES & LEMON CANDIES

### LEMON CUSTARD

| 7 | ounces lemon juice | 2 | ounces cream |
| 3 | egg yolks | 2 | ounces sugar |
| 1 | ounce flour | 2 | lemon zest |
| 3 | gelatin leaves | 7 | ounces sugar |
| 6 | egg whites | 2 | pints raspberries |

Boil together the lemon juice and the cream. Whisk together the egg yolks, the sugar and the flour. Then, pour the boiling lemon juice and cream over it. Put everything back into the pan to boil for 2 minutes. Add the gelatin leaves and the lemon zest. Whip the egg white and the sugar until the mixture is thick. Mix this mixture with the pastry cream. Pour into molds and keep in a cooler for 2 hours.

### LEMON CANDIES

| 3 | lemons | 4 | cups water |
| 2 | cups sugar | | |

Slice thinly the lemons. Cook them with the water and the sugar to a slow boil for 20 minutes. Separate the juice and the lemons.

### LEMON SAUCE

| 2 | cups whipped cream |

Whip the cream and add the cold lemon juice (lemon candies).

### RASPBERRIES SAUCE

| ¼ | cup sugar | 1 | pint raspberries |

Blend together raspberries and sugar. Strain.

### GARNISH

| 20 | leaves fresh mint julienne | 1 | pint strawberries |
| 1 | pint fresh raspberries | | |

In the middle of a soup plate, put the lemon mousse (remove the mold). Sprinkle with powdered sugar. Burn the top with a torch. Put the 2 sauces around the mousse. Add the berries, lemon candies and mint julienne.

Serves 14.

# VIKING CULINARY ARTS CENTER

## 119 South Main Street
## Suite 600
## Memphis, TN 38103

**Colleen DePete, Cooking School Director**
*Colleen is a seasoned professional with over 10 years of experience in the culinary field. She trained with Master Chef José Gutierrez of Chez Philippe, Peabody Hotel, where she was involved with events such as Julia Child's 80th Birthday Celebration and the James Beard Awards Dinner. Immediately before joining the Culinary Arts Center, Colleen owned Select A Chef, teaching cooking classes and organizing culinary events. As the Viking Culinary Arts Center Cooking School Director, Colleen develops each month's class roster, schedules guest chefs and teaches various cooking classes.*

## ROASTED VEGETABLE NAPOLEONS

| | | | |
|---|---|---|---|
| ½ | cup olive oil | ½ | pound mozzarella |
| 1 | pound eggplant (cut crosswise ⅓ inch thick slices) | | (cut into six ¼ inch slices) |
| 1 | pound zucchini (cut crosswise ⅓ inch thick slices) | 6 | sprigs fresh rosemary |
| ¾ | cup ricotta cheese | 2 | Yukon gold potatoes, sliced thin |
| 1½ | teaspoons fresh thyme, chopped | | |

Preheat oven to 450 degrees and brush 2 baking sheets with oil. Arrange as many vegetables as possible in 1 layer on sheets. Brush vegetables with some remaining oil and season with salt and pepper. Roast vegetables in middle and lower two-thirds of oven, switching position of sheets halfway through roasting until just tender and lightly browned, 10 to 15 minutes. Bring vegetables to room temperature before proceeding. In a small bowl stir together ricotta cheese, thyme and salt and pepper to taste. Put 1 eggplant slice on freshly oiled baking sheet.

Spread 1 teaspoon of ricotta mixture over eggplant. Cover ricotta mixture with 2 potato slices and layer with 2 zucchini slices, 1 slice mozzarella and 1 onion slice. Spread 1 teaspoon of ricotta mixture over onion and top with 1 eggplant slice. Make 5 more napoleons using remaining vegetables, ricotta mixture and mozzarella in same manner. Insert a metal or wooden skewer through center of each napoleon to make a hole from bottom to top. Trim rosemary sprigs to 1-inch taller than napoleons and remove bottom leaves from each sprig, leaving about 1-inch of leaves around the top. Insert 1 sprig into napoleon and bake in middle of oven 5 minutes or until mozzarella is melted and vegetables are heated through. Serve napoleons with orzo.

## TORTELLINI WITH PROSCIUTTO, PEAS & PEPPERS

| | | | |
|---|---|---|---|
| 1 | cup frozen baby peas, cooked | 1 | stick unsalted butter, softened |
| 4 | ounces prosciutto (sliced ¼ inch thick and cut into ¼ inch dice) | 1 | garlic clove, minced |
| 1 | large red bell pepper, sliced thin (or 3 large plum tomatoes – peeled, seeded and cut into ¼ inch dice) | ½ | teaspoon pepper, finely grated |
| | | ½ | teaspoon thyme (or) rosemary, chopped fine |
| 6 | tablespoons (plus more for serving) Parmesan cheese, freshly grated | 1½ | pounds cheese tortellini |

Bring a large pot of salted water to boil. Meanwhile, in a serving bowl, combine prosciutto, peas, peppers and sauté in pan with butter, garlic, salt, pepper and thyme. Cook pasta in water until al dente then drain well. Add pasta to mixture and toss with cheese. Season with salt and pepper to taste and additional cheese.

*A light cream sauce with shallots and rosemary can be an addition.*

Serves 6.

## AMARETTO BREAD PUDDING

| | | | |
|---|---|---|---|
| 1 | loaf French bread | 1½ | cups granulated sugar |
| 1 | quart half-and-half | | |
| 2 | tablespoons unsalted butter, room temperature | 2 | tablespoons almond extract |
| | | ¾ | cup golden raisins |
| 3 | eggs | ¾ | cup almonds, sliced |

Break up bread into small pieces. Place in medium-sized bowl and cover with half-and-half. Cover bowl and let stand for 1 hour. Preheat oven to 325 degrees. Grease a 9x13x2-inch baking dish with butter. In a small bowl, beat together eggs, sugar and almond extract. Stir into bread mixture. Gently fold raisins and almonds into bread mixture. Spread bread mixture evenly in buttered baking dish. Set on middle rack of oven. Bake for 50 minutes, until golden brown. Remove and let cool.

### AMARETTO SAUCE

| | | | |
|---|---|---|---|
| 8 | tablespoons butter, room temperature | 1 | egg, well-beaten |
| 1 | cup confectioners' sugar | 4 | tablespoons amaretto liqueur |

**To serve:** Preheat broiler. Cut pudding into 8 to 10 squares and place on decorative ovenproof serving dishes. Spoon Amaretto sauce over pudding and place under broiler until sauce bubbles. Serve immediately.

Serves 8 to 10.

CULINARY ARTS
CENTER

# McEwen's on Monroe

## *122 Monroe Avenue*
## *Memphis, TN 38103*

**Mac & Cindy Edwards, Owners**
**Chris Lee, Executive Chef**

*Chris Lee attended Johnson and Wales University in Charleston, South Carolina, majoring in Culinary Arts: he graduated from Le Cordon Bleu in London, England. He has been Executive Chef at the Clarksdale Country Club in Clarksdale, MS; Jackson-Madison County General Hospital in Jackson, TN; Café Society in Memphis, TN; Bonne Terre in Nesbit, MS; Café Samovar in Memphis, TN prior to joining McEwen's on Monroe as Executive Chef.*

## CHOCOLATE LAYER CAKE WITH MOCHA GANACHE

*(Melissa's Pie)*

| | |
|---|---|
| 2½ | cups flour, sifted |
| 1½ | teaspoons baking soda |
| 1 | cup water, boiling |
| ½ | cup yogurt, plain reg. or low fat |
| ¾ | cup water, cold |
| ⅔ | cup cocoa |
| 1⅛ | tablespoons vanilla extract |
| 6 | ounces butter, with salt, softened |
| 2½ | cups sugar |
| 3 | eggs at room temperature |

### GANACHE

| | |
|---|---|
| 24 | ounces chocolate, semisweet |
| 1 | cup cream |
| 2 | tablespoons cream |
| 3 | ounces butter |
| 1½ | teaspoons vanilla |
| 4½ | teaspoons espresso coffee, instant powder |

Preheat oven to 350 degrees. Grease and flour two 10-inch cake pans.

**Cake:** Combine the flour and baking soda. Sift 3 times and set aside. Place cocoa in a bowl, pour the boiling water over it and stir until smooth. Refrigerate to cool to lukewarm, stirring occasionally. Stir in the yogurt. Add the cold water and vanilla. Set aside. Cream the butter and sugar until light in texture, about 6 minutes on high speed. If using a heavy-duty mixer, use the paddle attachment as the whisk attachment will over-beat the cake. In a small bowl whisk the eggs lightly. Dribble them slowly into the butter mixture at medium low speed, stopping to scrape down the bowl and beaters as needed. Stop the mixer and place ⅓ flour into the bowl. Beat at low speed until just incorporated. Pour in ½ of the cocoa mixture and beat on low speed until just combined. Scrape the bowl. Repeat this step until all ingredients are incorporated, ending with flour. Divide batter evenly among the prepared cake pans. Bake until the cake begins to shrink from the sides of the pan and a toothpick inserted in the center comes out clean, about 30 minutes. Cool cakes for 10 minutes and remove from pan. Cool completely before icing cake.

**Ganache:** Put the chocolate, butter and espresso powder in a bowl and set aside. Bring cream to boil. Add chocolate mixture. Reduce heat to very low and stir until smooth about 1 to 2 minutes. Remove from heat and stir in vanilla. Put ½ of ganache into a small bowl and refrigerate until spreadable but not set. Place a generous portion on top of the bottom layer of the cake. Spread evenly. Place the top layer of the cake over the bottom layer. Use remaining cool icing to even out and smooth where the 2 layers meet. Set the cake on a revolving cake platter or on a wire rack. Pour the remaining ganache over the top of the cake (you may have to reheat the ganache but must do so on very low heat for just a minute). Use a metal spatula to direct the icing to flow over the sides of the cake. Let sit at room temperature to cool.

This cake is best served at room temperature. It freezes very well if triple wrapped in plastic wrap. Remove plastic before thawing. For a decadent midnight snack, microwave a slice for 30 seconds or until warm (icing will melt) and serve with a big scoop of vanilla ice cream.

Serves 10 to 14.

# WILD MUSHROOMS & OVEN-DRIED TOMATO CHEESECAKE WITH SMOKED GARLIC CREAM SAUCE

### FILLING

| | | | |
|---|---|---|---|
| 2½ | pounds cream cheese | 1 | cup sautéed oyster shiitake, crimini mushrooms, mixed |
| 3 | tablespoons pesto | | |
| ½ | cup oven-dried tomatoes | 1 | teaspoon black pepper |
| 6 | large eggs | ½ | teaspoon kosher salt |

Blend in food processor until well mixed but not smooth.

### CRUST

Grind approximately 6 muffins (or one loaf) of cornbread in food processor. Melt ½ pound butter and add to processor and continue processing until thoroughly blended. Press cornbread mixture into 9-inch springform pan to cover sides and bottom. Wrap outside of pan (bottom and sides) with aluminum foil. Pour cheesecake mixture into crust-lined pan. Bake cheesecake in water bath approximately 1 hour or until firm and lightly browned. Cool and slice.

### SAUCE

Smoke 1 cup peeled whole garlic cloves until brown. Purée garlic in food processor. In a 2-quart saucepan, reduce 375ml. dry white wine with puréed garlic until reduced by half. Add 1 quart heavy cream and the juice of one lemon. Reduce to sauce consistency. Season to taste with kosher salt, white pepper and cayenne.

**To serve:** Reheat individual slice of cheesecake in 400 degree oven for 5 minutes. Pour approximately 2 tablespoons of warm garlic sauce on a small plate. Place one slice of cheesecake on sauce. Garnish as desired.

Makes one 12-slice cheesecake.

# SEKISUI, INC.
## 50 Humphreys Boulevard Memphis, TN 38120

### Jimmy Ishii, Chef/Owner

*Jimmy Ishii's three Sekisui restaurants, in Memphis, prove that Memphians have fallen head-over-heels for Japanese sushi and other traditional foods. The East Memphis location opened in 1989. Jimmy has since opened locations in Midtown and Downtown. Sekisui offers Japanese food at its best. Food selections include sushi and sashimi, robata grilled items, tempura, teriyaki, dumplings and more. Every year since opening **Memphis Magazine** has named Sekisui of Japan "Best Japanese Restaurant" and in 1988, the Memphis Restaurant Association named Jimmy Ishii its "Distinguished Restaurateur of the Year." Mr. Ishii also has other restaurant holdings in the Memphis area.*

# SHRIMP IN CHAMPAGNE MUSTARD SAUCE

### FOR THE SHRIMP

| | | | |
|---|---|---|---|
| 36 | large shrimp (26 to 30 count) | 2 | to 3 tablespoons chopped garlic |
| 1 | cup olive oil | 2 | cups plain bread crumbs |

### FOR THE SAUCE

| | | | |
|---|---|---|---|
| 6 | ounces champagne | 1¾ | cups ketchup |
| 1 | cup butter, softened | 1½ | tablespoons hot Japanese mustard |

### FOR THE GARNISH

| | | | |
|---|---|---|---|
| 12 | lemon wedges | 1 | cup chopped parsley |

Peel and devein the shrimp, leaving tails on. Marinate in olive oil and garlic for at least 3 hours, or preferably overnight in the refrigerator. Heat champagne in non-corrosive pan, bring to a boil and reduce to ½ of original volume. Let cool. Combine champagne, softened butter, ketchup and mustard in blender. Blend at high speed for 30 seconds. Heat a broiler or grill. Remove shrimp from marinade and roll in bread crumbs. Grill until shrimp turn pink. For each serving, place 3 shrimp on small plate, pour a little of the sauce over each shrimp. Garnish with a lemon wedge and sprinkle with chopped parsley. Yield: 12 appetizers.

*Note: Leftover sauce may be refrigerated up to 2 weeks.*

# RIVER TERRACE ON MUD ISLAND
## 280 North Mud Island Drive Memphis, TN 38103

### Mike Patrick, Chef de Cuisine

*This is a great downtown spot to meet for an end-of-the-day cocktail. Drive over the Auction Avenue Bridge, make a left – and within a few yards – you'll be right at the door of the "new" River Terrace.*

*Recently acquired by one of Memphis' most successful restaurateurs – Jimmy Ishii – River Terrace's menus combine the culinary talents of Jimmy Ishii and Chef de Cuisine, Michael Patrick.*

## PECAN ENCRUSTED PORK MEDALLIONS WITH MAPLE APPLE CHUTNEY

### MARINADE FOR 2 TENDERLOINS

| | | | |
|---|---|---|---|
| ½ | cup olive oil | 1 | tablespoon chopped garlic |
| ¼ | cup white wine | | |

### MAPLE APPLE CHUTNEY

| | | | |
|---|---|---|---|
| 2 | red delicious apples | 1 | teaspoon dry nutmeg |
| 1 | yellow onion (fine dice) | 1 | teaspoon cinnamon |
| 1 | red bell pepper (fine dice) | 1 | teaspoon cayenne pepper |
| 1 | yellow bell pepper (fine dice) | ¼ | cup rice wine vinegar |
| 1 | green bell pepper (fine dice) | ¼ | cup brown sugar |
| 1 | tablespoon chopped garlic | ¼ | cup honey |
| 1 | finger of ginger (fine dice) | | Kosher salt and white pepper to taste |

### BREAD CRUMBS WITH PECANS

| | | | |
|---|---|---|---|
| 2 | cups fine chopped pecans | 1 | cup all-purpose flour |
| 1 | cup finely grated bread crumbs | 4 | eggs with ½ cup milk (egg wash) |
| ¼ | cup fresh chopped parsley | | |

**Make Marinade:** Combine all ingredients listed for marinade.

**Marinate Pork:** Trim tenderloins well, removing all silver skin and fat. Slice pork into 2 ounce medallions and place in non-reactive shallow pan. Pour the marinade over medallions and refrigerate up to 4 hours.

**Make Mango-Apple Chutney:** Combine all ingredients in a saucepan and bring to a boil. Turn the sauce down to a simmer and continue to simmer for about 20 minutes or until slightly thickened.

**Complete Breading of Pork Medallions:** Remove pork medallions from refrigeration. Use three shallow pans. Add all-purpose flour to first pan. Combine eggs and milk for egg wash in second pan. Add pecan bread crumb mixture in third pan. Coat pork medallions in flour, then egg wash, then bread them. Continue the process until all pork is breaded.

**Final Assembly:** Preheat oven to 350 degrees. Season Pecan Encrusted Pork Medallions with kosher salt and ground white pepper. Pour 1 tablespoon of olive oil on baking sheet pan and coat the entire pan. Place pork medallions on pan and place in the oven. Cook at 350 degrees for approximately 8 minutes or until desired doneness. Remove from oven and set aside. On a dinner plate, take approximately 2 ounces of maple chutney and pour on plate. Place 4 to 6 Pecan Encrusted Pork Medallions over the sauce.

**Serving Suggestions:** At River Terrace, this dish is served with sweet potatoes and sautéed fresh seasonal vegetables. The dish is then garnished with very thinly sliced and fried sweet potato chips.

# THE HALF SHELL
## 688 South Mendenhall
## Memphis, TN 38117

**Danny Summerall, Owner**
*Only the freshest in seafood make it to the plates and to our customers. Yellow fin tuna, crab cakes, seafood gumbo – the best in town, hand-cut steaks and great burgers are some of the selections available on the menu.*

## CRAWFISH CAKES

### STAGE 1

| | |
|---|---|
| 6 | pounds crawfish tail meat, diced |

### STAGE 2

| | | | |
|---|---|---|---|
| 1 | red bell pepper, chopped | 6 | tablespoons prepared horseradish |
| 1 | green bell pepper, chopped | | Lemon juice from 3 lemons |
| 6 | tablespoons Dijon mustard | 3 | eggs |
| | | ¾ | cup heavy cream |

### STAGE 3

| | |
|---|---|
| 2¼ | cups Japanese bread crumbs |

Drain all the juice from the tail meat. Dice the tail meat and place in a large stainless steel bowl. Add all Stage 2 ingredients and mix well. Add bread crumbs, mix well and form into 3-ounce patties. Sauté cakes until browned on both sides. Serve with either a remoulade sauce or choron sauce.

Yield: approximately 30 crawfish cakes.

## CORN & CRAB BISQUE

### STAGE 1

| | | | |
|---|---|---|---|
| 1 | ounce olive oil | ⅔ | ounce garlic purée |
| 3 | bay leaves | 4 | ears corn, cut and scraped |
| 1 | cup onions, chopped | | |
| ⅔ | cup celery, chopped | | |

### STAGE 2

| | | | |
|---|---|---|---|
| 2 | cups shrimp | ⅓ | teaspoon cayenne pepper |
| ⅓ | teaspoon white pepper | ⅔ | ounce Worcestershire sauce |
| ⅓ | teaspoon black pepper | | |

### STAGE 3

| | |
|---|---|
| 2 | quarts half-and-half |

### STAGE 4

| | | | |
|---|---|---|---|
| ⅓ | pound butter | ⅔ | cup flour |

Sauté all Stage 1 ingredients until soft. Add all stage 2 ingredients and let simmer 20 minutes. Add half-and-half and bring to a boil. In a small saucepan, melt butter and add flour. Mix well and let cook for 5 minutes. Add the butter/flour mixture to the soup, stir well and cook until soup thickens. Remove from heat.

*NOTE: You can substitute corn stock for shrimp stock.*

Yield: 1 gallon

## BRAVO! RESTAURANTE ADAMS MARK HOTEL
### I-240 at Poplar
### Memphis, TN 38120

**Edward Nowakowski, Executive Chef**
*At dinner, singing servers perform arias and show tunes while serving delicious Italian and other Mediterranean specialties. The restaurant is also the setting for its popular Sunday brunch. A Southern-style lunch buffet is available Monday through Friday.*

## CHICKEN, VEAL & SHIITAKE MUSHROOM TERRINE

| | | | |
|---|---|---|---|
| 2 | teaspoons canola oil | | Salt & pepper |
| 1 | shallot, finely diced | 1 | pound lean trimmed veal, cut into small cubes |
| 1½ | cups shiitake mushrooms, stems removed, fine julienne | | Mixture of cayenne pepper, paprika and black pepper to taste |
| 2 | pounds boneless, skinless chicken breasts | 1 | pound caul fat* |
| ⅓ | pound unsalted fatback | 2 | bay leaves |
| | | 1 | large sprig rosemary |
| ⅓ | cup cream | | |
| 1 | egg | 2 | sprigs thyme |

Preheat oven to 400 degrees. Heat oil to hot in a sauté pan. Sauté shallot and mushrooms until juices are released. Remove from heat and let cool. In a food processor, purée chicken, fatback, cream and egg until smooth. Be careful not to overwork the mixture. Season with a pinch of salt and pepper. Place chicken mixture in a large bowl. Fold in mushrooms and shallots. Season all sides of veal cubes with cayenne mix. Then fold veal cubes into chicken mixture. Line a 1½-quart terrine mold with caul fat leaving enough excess to cover the top of the terrine. Carefully fill the mold. Use a spatula to pack corners and smooth top. Cover the terrine with caul fat making sure to get a good seal. Place bay leaves, rosemary and thyme on top of terrine. Bake 45 minutes or until just firm to touch. Remove from oven and allow to cool, approximately 30 minutes. Refrigerate overnight. Unmold to serve. Serves 10.

*\*Chef's Note: Caul fat can be purchased from your butcher.*

## FRESH TOMATO BISQUE WITH KIWI SORBET

*This is one of those seasonal dishes that should only be made in summer or early fall when the tomatoes are fresh & fabulous.*

| | | | |
|---|---|---|---|
| 2 | tablespoons olive oil | 2 | dozen fresh basil leaves |
| ½ | pound chopped onions | 2 | cups chicken stock Kosher salt to taste Freshly ground white pepper |
| 1 | celery rib roughly cut up | | |
| 2 | garlic cloves | 1 | cup heavy cream |
| 2½ | pounds ripe beefsteak tomatoes (cored, seeded and cubed) | 6 | scoops Kiwi sorbet or any other sorbet as you desire |

Heat the olive oil in a skillet. Add the onion, celery and garlic. Cook over low heat for about 10 minutes, or until the vegetables are soft but not brown. Add tomatoes and half the basil and stir to blend. Cook slowly for about 10 minutes. Stir in the chicken stock and salt to taste. Bring to boil, lower the heat. Simmer about 1 hour or until everything is very soft. Purée the mixture in blender and then push it through a fine sieve to give a smooth purée. Place in the refrigerator for minimum of one hour or until cold. Stir in the cream: adjust the seasoning and chill. Serve in chilled bowls, garnish with scoops of Kiwi sorbet and remaining basil leaves.

Serves 6.

## SAUTÉED SCAMPI WITH MUSTARD & TARRAGON

| | | | |
|---|---|---|---|
| 5 | ounces scampi shrimp | ½ | ounce mustard |
| 1 | ounce sherry | 6 | fresh tarragon leaves |
| 1 | ounce white wine sauce | ½ | of 1 shallot |
| 1 | ounce heavy cream | 3 | sprigs of parsley |

Season the shrimp using a large sauté pan, heat the oil until it begins to smoke. Over very high heat, sauté the shrimp for about 5 minutes, remove shrimp and keep warm. Add shallots and tarragon, sauté for 2 minutes and deglaze the pan with sherry, add the cream and reduce the sauce until it coats the back of a spoon. Whisk in the butter, one small piece at a time (do at the last minute). Do not let the sauce boil. Correct seasoning to taste. Garnish with chives.

Yield: 6 servings

## LA MONTAGNE
### 3550 Park Avenue
### Memphis, TN 38111

**Rob Sangster, Owner**
**Terry Cox, General Manager**
**Gregory Reid, Executive Chef**

*La Montagne celebrates its 20th anniversary this year in their newly renovated facility. La Montagne which means "the mountain," takes the concept of healthful cooking to "new heights" according to most food critics. This restaurant offers fresh seafood, pastas, poultry and vegetarian specials from around the world – 150 specialties from more than 20 countries!* **Memphis** *magazine rates La Montagne as one of the best seafood restaurants in Memphis.*

## SPINACH, SUN-DRIED TOMATO & CHEESE TORTE

| | | | |
|---|---|---|---|
| 1 | cup long-grain rice | 1 | cup part skim ricotta cheese |
| ½ | teaspoon salt | | |
| 1 | cup sundried (not oil-packed) tomatoes | 2 | tablespoons grated Parmesan cheese |
| 2 | cups boiling water | 2 | whole eggs |
| 1 | teaspoon olive oil | 3 | egg whites |
| 10 | ounce package frozen chopped spinach, thawed | 1 | cup packed fresh basil leaves |
| 2 | cups low-fat (1%) cottage cheese | 2 | tablespoons pine nuts |

In a medium saucepan, bring 2¼ cups of water to a boil. Add the rice and ¼ teaspoon of the salt, reduce to a simmer, cover and cook until the rice is tender, about 17 minutes. Cool to room temperature. Meanwhile, in a small bowl, combine the sun-dried tomatoes and boiling water and let stand for 15 minutes, until softened. Drain and coarsely chop the tomatoes. Preheat the oven to 375 degrees. Spray a 9-inch springform pan with nonstick cooking spray. Spoon the rice into the bottom of the pan and cover with plastic wrap or waxed paper. Use a measuring cup to press the rice into an even layer on the bottom of the pan and to make it come up about a ½ inch on the sides. Set aside. In a small bowl, combine the oil and spinach. In a food processor, combine the cottage cheese, ricotta, Parmesan, whole eggs, egg whites, basil and the remaining ¼ teaspoon of salt. Process until smooth. Add the sun-dried tomatoes and pine nuts and process just to combine. Pour ½ of the cheese mixture over the rice in the prepared pan. Top with a layer of the spinach mixture and pour the remaining cheese mixture on top. Place on a baking sheet and bake for 50 to 60 minutes, or until just set. Cool to room temperature, cut into wedges and serve.

Serves 6.

## ENCRUSTED SALMON

*This La Montagne signature dish is a fresh filet of salmon encrusted in herb bread crumbs & Parmesan cheese topped with lemon dill & spinach pesto sauce. Serve over angelhair pasta or brown & wild rice.*

| | | | |
|---|---|---|---|
| 1 | 8-ounce salmon filet | 2 | ounces bread crumbs |
| 1 | egg | | Dashes of oregano, crushed red pepper, garlic, basil, rosemary |
| 1 | cup milk | | |
| 1 | ounce Parmesan cheese | | |

### LEMON DILL SAUCE

| | | | |
|---|---|---|---|
| 3 | teaspoons lemon juice | 1 | ounce mayonnaise |
| 3 | tablespoons buttermilk | | Dash of minced dill |
| | | ½ | teaspoon corn oil |

### SPINACH PESTO SAUCE

| | | | |
|---|---|---|---|
| ½ | cup spinach | 3 | tablespoons pine nuts |
| ½ | ounce Parmesan cheese | | |
| 1 | teaspoon basil | 2 | tablespoons olive oil |
| 1 | teaspoon granulated garlic | | |

Blend in a Cuisinart.

**Preparation:** Dust the salmon filet with flour then encrust it with a blend of milk, beaten egg, Parmesan herbs and bread crumbs. Bake at 350 degrees for 8 to 9 minutes. Top the salmon first with spinach pesto sauce and then with lemon dill sauce. Garnish with sprigs of fresh dill. Serve over your favorite pasta or rice.

Single Serving.

# THE CUPBOARD
### 1400 Union Avenue
### Memphis, TN 38104

# THE CUPBOARD TOO
### 149 Madison Avenue
### Memphis, TN 38103

**Charles Cavallo, Owner**

*The Cupboard's fresh vegetables are cooked to perfection. The menu features homemade rolls and cornbread, an array of Southern favorites including chicken-fried steak, meat loaf and fried pork chops. The desserts are made from scratch daily. The Cupboard is the perennial winner of **Memphis** Magazine's "Best Down-Home Cooking" award.*

## THE CUPBOARD'S FAMOUS CORN PUDDING

| | |
|---|---|
| 3 | cans cream corn |
| 1 | can whole kernel corn |
| 8 | eggs |
| 1½ | cups margarine |
| 1½ | cups all-purpose flour |
| 1½ | cups sugar |
| | Salt to taste |

Place cream corn in a buttered 2-quart baking dish. Mix in eggs, sugar, flour and margarine than add whole kernel corn. Mix thoroughly. Bake at 325 degrees for approximately 1 hour until light brown.

Yield: 8 to 10 servings

## CUPBOARD'S CORNBREAD

| | |
|---|---|
| 1 | cup vegetable oil |
| 1 | cup buttermilk |
| 6 | eggs |
| 1 | pound self-rising cornmeal |
| ½ | cup all-purpose flour |
| | Salt to taste |

Sift the cornmeal and flour together. Mix all of the above ingredients thoroughly into a mixing bowl. Preheat oven to 400 degrees. Pour mixture into a greased muffin pan. Bake for 20 to 25 minutes until golden brown.

# THE SIDE PORCH STEAK HOUSE
### 5689 Stage Road
### Bartlett, TN 38135

**Bill & Donna Yancey, Owners**

*The Side Porch Steak House, family-owned and operated, was established in 1976. It serves a variety of entrées, but steaks are their specialty, served in a "secret" marinade. In 1999, and again in 2000, The Side Porch was voted the #1 steak house in the city by **The Bartlett Express** Reader's Poll. In 1998 it was awarded "Best Restaurant" in Bartlett by **The Memphis Flyer**.*

## CHOCOLATE CHIP PECAN PIE

| | | | |
|---|---|---|---|
| | Piecrust in pan | ½ | cup dark corn syrup |
| 6 | ounces semisweet chocolate chips | 3 | eggs |
| 2 | cups broken pecans | 1 | teaspoon vanilla |
| ½ | cup firmly packed brown sugar | 1 | teaspoon soft margarine |

Sprinkle chocolate chips over bottom of piecrust. Top with pecans. In small bowl, combine brown sugar, corn syrup, eggs, vanilla and margarine. Beat well. Pour over pecans. Bake at 375 degrees for 35 minutes. Garnish with ice cream and whipped cream. Store in refrigerator.

Serves 6.

*The Side Porch Steak House*

## LAKEVIEW DINING ROOM
### Rt. 1, Box 980
### Tiptonville, TN 38079

**Dottie Downing, Owner**

## EARTHQUAKE CAKE

| | | | |
|---|---|---|---|
| 1 | box chocolate base cake mix | 1 | (8 ounce) package cream cheese |
| 1 | cup coconut | 1 | box powdered sugar |
| 1 | cup pecans, chopped | 1 | stick melted margarine |

Mix coconut and pecans. Press into one 9x13 inch pan. Mix box of cake mix, pour into pan on top of pecan mixture. Mix cream cheese, sugar and margarine. Stir until cream. Take a teaspoon and drop cheese mixture on top of cake mix and bake at 350 degrees for 45 minutes.

## MISSISSIPPI MUD CAKE

| | | | |
|---|---|---|---|
| 1¾ | cup sugar | ⅓ | cup cocoa |
| 1 | cup vegetable oil | 4 | eggs |
| 1 | to 2 teaspoons vanilla | 1⅓ | cups flour Jar marshmallow cream |
| 1 | cup chopped pecans | | |

Place sugar in mixing bowl. Add cocoa and mix. Add vegetable oil. Add 4 eggs, one at a time, beating well after each addition. Add vanilla, flour and pecans. Pour into greased and floured 9x13-inch pan. Bake at 350 degrees until done, but not overdone. Remove from oven, put jar of marshmallow cream over cake while still warm.

Yield: 1 cake

## MISSISSIPPI MUD ICING

| | | | |
|---|---|---|---|
| ½ | stick margarine, softened | 1 | teaspoon vanilla |
| 1 | box powdered sugar | ¼ | cup evaporated milk, or more to soften |
| ½ | cup cocoa | 1 | cup pecans |

Mix powdered sugar, oleo and cocoa. Cream. Add milk. Add remainder of ingredients. Mix well. Spread over hot cake.

*Eagles winter at Reelfoot Lake*

## BOYETTE'S
### Hwy. 21 South
### Tiptonville, TN 38079

### SHRIMP MOLD

1 (10½ ounce) can tomato soup, undiluted
1 envelope unflavored gelatin
¼ cup warm water
1 (8 ounce) package cream cheese
1 cup celery, chopped
1 cup pecans, chopped (optional)
¼ cup onion, chopped
1 cup mayonnaise
2 cans small size shrimp, drained and mashed

Heat soup in saucepan. Dissolve gelatin in water and add to hot soup. Stir in cream cheese and heat until melted. Add celery, pecans, onion, mayonnaise and shrimp. Mix well. Pour into mold and refrigerate. Serve with assorted crackers.

### BOYETTE'S GARLIC GRIT CASSEROLE

1 cup grits
1 stick butter
1½ rolls garlic cheese or garlic powder
2 eggs, slightly beaten
⅔ cup milk
1 cup corn flakes, crushed

Cook grits according to package directions. Add butter, cheese and eggs and heat until melted. Stir in milk. Put in greased Pyrex pan. Cover with corn flakes. Bake at 350 degrees for about 45 minutes or 1 hour. Great with Tennessee ham!

## KELLEY'S KATCH CAVIAR
### 140 Jaggers Lane
### Savannah, TN 38372

**Mike & Vickie Kelley, Owners**
*Paddlefish caviar is harvested in the fresh waters of Tennessee and other American states. Paddlefish is quickly becoming a standard delicacy among those who have discovered it. Kelley's Katch proudly offers smoked paddlefish that has a savory mild flavor and wonderful texture. It is all natural with no preservatives. Call 888-681-8565 for prices and shipping information.*

### CAVIAR RECIPE

*This is the traditional way of serving caviar with toast points and other accompaniments.*

2 eggs
2 tablespoons, finely chopped parsley
1 large red onion, very finely chopped
4 to 5 teaspoons Kelley's Katch Caviar
1 lemon, quartered (optional)

First make your toast points, you can do this by cutting out your bread with a cookie cutter and toasting in the oven. Put your eggs in a saucepan of cold, salted water. Bring to a boil, reduce the heat and simmer for 10 minutes, then drain, cool under cold running water and draining again. Set aside. Shell the eggs and carefully remove the yolks. Chop both whites and yolks finely, keeping them separate. Arrange the hard-cooked egg white, yolks, parsley and onion around the rim of four individual plates, leaving the center free for the caviar, which should be added just before serving. The sour cream may be put on the plate or passed around in a bowl. If you must, add a lemon wedge to each portion.

Serves 4.

## BROOKS SHAW & SON OLD COUNTRY STORE

### Casey Jones Village
### 56 Casey Jones Lane
### Jackson, TN 38305

**Anne L. Shaw**     **T. Clark Shaw**
**Deborah Shaw Laman**     **Norwood Jones**
**Lawrence Taylor, Owners**

*Brooks Shaw & Son Old Country Store opened in April 1965 as a museum and later added a full operation store, ice cream parlor and restaurant. The operation now encompasses a 500-seat restaurant with three country-style buffets daily, an 1890's Ice Cream Parlor, and a 6,000 square foot gift shop. In addition, Brooks Shaw & Son is the operator of the Casey Jones Home and Railroad Museum and Train Store. This tourist attraction hosts over 800,000 visitors a year and is listed in the Top 10 tourist attractions in the state of Tennessee.*

## DONNIE'S HOMEMADE BISCUITS

| | | | |
|---|---|---|---|
| 2 | cups self-rising flour | ¼ | cup shortening |
| | | ¾ | cup buttermilk |

Preheat oven to 450 degrees. Cut shortening into flour, add milk. Turn out dough onto lightly floured board and knead until smooth. Roll dough ¼ inch thick and cut with 2-inch biscuit cutter. Place biscuits onto lightly greased pan. Bake 10 to 12 minutes or until brown.

*(Original recipe from Chef Donnie Newble, employee of the Old Country Store since 1965)*

Yield: 12 to 14 biscuits

## COLE SLAW FOR A GREAT PICNIC

| | | | |
|---|---|---|---|
| 1 | large head fresh cabbage – chopped finely | 1 | cup sugar |
| | | 1 | tablespoon mustard seed |
| 1 | large green bell pepper – chopped finely | 1 | tablespoon turmeric |
| | | 1 | tablespoon salt |
| 1 | cup apple cider vinegar | 1 | tablespoon celery |

Mix vinegar, sugar, mustard seed, turmeric, salt and celery seed thoroughly and heat to boiling point. While hot, pour over cabbage and pepper mixture and mix all thoroughly. Chill and serve.

Serves 12 to 15 people.

## OLD COUNTRY STORE FRIED GREEN TOMATOES

| | | | |
|---|---|---|---|
| 2 | green tomatoes (sliced ½ inch thick per slice) | 1 | cup cornmeal |
| | | ¼ | cup flour |
| | | 1 | teaspoon salt |
| 4 | eggs, beaten | 1 | dash black pepper |

Mix all dry ingredients thoroughly. Dredge tomatoes in egg. Dust with cornmeal mix. Fry in 350 degree oil until golden brown on both sides.

Serves 2.

## OLD COUNTRY STORE CHESS PIE

| | | | |
|---|---|---|---|
| 1½ | cup sugar | ¼ | cup milk |
| 1½ | tablespoon flour | 3 | eggs |
| 1½ | tablespoon cornmeal | 1 | stick butter – melted |
| 1 | teaspoon vinegar | 1 | teaspoon vanilla |

Beat eggs. Add sugar, flour and meal to eggs. Stir. Add vanilla, vinegar and milk. Lastly, add the melted butter. Stir all ingredients well. Put into unbaked pie shell. Bake at 350 degrees for 45 to 50 minutes until firm in the middle.

*(Original recipe of Anne L. Shaw, Chairman of the Board)*

Serves 6 to 8.

## DAVIS-KIDD CAFÉ

### At Davis-Kidd Booksellers 869 North Parkway Jackson, TN 38305

**Rodney Goldy, Café General Manager**

*This is your classic bookstore café — complete with subtle classical music, a variety of espresso based coffee drinks, displays of desserts and bakery and a casual American menu of salads, sandwiches, pot pies and homemade soups.*

## QUICHE DI NAPOLI

| | | | |
|---|---|---|---|
| ¼ | cup diced small yellow onion | ¾ | teaspoon dried basil |
| 4 | sliced thin button mushrooms | ¾ | teaspoon dried oregano |
| 1 | cup shredded boneless skinless chicken breasts | ⅓ | cup diced tomatoes |
| | | 3 | large eggs |
| ½ | cup crumbled feta cheese | 1 | egg yolk |
| | | 1 | teaspoon salt |
| ½ | teaspoon dried rosemary | 1 | teaspoon pepper |
| | | 1½ | cups heavy cream |
| ½ | teaspoon dried thyme | 1 | 9-inch partially baked pie shell |

Preheat oven to 375 degrees.

**For the filling:** Combine onion, mushrooms, chicken breasts and dried herbs and tomatoes and spread on the bottom of the pie crust.

**For the custard filling:** In bowl, blend the cream and eggs together with salt and pepper. Pour mixture over ingredients in pie crust. Bake at 375 degrees for about 35 minutes, until filling is set and golden.

Serves 4 to 6.

## DILL POTATO SALAD

| | | | |
|---|---|---|---|
| 1 | ounce Dijon mustard | 4 | ounces cider vinegar |
| ½ | tablespoon sugar | ¼ | cup fresh dill minced fine |
| ½ | cup peeled garlic | | |
| ½ | tablespoon salt | ½ | cup fresh parsley minced fine |
| ¼ | teaspoon cracked black pepper | 1 | teaspoon dry dill weed |
| ¼ | quart olive oil | | |
| 1 | cup vegetable oil | 1½ | pounds red potatoes |

**Dressing:** Chop garlic finely in bowl of food processor. Add mustard, sugar, salt and pepper and process. Combine oils in large bowl. Add the mustard garlic mixture from above to bowl and mix ell with a wire whip. Add vinegar to bowl and continue to mix. Add dill and parsley to the dressing and mix.

**To cook potatoes:** Place potatoes in large pot and cover with water by one inch. Add 2 tablespoons salt and bring to a boil. Turn down the heat and simmer for approximately 10 to 12 minutes. Potatoes should be firm but not hard. Gently drain the potatoes. When the potatoes are cool enough to handle, cut into quarters.

**To finish the salad:** While the potatoes are still warm, pour the dressing on the potatoes and toss together. Let stand at room temperature until cooled. After potatoes have cooled, place into a container and refrigerate.

Yield: 6 to 8 servings

NASHVILLE, Tennessee's state capitol, is one of the fastest growing cities in the nation. Because of the Grand Ole Opry, Nashville is a primary destination point for country music lovers. Nashville is affectionately called "Music City USA." The International Country Music Fan Fair is held each June. More than nine million visitors arrive in Nashville annually. The area known as Music Row is the heart of Nashville's recording industry. Music Row is the home of more than a dozen major record labels and many music publishing companies. Nashville is also known as the "Athens of the South" because of the full-size replica of the Parthenon and the fact that sixteen institutions of higher learning, including Vanderbilt University, are located here. The Hermitage, home of President Andrew Jackson, is located in east Nashville. The AFC champion Tennessee Titans of the NFL and the NHL Predators call Nashville home.

BRENTWOOD, located south of Nashville in Williamson County, is an upscale community. Williamson County, the fastest growing community in the state, has the highest per capita income. Brentwood has some of the finest residential construction in the area.

FRANKLIN, another upscale community, is the county seat of Williamson County. It is located south of Brentwood. Franklin retains its small-town charm but because of its proximity to Nashville, offers a wide variety of antique and specialty shopping. Franklin's historic downtown is listed in the National Register of Historic Places. Many of Franklin's specialty shops line the downtown area.

MURFREESBORO was the capitol of Tennessee from 1819 to 1825. It is one of the fastest growing cities in the Southeast. The Stones River National Military Park was established in 1927 to preserve the relics of the battle of Stones River during the Civil War. Middle Tennessee State University, the third largest university in Tennessee, is located in Murfreesboro.

COLUMBIA is the county seat of Maury County. The eleventh president of the United States, James K. Polk, lived here. Polk was governor of Tennessee for one term and also served in the U.S. House of

Representatives for seven terms. Columbians celebrate Mule Day every year. In the mid-1800's Columbia became a crossroads for mule traders.

CLARKSVILLE was established in 1784. It is the fifth-largest city in Tennessee. The Clarksville-Montgomery County Museum is located at 200 South Second Street. Information on walking and driving tours are available at the museum. Within the city the River Walk has an amphitheater, river dock and riverboat that offers cruises on the Cumberland River daily. Bed and breakfasts in the area include the Hachland Hill Inn, which has seven rooms with private baths as well as three log cabins.

SHELBYVILLE is known as the Walking Horse Capital of the World. The Southern plantation walking horse, better known as the Tennessee Walking Horse, was derived from the horses used on the plantations in middle Tennessee during the nineteenth century. The annual Tennessee Walking Horse show is held during a ten-day period and the grand champion is named at the conclusion of the event.

LYNCHBURG is the county seat of Moore County. Jack Daniel was born near here in 1848. Jack discovered that the iron-free spring water from Cave Spring would be needed to make good whiskey, so he bought the spring. In 1866, Jack's distillery was the first in the country to receive a federal license.

McMINNVILLE is the county seat of Warren County. Because of its elevation and variety of soils on the Highland Rim, Warren County is known as "the nursery capital of the world." It is one of the largest nursery producers in the nation. Cumberland Caverns, the largest cave in Tennessee and the second largest in the United States, is located 7 miles from here.

SPARTA is the county seat of White County and is located near the Cumberland Plateau on the Eastern Highland Rim. Bluegrass musician Lester Flatt grew up near Sparta and an annual gospel and bluegrass festival is held in his honor at the Foggy Mountain Music Park. Fall Creek Falls, the highest waterfall in the eastern United States, is located about thirty miles from Sparta.

# HACHLAND HILL DINING INN

## 1601 Madison Street
## Clarksville, TN 37043
## 931-647-4084

*A secluded dining inn located 45 minutes from Nashville seems an unlikely place to find Châteaubriand, Oysters Rockefeller, or other celebrated dishes. But such surprises are a common occurrence at Hachland Hill Dining Inn. The overnight guests will long remember* **true Southern Hospitality!**

**Phila Rawlings Hach**
**Inn Keeper, Gourmet & Renowned Author**

*Phila Hach, a lady of incredible diversity and multi-faceted talent deservedly has earned the reputation as one of the South's favorite speakers and chefs. Phila has served editors and staffs of leading magazines,* **Bon Appetit, Gourmet Food & Wine,** *and* **Better Homes & Gardens** *in her beautiful and famous Hachland Hill Dining Inn. In the early 50's Phila Hach did the first cooking show in the South over WSM-TV in Nashville!*

*The following recipes are from Phila Hach's* **1982 World's Fair Cookbook.**

## CRACKER BALL SOUP

| 2 | cups cracker crumbs | 4 | half-egg shells of water |
|---|---|---|---|
| 4 | eggs | | Salt, pepper and |
| 3 | tablespoons chicken fat | | minced parsley |
| | | | Dash nutmeg |

Beat eggs, then add chicken fat, water and seasoning to taste. Add sufficient cracker crumbs to make stiff dough. Shape into small balls and drop into boiling chicken broth that has been flavored generously with parsley. Let boil for 30 minutes.

## COQ AU VIN

Place chicken breast (skin side down) in baking pan. Sprinkle with:

| ½ | teaspoon dry mustard | ½ | teaspoon dried sage |
|---|---|---|---|
| ½ | teaspoon onion powder | ½ | teaspoon dried oregano |
| ½ | teaspoon dried basil | | |

Dot with butter – ¼ cup. Add 1 cup water and 1 cup good sherry wine. Cover and bake in 350 degree oven for 1 hour. Remove cover and allow chicken to brown. Drain juice from chicken and thicken with cornstarch. Add ¼ cup red wine and 1 small can sliced mushrooms. Correct seasoning and serve with: Orange Rice. (Rice cooked in ½ water and ½ orange juice – this is grand!) Season with salt, pepper and plenty of butter.

Single serving

## CHESS PIE

| 1 | cup sugar | 1 | teaspoon almond flavoring |
|---|---|---|---|
| ½ | cup butter | | |
| 3 | eggs | ½ | cup ground almonds (optional) |
| 1½ | teaspoons vinegar | | or 1 tablespoon cornmeal |
| 1 | teaspoon vanilla flavoring | | |

Cream butter; add sugar gradually and blend thoroughly. Add eggs and beat well. Stir in vanilla and almond flavoring. Sprinkle unbaked pie shell with ground almonds then pour in the above mixture and bake in 400 degree oven for 12 minutes. Reduce heat to 350 degrees and bake for 15 minutes longer until done.

Yield: 1 pie

Hachland Hill Inn
Joe & Phila Hach
Owners

## FLUFFY HOT CAKES

| | | | |
|---|---|---|---|
| 1 | egg | 1 | cup flour, sifted |
| ¾ | cup and 2 tablespoons milk | ½ | teaspoon salt |
| 2 | tablespoons melted shortening | 2 | tablespoons baking powder |
| | | 2 | tablespoons sugar |

Beat all ingredients until smooth. Bake on griddle until fluffy and brown. Turn only once.

## SOUTHERN SQUASH SUPREME

| | | | |
|---|---|---|---|
| 1 | gallon shredded squash | 1 | cup melted butter |
| 1 | cup shredded onion | 1 | cup flour |
| 2 | teaspoons black pepper | ¼ | cup cornstarch |
| 1 | tablespoon salt | 2 | tablespoons sugar |
| | | 4 | cups milk |
| | | 8 | eggs, slightly beaten |

Mix all ingredients in order given. Pour into 12x20 inch pan. Bake 45 to 50 minutes at 350 degrees.
30 Servings

## ROAST PORK

| | |
|---|---|
| 1 | pork loin (rub with salt, pepper and oregano) |

**Sauté:**

| | | | |
|---|---|---|---|
| ½ | cup chopped onions | 2 | chopped bell peppers |
| 2 | cloves garlic | 6 | tablespoons oil |

**Add:**

| | | | |
|---|---|---|---|
| ½ | cup honey | 1½ | teaspoons salt |
| ½ | cup tomato purée | | Dash of cayenne pepper |
| ½ | cup wine vinegar | | |
| 1 | teaspoon dried oregano | | |

Pour over roast and bake covered for 1 hour at 350 degrees, basting frequently. Serve with boiled onions and green rice (rice to which lots of butter and fresh chopped parsley has been added).

Serves 6 to 8.

## SHRIMP DIJON

| | | | |
|---|---|---|---|
| ½ | cup chopped shallots | | Salt and pepper to taste |
| 1 | teaspoon minced garlic | 2 | pounds boiled shrimp |
| 4 | tablespoons butter | | Cornstarch and water to thicken |
| 1 | teaspoon thyme | 1 | cup cracker crumbs |
| 1 | teaspoon basil | | Butter |
| 1 | cup sauterne | | |
| ¼ | cup sherry | | |
| 1 | tablespoon Dijon mustard | | |

Sauté shallots and garlic in butter for 5 minutes. Add thyme, basil, wines, mustard, salt and pepper. Bring to a boil and thicken with cornstarch and water. Stir in shrimp. Put in casserole and top with crumbs. Dot with butter and bake in 350 degree oven until brown, about 20 minutes.

# THE ROSE GARDEN TEA ROOM

### 512 Madison Street
### Clarksville, TN 37040

**Mary Higgs Beach, Owner**
*This beautiful Victorian mansion was built in 1886 in historic downtown Clarksville. It features 5 elegant dining areas and a Courtyard Garden shop. The Rose Garden Tea Room has been featured in **Southern Living** Magazine in October, 1999 and June, 2000. It has also been featured in **Nashville Lifestyles** and **Clarksville** Magazine. It will also be featured in an upcoming issue of **Victoria** Magazine!*

## THE ROSE GARDEN SPINACH SALAD WITH HOUSE VINAIGRETTE DRESSING

**Dressing:**

| | | | |
|---|---|---|---|
| ¼ | cup sugar | 1 | tablespoon parsley |
| ¼ | cup apple cider vinegar | 1 | tablespoon chives |
| 2 | tablespoons canola oil | 1 | teaspoon Worcestershire sauce |
| 1 | tablespoon green onion | 1 | teaspoon mustard |
| | | 1 | ice cube |

Shake and chill.

**Salad fixings:**

| | |
|---|---|
| Fresh spinach | Nuts |
| Bacon | Raisins |
| Mushrooms | Red onions |
| Mandarin oranges | |

# CHICKEN ARTICHOKE CASSEROLE*

| | | | |
|---|---|---|---|
| 5 | boiled chicken breasts (cut up) | ¾ | can (16 ounces) mushrooms (drained) |
| 1 | cup butter | | |
| ½ | cup flour | 3 | cups artichoke hearts (drained and cut) |
| 3½ | cups milk | | |
| 1 | cup grated cheddar cheese | ½ | teaspoon garlic powder |
| 3 | ounces Gruyère cheese chunks | ½ | teaspoon cayenne pepper |

Preheat oven to 350 degrees. Melt butter in a saucepan. Slowly, add flour, stir until smooth. Slowly blend in milk, cayenne pepper, Accent and garlic powder until dissolved. Next, add grated cheddar cheese and Gruyère cheese chunks. Stir over medium heat until mixture thickens. Now, mix together cut-up chicken, mushrooms, artichokes and sauce. Pour into a 3-quart casserole dish and cook for 45 minutes at 350 degrees.

*This is a home recipe of Annette Shrader, a Clarksville Southern Belle, who was The Rose Garden's chef during its first year. This is still a very favorite entrée at The Rose Garden Tea Room.*

Serves 14.

# ROSE GARDEN FUDGE PIE*

| | | | |
|---|---|---|---|
| **Combine and mix:** | | 1½ | cup butter, melted |
| 3 | beaten eggs | ½ | cup flour |
| 1½ | cups sugar | 2 | teaspoons vanilla |
| 1 | cup Hershey's cocoa | 2 | handfuls pecans |

Preheat oven to 350 degrees. Pre-bake crust 10 minutes. Bake 20 minutes (no longer). Yes!..It will look muddy; take out and cool. Serves 8.

*This recipe originated from the Pan Am Grill which was Clarksville's first home restaurant. The owner of the Pan Am Grill lived in this house at 512 Madison Street and was Irene Johnson Beach - great grandmother to Mary and John Beach's children who live here now.*

## CRANBERRY-APPLE CRISP

*The Rose Garden Tea Room serves this hot in the winter as a side dish to the chicken casseroles.*

Preheat oven to 350 degrees. Preparation time: 45 minutes.

**Combine:**

| | | | |
|---|---|---|---|
| 3 | cups peeled, chopped apples | 2 | tablespoons all-purpose flour |
| 2 | cups fresh cranberries | | |

Pour into the casserole dish.

**Add:**

1 cup sugar and toss to coat

**Topping:**
**Combine:**

| | | | |
|---|---|---|---|
| 4 | ounces oatmeal | ½ | cup firmly packed brown sugar |
| ¾ | cup chopped pecans | ½ | cup butter, melted |
| ½ | cup flour | | |

Mix well and spoon over the fruit mixture. Bake uncovered at 350 degrees for 45 minutes.

Serves: 8 to 10

*The Rose Garden Tea Room*

## VALENTINO'S RISTORANTE

### 1907 West End Avenue Nashville, TN 37203

**Kevin Beitter, General Manager**
**Sime Glavan, Executive Chef**
*Chef Glavan is a native of Croatia. His culinary training was in Europe prior to coming to the United States as a chef 25 years ago. Chef Glavan's culinary experiences include 14 years on a luxury cruise ship.*

## SHRIMP SCAMPI

| | | | |
|---|---|---|---|
| 20 | pieces of 16/20 count shrimp, peeled | 1 | tablespoon lemon juice |
| 12 | ounces butter | 1 | tablespoon A1 sauce |
| 1 | teaspoon minced garlic | 1 | tablespoon Worcestershire sauce |
| 1 | teaspoon minced parsley | 1 | tablespoon white wine |

Mix (with a mixer) butter, garlic, white wine, lemon juice, A1 sauce and Worcestershire sauce until it is nice and fluffy. In the meantime, bake shrimp in the oven at 450 degrees for 3 to 5 minutes. In a large skillet heat the butter mixture over medium heat, add shrimp and serve.

Serves 3 to 4 as appetizer.

## GROUPER WITH TOMATO SAUCE

| | | | |
|---|---|---|---|
| 4 | pounds of fresh grouper in 4 pieces | 2 | cups seafood stock |
| 1 | large onion, minced | 1 | cup milk or sour cream |
| 1 | tablespoon olive oil | 12 | medium shrimp |
| 1 | cup white wine | ½ | teaspoon hot pepper sauce |
| 1 | tablespoon butter | 1 | tablespoon tomato paste |
| ½ | lemon juice | | |
| 1 | teaspoon seafood base | | |

In a large skillet, add minced onions and sauté (stirring until lightly colored). Add fish, white wine, lemon juice, fish base, tomato paste and fish stock. Cover and simmer slowly for 20 minutes. Take fish out and add milk or sour cream to the fish sauce. Add shrimp and cook for 3 to 5 minutes or until shrimp are red in color. Serve the sauce over the grouper along with a green vegetable.

Serves 4.

VALENTINO'S
RISTORANTE

## RICOTTA CHEESECAKE

| | | | |
|---|---|---|---|
| 1 | cup superfine sugar | 8 | ounces chilled unsalted butter, in small pieces |
| 3 | tablespoons water | | |
| 5 | tablespoons pine nuts | 1 | egg |
| 4 | tablespoons golden raisins | 1 | teaspoon vanilla |
| 2 | tablespoons rum | 1½ | pounds whole-milk ricotta |
| 3½ | cups flour | 1 | teaspoon grated lemon rind |
| ½ | cup dark brown sugar | 2 | ounces milk chocolate, coarsely chopped |
| 1¼ | cups ground almonds | | |

In a 1-quart saucepan, heat ¼ cup of the superfine sugar and the water over high heat. When the mixture boils and sugar dissolves, add pine nuts. Continue cooking, swirling pan often, until sugar turns a light brown. Turn out mixture onto an oiled baking sheet and let cool. Break up into small chunks. Combine raisins and rum in a small bowl and set aside for 1 hour. To make dough in a food processor: combine flour, baking powder, brown sugar and almonds in a work-bowl of the food processor. Process for 2 seconds. Add butter and process until mixture resembles coarse meal (about 10 seconds). Whisk egg and vanilla together, then add to food processor with motor running. Process just until dough nearly hold together. Turn out dough onto a board and gather into a ball. Do not knead or work the dough, even if it doesn't hold together well. Wrap in plastic and refrigerate for at least 1 hour.

In a large bowl, combine ricotta, the remaining sugar, lemon rind, raisins and rum. Add chocolate pieces and pine-nut brittle; mix well. Preheat oven to 350 degrees F and line bottom and sides of a 10-inch springform baking pan with foil. Place a little more than half of the dough on the pan patting it into place and pushing it into place and part way up the sides. Spoon in the ricotta filling; roll out remaining pastry into a 10-inch round and lay it over the top of the filling. Bake 50 to 55 minutes until top colors slightly. Transfer cheesecake to a rack and cool in the pan. Release sides of the springform pan and gently peel back the foil from the sides. Lift the bottom of the cake gently with a spatula and pull out the foil.

Yield: 1 10-inch cheesecake

## BASANTE'S RESTAURANT

### 1800 West End Avenue
### Nashville, TN 37203

*Basante's Restaurant received the writer's choice award for Best New Restaurant in 1998 from* **In Review** *Magazine. Basante's has also received numerous other great reviews from food writers in the area.*

**Luis A. Fonseca, Jr., Chef/Owner**
**Chef Steve Chapman**

*Steve Chapman is a native of Fairfield, California and is married with 3 children. Chef Steve is a 1994 honors graduate from the California Culinary Academy in Sacramento. Previous cooking stints include the Sunset Grill and the Bound'ry in Nashville.*

## ASIAN VINAIGRETTE WITH SEARED SCALLOPS

### ASIAN VINAIGRETTE

| | | | |
|---|---|---|---|
| ¾ | cup soy sauce | ¼ | bunch chopped cilantro |
| 1½ | cups rice wine vinegar | ¼ | bunch chopped green onion |
| 1¼ | cups olive oil | ¾ | teaspoon garlic, minced |
| 2 | tablespoons sesame oil | ¾ | teaspoon shallot, minced |
| ¾ | tablespoon fresh lemon juice | 1 | tablespoon basil, chopped |
| ½ | tablespoon fresh lime juice | | |
| ½ | tablespoon fresh orange juice | | |

For dressing mix all together. Make sure to shake the dressing well to incorporate all the flavors. Sear 2 large scallops (per serving) until golden on both sides. Use Diver or U-10 Dry-Pack Scallops. Prepare the plate with the mixed greens in dressing. Drizzle a little vinaigrette over the scallops and garnish with julienne carrots and chopped parsley.

## BLACK PEPPER TUNA WITH PINOT NOIR SAUCE & BALSAMIC SYRUP

| | | | |
|---|---|---|---|
| 2 | pounds sushi grade tuna (ahi or yellow fin) | 1 | cup Pinot Noir |
| | | 1 | tablespoon shallots |
| 4 | tablespoons black peppercorns | 1 | ounce heavy cream |
| | | ¾ | pound unsalted butter |
| 2 | cups balsamic vinegar (reduced to syrup) | | Salt to taste |

Cut tuna into 7 to 8 ounce pieces. Crack pepper with a grinder or if a grinder is unavailable, use the back of a frying pan. Lightly coat the tuna with the pepper and salt to taste. Grill medium rare. To make sauce, reduce wine and shallots until the liquid is almost gone. Add the cream and bring to boil and reduce until cream thickens, lower heat, and slowly add butter whisking to incorporate. Season with salt and pepper to taste.

**Serving idea:** Serve tuna on mashed potatoes with Brie or boursin cheese.

**Note:** To garnish plate place potatoes in the middle, tuna on potatoes and drizzle 2 ounces of pinot sauce over top. Drizzle balsamic next (use sparingly since balsamic will overpower the flavors). Place your favorite vegetables around the plate.

Serves 4.

## FLOURLESS CHOCOLATE CAKE WITH PORT WINE RASPBERRY SAUCE

| | | | |
|---|---|---|---|
| 1½ | pounds bittersweet chocolate | 12 | large eggs (separate out yolks) |
| 8 | ounces butter | | |
| 1½ | ounces cocoa powder | 6 | ounces granulated sugar |

Preheat oven to 350 degrees. Melt the chocolate and butter together in a double boiler, and then add the cocoa. Set aside. Whip egg yolks till frothy, set aside. Whip whites and 4½ ounces of sugar until it peaks easily. Add egg yolks to the chocolate mixture and then gently fold in the egg white mixture. Pour mixture into the baking pan and bake in center of oven at 350 degrees for 40 to 45 minutes. Center should be slightly wet. Make sure pans are floured and buttered before starting.

## GLAZE FROSTING FOR FLOURLESS CHOCOLATE CAKE

| | | | |
|---|---|---|---|
| ½ | pound bittersweet chocolate | ½ | cup toasted almonds (in the middle layer) |
| 4 | ounces butter | | |
| ¼ | cup dark corn syrup | | |

To make glaze, melt all together over a double-boiler. Pour glaze into the middle of cake to hold together, then glaze the top and sides.

## PORT WINE SAUCE

| | | | |
|---|---|---|---|
| 3 | cups port wine | 1 | cup fresh raspberries as garnish |
| 2½ | cups sugar | | |
| 1 | cup raspberries | | |

Cook wines until alcohol is gone, then add sugar and berries, simmer until sugar is dissolved. Add berries when sauce is cooled as a garnish.

## SUNDRIED TOMATO SPAGHETTI WITH EXTRA VIRGIN OLIVE OIL, TOASTED GARLIC & FRESH ITALIAN PARSLEY

| | | | |
|---|---|---|---|
| 1 | pound fresh sundried tomato spaghetti | 2 | dried red chilies |
| | | ½ | cup Italian parsley, roughly chopped |
| 6 | tablespoons extra virgin olive oil | ⅓ | cup freshly grated aged asiago cheese |
| 4 | medium garlic cloves, chopped | | |

In a heavy skillet over low heat, cook garlic and red pepper very gently in the olive oil until garlic is lightly browned. Remove chile and use in your favorite recipe. While this is cooking, cook pasta in rapidly boiling heavily salted water for 2 to 3 minutes until just cooked. Pasta should be firm. Drain and immediately toss with the asiago cheese, fresh parsley and garlic oil mixture. Garnish with additional asiago cheese and enjoy!

Serves 2.

## CONCHIGLIE SALAD WITH ROASTED FENNEL & SESAME GINGER VINAIGRETTE

### SALAD

| | | | |
|---|---|---|---|
| 2 | pounds fresh conchiglie (sea shells) pasta | 1 | cup roughly chopped fresh Italian parsley |
| 4 | large heads fresh fennel bulb | 1 | cup carrot julienne into ½ inch strips |
| 1 | cup roughly chopped rinsed Kalamata olives | 1 | bunch chopped green onions |

### VINAIGRETTE

| | | | |
|---|---|---|---|
| 2 | teaspoons tangerine zest | 4 | tablespoons safflower oil |
| 4 | tablespoons tangerine juice | 2 | tablespoons Tamari |
| 4 | teaspoons finely grated ginger | 2 | tablespoons toasted sesame oil |
| 5 | tablespoons seasoned rice wine vinegar | | Pinch sea salt |

Wash and trim fennel bulbs, rub with olive oil and season with sea salt and freshly ground black pepper. Roast in a 450-degree oven for 20 minutes or until fennel is tender but not overcooked. Cool and julienne into ½ inch strips. Whisk all the ingredients for the dressing and let sit for 1 hour at room temperature. Cook the pasta in rapidly boiling salted water for 2 to 3 minutes or until just cooked. Pasta should still be firm. Drain but do not rinse and immediately toss with remaining ingredients and the vinaigrette. Chill for 1 hour. Enjoy!

*This is a wonderful summertime salad and served with freshly baked Tuscan bread and a crisp white wine makes a delicious lunch.*

Serves 6 guests.

## PENNE WITH SHRIMP & ARTICHOKES

| | | | |
|---|---|---|---|
| 1 | pound of fresh penne pasta | 4 | tablespoon extra virgin olive oil |
| 5 | baby globe artichokes | 1 | teaspoon lemon juice |
| 12 | large 16/20 count shrimp | ¼ | cup roughly chopped fresh Italian parsley |
| 2 | large minced garlic cloves | ¼ | cup water |
| 1 | tablespoon butter | ¼ | cup finely grated Pecorino cheese |

Add a little lemon juice to a bowl of cold water. Clean and quarter the artichokes and place in the water. Drain and dry. Peel and de-vein shrimp. In a heavy skillet over medium heat, sauté the artichokes and garlic gently in the olive and butter for 10 minutes or until tender. Add the shrimp, lemon juice and water and cook over medium–high heat until the shrimp are cooked. Sprinkle with fresh parsley. Cook pasta in rapidly boiling salted water for 2 to 3 minutes until just cooked. Pasta should be firm. Drain and immediately toss the pasta with the artichokes and shrimp and sprinkle with Pecorino cheese.

Serves 3 to 4 guests.

## AMERIGO, AN ITALIAN RESTAURANT

*Park Place Centre
Memphis, TN 38119*

*1920 West End Avenue
Nashville, TN 37203*

*1656 Westgate Circle
Brentwood, TN 37027*

**Al Roberts & Bill Latham, Proprietors**

*Amerigo was voted #1 Italian restaurant by The Reader's Poll in **Nashville Scene** Magazine!*

## GRILLED PORTOBELLA MUSHROOM SALAD

| | | | |
|---|---|---|---|
| 8 | ounces fresh baby greens | 4 | large portobella mushrooms, stems removed |
| 4 | ounces roasted walnuts | | Olive oil |
| 4 | ounces goat cheese | | Salt & pepper |
| 8 | ounces balsamic vinaigrette | | |

Rub mushrooms with olive oil and season with salt and pepper. Grill until desired doneness. While mushrooms are cooking, arrange mixed greens on 4 plates. Remove mushrooms from grill and slice each one into 6 to 8 slices. Place slices on side of lettuce mix. Top with balsamic vinaigrette, goat cheese and roasted walnuts. Salad can be served with cheese toast or garlic crostinis.

**For vinaigrette:** Utilizing any good quality dried Italian dressing mix, substitute balsamic vinegar for red wine vinegar. Hold in refrigerator until ready to use.

## BOWTIE PASTA CAESAR SALAD

| | | | |
|---|---|---|---|
| 1 | pound chopped romaine lettuce, rinsed and drained | 1 | pound cooked bowtie pasta |
| 8 | ounces Caesar salad dressing | 4 | ounces walnut pesto (recipe follows) |
| 3 | 5-ounce chicken breasts, seasoned and oven roasted, then cooled and sliced thinly | 4 | ounces balsamic vinaigrette |
| | | 2 | ounces diced sundried tomatoes |

Toss salad and Caesar dressing. Separate onto 4 plates. Toss remaining ingredients and place equal portions over Caesar salad. Top with croutons and Parmesan cheese if desired.

## BASIL & WALNUT PESTO

| | | | |
|---|---|---|---|
| 3 | ounces fresh whole basil leaves | 2 | tablespoons chopped fresh garlic |
| 1 | cup extra-virgin olive oil | 1 | teaspoon salt |
| 1/3 | cup chopped walnuts | 1/2 | cup finely grated Parmesan cheese |

Place all ingredients into food processor and purée until smooth. Store in airtight container in refrigerator.

# SUNSET GRILL

## 2001 Belcourt Avenue
## Nashville, TN 37212

**Randy Rayburn, Owner**
**Brian Uhl, Executive Chef**

*This upscale restaurant lives up to its reputation as one of the best restaurants in Nashville. It has won numerous awards such as **Wine Spectator Award of Excellence, Nashville Scenes** Reader Poll Award "For Best Dessert 1st place," "Best Place for a Business Lunch 3rd place" and "Best Wine List at a Restaurant 1st place!"*

## CHOCOLATE DECADENCE CAKE

| | | | |
|---|---|---|---|
| 1 | pound chocolate – bitter sweet | 1½ | ounces espresso |
| 1 | pound butter | 1½ | ounces liqueur (Frangelico, Kamura, etc.) |
| 4 | eggs | | |
| 6½ | ounces sugar | | |

Melt chocolate and butter in double boiler. Combine eggs and sugar. Temper chocolate into eggs. Whisk in espresso and liqueur. Butter and sugar 9" spring pan. Fill to approximately ¾ full. Cover with parchment paper. Bake in steam bath covered with foil at 350 degrees for 45 minutes. Uncover and bake additional 10 minutes.

Yield: 1 cake

# HABANERO BREAD PUDDING

| | | | |
|---|---|---|---|
| 1¼ | cup heavy cream | ¼ | teaspoon habanero sauce |
| 2 | cups milk | | |
| 5 | eggs | 2 | cups butterscotch chips |
| ⅓ | cup sugar | | |
| ½ | teaspoon vanilla | | Bread |

Sprinkle 4 ounces of butterscotch on top of each pan. Melt 12 ounces into mix.

Cube bread into 1 inch cubes. Scald milk and pour over 2 packages of butterscotch chips. Combine eggs and sugar. Temper scalded milk into egg mix. Add cream, vanilla, habanero sauce. Add mixture into bread. Portion into pans and mix in ½ package of chips per pan. Bake at 350 degrees in steam bath covered with foil for 50 minutes. Remove foil and bake an additional 10 minutes to brown top and melt chips.

## BOUND'RY

### 911 20th Avenue South
### Nashville, TN 37212

**Guillermo "Willie" Thomas**
**Executive Chef/Owner**
**Sue Parnell, Office Manager**

*Chef Guillermo "Willie" Thomas was born in Gijon, Spain, raised in the Pittsburgh area and is a 1987 graduate of Johnson and Wales University. Chef Thomas was selected by the James Beard Foundation as one of five Tennessee chefs to prepare a dinner at the Beard House in October of 1996 in celebration of the Tennessee Bicentennial. He was featured on the "Great Chefs of the South" series on the Discovery Channel and was named the city's best chef in the 1996 Nashville Scene's Reader's poll.*

**Jason Krell, Sous Chef**

*Chef Krell was born and reared in Buffalo, NY where he started his first restaurant job at the age of 13. Later his family moved to Tennessee. In 1994, Jason graduated from Opryland Culinary Institute as the youngest in his class. Shortly after culinary school he became the executive chef of the Belle Meade Brasserie and stayed there for a period of three years. In 1996 he won first place in the "Taste of Elegance" Tennessee Port Competition and second place in 1997.*

## SAUTÉED SCALLOPS WITH LOBSTER CORN CRÈME BRÛLÉE & TOMATO VANILLA BEAN SAUCE

### LOBSTER CORN CRÈME BRÛLÉE

| | | | |
|---|---|---|---|
| 2 | ounces grated Parmesan | ½ | pound lobster meat, diced (tail and/or claw) |
| 6 | (6 ounce) ceramic soufflé cups | | |
| 1 | cup milk | 1½ | teaspoon salt |
| 1 | cup heavy cream | ½ | teaspoon black pepper |
| 4 | eggs | | |
| 1 | cup fresh corn puréed (frozen is acceptable) | | |

Preheat oven to 275 degrees. In a sauce pot combine milk, cream, corn purée, salt and pepper, bring to a boil. Add the lobster, simmer for 5 minutes. Blend egg well in a mixing bowl, then slowly pour the mixture in while quickly stirring the hot liquid. This prevents the mixture from scrambling. Place the soufflé cups in a two-inch deep casserole dish and spray non-stick vegetable spray, fill the dish ½ way with water. Ladle the mixture into the soufflé cups. Cover the entire top with aluminum foil and bake 45 minutes to 1 hour.

Yield: 6 servings

### TOMATO VANILLA BEAN SAUCE

| | | | |
|---|---|---|---|
| 1 | cup sherry wine | 1 | small onion sliced |
| 1 | vanilla bean | 1 | (28 ounce) can crushed tomatoes |
| 4 | Roma tomatoes, cored and cut in half | | Salt and pepper to taste |

Split vanilla bean and scrape pulp into a pot with sherry, reduce ½ way. Char tomatoes and onions on the grill then add to the sherry along with the canned tomatoes. Simmer for 20 minutes. Remove the vanilla bean and blend in the blender. Season to taste.

### SCALLOPS

| | | | |
|---|---|---|---|
| 24 | to 36 quarter size scallops | | Black pepper |
| | Kosher salt | 1 | tablespoon olive oil |

Place sauté pan on high heat. Season the scallops with salt and pepper. Place in the sauté pan browning the top and bottom 1minute on each side. Ladle the sauce on the plate with the brûlée in the center, then place the scallops around it. Check the brûlée by sticking a paring knife in the center. If it's dry, it's finished. When it's finished, pull out of the oven and chill until needed. Before serving sprinkle Parmesan cheese on top and re-heat under a broiler. Pop it out of the soufflé cup and serve cheese side up.

## BOUND'RY

### 911 20th Avenue South
### Nashville, TN 37212

**Callie Johnson, Pastry Chef**

## MILK CHOCOLATE BANANA CRÈME BRÛLÉE

| | | | |
|---|---|---|---|
| 2 | cups heavy cream | ¼ | teaspoon cinnamon |
| 2 | cups milk | 5 | ounces milk |
| 3 | ounces sugar | | chocolate |
| ½ | cup rum – boiled | | (chopped) |
| | and reduced by | 10 | egg yolks |
| | half | 3 | bananas |
| ¼ | teaspoon mace | | |
| | (nutmeg spice) | | |

Combine milk, cream and sugar and bring to a boil. Reduce rum in separate pan, set aside. Whisk until blended. Add spiced rum reduction to cream mixture. Whisk until blended. Temper in egg yolks. Slice bananas and place in bottom of ramekins. Pour custard into ramekins. Bake in a water bath at 275 degrees for about 25 minutes or until set in center. After custard is complete, chill for approximately 3 hours. Sprinkle top of custards with granulated sugar and burn with a blow torch or put under broiler for approximately 15 seconds. Serve immediately.

*Note: This custard is best served the day it is made so the bananas do not brown from exposure.*

Serves 4 to 6.

## MIDTOWN CAFÉ

### 102 19th Avenue South
### Nashville, TN 37203

*Midtown Café has been in business for over 10 years. In September, 1997, Randy Rayburn purchased Midtown and has an impressive culinary management team in place. Midtown recently was honored with an award from the International Restaurant and Hospitality Rating Bureau as one of the Top 25 Restaurants in America in its category. The **Nashville Scene** Readers Poll voted Midtown "The Best Place for Romantic Dining" and "The Best Place for a Business Lunch."*

**Gary Tunks, Executive Chef**

*Chef Gary is a native of Fort Lauderdale, Florida. He has 15 years culinary experience, the last 3 years as executive chef at Midtown Grill.*

## SEA SCALLOPS & PRAWNS OVER CRAWFISH SAFFRON RISOTTO

| | | | |
|---|---|---|---|
| 8 | large sea scallops | 10 | cups fish or |
| 8 | prawns | | chicken stock |
| 1 | red bell pepper, | ½ | pound butter |
| | diced | 1½ | cup Parmesan |
| 1 | green bell pepper, | | cheese |
| | diced | | Pinch of saffron |
| 1 | red onion, diced | 1 | pound crawfish |
| ½ | cup olive oil | | tails |
| 4 | cups arborio rice | | Salt and cracked |
| | | | black pepper |

**Risotto Preparation:** Heat olive oil in a large saucepan and cook the onions and peppers, very gently without browning. Then add rice and stir the grains until they absorb oil and become translucent. Add stock and stir until the rice begins to absorb. Add crawfish tails, butter, salt, pepper & saffron. Allow to cook on low heat for 15 minutes. Stir. (Rice should be soft). Add Parmesan cheese and adjust seasoning. Grill or pan-sear scallops and prawns. Place on top of risotto. Garnish with roasted Roma tomatoes and chives.

Serves 4.

## ZOLA RESTAURANTE

### 3001 West End Avenue
### Nashville, TN 37203

**Debra Paquette, Executive Chef/Owner**

*Chef Paquette is a graduate of the Culinary Institute of America and a nationally-recognized chef. Her twenty year culinary experiences include a stint as Executive Chef at the Bound'ry and 2½ years at Zola. The 1999 Reader's Poll at the* **Nashville Scene** *voted Zola one of the top three "Best New Restaurants" opened since January 1998. It also received the #2 ranking in the same poll for "Best (Most Original) Menu" for the* **Nashville Scene** *Reader's Poll. A recent article in the* **New York Times** *featured Zola's as one of the top new restaurants in the Nashville area.*

*John Mariami of* **Spirit Magazine** *wrote an article last year on the "Eleven Modern Master Chefs" of the year — and Debra was one of them. Also, she can be seen on the "Great Chefs of the South" on the Discovery Channel.*

## CHORIZO & MANCHEGO EGG ROLLS

### CHORIZO

| | | | |
|---|---|---|---|
| 3 | pounds of ground pork | ⅓ | cup chili powder |
| 1 | to 2 tablespoons fresh chopped garlic | 1 | tablespoon ground cumin |
| ¾ | cup red wine vinegar | 2 | tablespoons paprika |
| 1 | tablespoon salt | 2½ | tablespoons oregano |

Mix very well. Cook a small patty to see if the flavor suits you. If o.k., place on cookie sheet pan, press to ½ inch thick and bake at 350 degrees for 15 to 20 minutes. Remove from oven carefully, let sit with fat for 15 minutes and then pour it off. Cool.

### OLIVE PASTE

| | | | |
|---|---|---|---|
| 8 | to 10 green olives (rinse) | 1 | teaspoon honey |
| ½ | cup golden raisins | | Pinch of salt |
| ¼ | cup roasted almonds | | if needed |

Mince to make a paste. (Almonds should be slightly broken to give a crunchy texture)

You'll need ¼ pound of manchego (sheep's milk cheese) or other good milk cheese. Cut in slivers 3 inch long by ¼ inch wide. Let out egg roll wrappers (never leave uncovered). Make an egg wash (1 egg with water). Place ⅓ cup chorizo sausage at one end of wrapper and press to a long thin rectangle. Lay 2 tablespoons of olive paste and 2 slices of cheese on top. Carefully fold egg roll and seal with egg wash. Dust with cornstarch so that egg rolls will not stick to one another. Deep fry for 2 minutes or sear in 1 inch of oil in sauté pan, turning to brown all sides. (You can also spray with vegetable oil (Pam) and bake in 350 degree oven for 10 minutes.)

Serve with aioli verde!

### AÏOLI

| | | | |
|---|---|---|---|
| ½ | bunch parsley tops | ¼ | cup olive oil |
| ⅛ | cup capers | | Pinch salt |
| 3 | garlic cloves | | Pinch cayenne |
| 1 | spring onion | | |

Place in blender or Cuisinart and blend until smooth. Blend or hand stir in 1½ cups mayonnaise.

**Restaurante**

*Zola*

## APPLE SQUASH PEANUT CRISP

*People love a great pork loin and the South loves their peanuts. The following recipe goes great with pork chops, roast of tenderloin and maybe a little sorghum butter.*

### FILLING

| | | | |
|---|---|---|---|
| 2 | medium onions, medium dice | ¼ | cup honey |
| 2 | medium butternut or acorn squash, medium dice | ⅛ | cup flour |
| | | 2 | teaspoons black pepper (coarse grind) |
| 3 | Granny Smith apples, peeled and medium dice | 1 | teaspoon salt |
| | | ¼ | cup vegetable oil |

### CRISP

| | | | |
|---|---|---|---|
| 1 | cup cornmeal | 1 | teaspoon cinnamon |
| 1 | cup all-purpose flour | | Pinch of cayenne |
| 1 | cup oats | ½ | pound melted butter |
| 1 | tablespoon thyme | ¾ | cup sugar |
| 1 | tablespoon coarse black pepper | 2 | cups rough chopped peanuts (no skins) |
| 1 | tablespoon salt | | |

Sauté onions in oil till soft. Add squash and cook till tender (not mushy). Place filling in an 8x11 pan and smooth from edge to edge evenly. Place all crisp ingredients in bowl, add melted butter and toss very gently to form small clumps. Lightly press crisp topping over filling. Bake at 350 degrees for ½ hour (lightly brown on top) Cool!

## TOASTED ALMOND BREAD PUDDING

| | | | |
|---|---|---|---|
| 6 | croissants, cut into large cubes | 1 | tablespoon almond extract |
| 6 | egg yolks | 1 | cup toasted almonds |
| ½ | cup sugar | | |
| ½ | quart cream | | |

In a large bowl, whisk egg yolks, sugar, cream and extract. Add cubed croissants and let sit to allow to absorb liquid. Fold in almonds. Pour mixture into 2-inch deep baking pan and bake at 350 degrees until golden brown. (approximately 30 to 45 minutes) Serves 6.

## SAUTÉED CHICKEN LIVERS ON BRIOCHE TOAST WITH BRANDY, BACON & CARAMELIZED ONIONS

| | | | |
|---|---|---|---|
| 16 | clean chicken livers | 3 | tablespoons butter |
| 2 | cups milk | 3 | tablespoons brown |
| 1 | cup flour | | sugar |
| 1 | large yellow onion | 3 | tablespoon red |
| 1 | cup cooked diced | | wine |
| | bacon | 1 | loaf brioche, sliced |
| ½ | cup brandy | | and toasted |
| 1 | cup cream | | |

Caramelize onion. Slice thinly and sauté with butter until soft and lightly brown. Add wine and brown sugar and cook slowly until moisture has evaporated and onions have rich brown hue. Remove and set aside. Soak livers in milk. Remove and lightly dredge in flour. Place in sauté pan over medium heat and cook until nicely browned on both sides. Season with salt and pepper. Add onions and bacon. Deglaze with brandy. Add cream and reduce until sauce-like consistency. Arrange brioche on plate and pour livers and sauce on top.

Serves 4.

**F. SCOTT'S**

## BAKED FLOUNDER WITH OYSTER STUFFING & OYSTER CREAM SAUCE

| | | | |
|---|---|---|---|
| 4 | flounder fillets (10 to 12 ounces) | 1 | teaspoon Old Bay seasoning |
| 2 | pints oysters (remove and save liquor) | 1 | rib of celery, small dice |
| ½ | pound butter | 1 | yellow onion, small dice |
| 3 | tablespoons butter (for roux) | 1 | tablespoon chopped fresh |
| 3 | tablespoons flour (for roux) | | parsley |
| 1 | tablespoon Worcestershire sauce | 1 | sleeve Ritz brand crackers, crushed |
| | | 1 | quart cream |

Place crushed crackers in large bowl. In saucepan melt ½ pound of butter. Add onion and celery and sauté until translucent. Add 1 pint of oysters (save liquor for later) and cook through. Remove from heat and add to crackers. Toss to coat and add parsley. When cool place ½ cup of mixture in center of each flounder fillet (skin side up) and roll up each fillet. Bake in 375-degree oven for 8 to 12 minutes.

**Oyster Cream Sauce:** Place saucepot on medium-low heat and make a roux with the butter and flour. Stir constantly. You only want to incorporate the ingredients and cook out the flour no more than 5 minutes. Be careful not to burn. The mixture should not have any color. Add all of the reserved oyster liquor and 1 quart of cream. Cook slowly and stir frequently to prevent lumps. Add Old Bay seasoning, Worcestershire and salt and pepper to taste. Add 1 pint of oysters and cook though. Serve over cooked flounder.

Serves 4.

# DAVIS-KIDD CAFÉ

*At Davis-Kidd Booksellers*
*Grace's Plaza*
*4007 Hillsboro Road*
*Nashville, TN 37215*

**Charles F. Latham, Café General Manager**
**Matt Emerine, Executive Chef**

## CHICKEN POT PIE

| | | | |
|---|---|---|---|
| ¼ | cup margarine | 2¼ | cups heavy cream |
| ¾ | cup yellow onion | 4 | cups mixed frozen |
| 6 | tablespoons all- | | vegetables |
| | purpose flour | 4 | boneless skinless |
| 2¼ | cups chicken stock | | chicken breasts |
| 3 | ounces white wine | | diced small |
| ½ | teaspoon ground | 2 | bunches broccoli |
| | white pepper | 8 | puff pastry |
| ½ | teaspoon fresh | ½ | cup shredded Swiss |
| | thyme | | cheese |
| ¼ | teaspoon curry | ½ | cup sliced almonds |
| | powder | | |

Pre-heat oven to 350 degrees.

**Sauce:** Place the margarine into the steam kettle and melt. Add the onions and sauté until soft, about 10 minutes. Add the flour to the onion mixture and stir with a whip to incorporate. Cook the roux for 10 minutes. In a large bowl, combine the stock, wine, pepper, thyme and curry. Mix these ingredients together and slowly add to the cooked roux, whipping constantly. Bring mixture to a boil, turn down kettle and simmer for 10 minutes. After the sauce has simmered for 10 minutes, add the cream and bring to one boil. Remove from heat and cool immediately.

**To complete pies:** Blanch frozen vegetables for 3 minutes. Combine vegetables, chicken and broccoli in a large bowl. **To assemble pies:** (using 8 small individual casserole dishes (about 10 to 12 ounce size) layer 1¼ cups of vegetable and chicken mixture with ¾ cup sauce, starting with sauce. Top with puff pastry, 1 tablespoon shredded Swiss cheese and 1 tablespoon almonds. Bake at 350 degrees for 18 minutes, until pastry is puffed and golden.

Yield: 8 pot pies

## LEMON TARRAGON CHICKEN SOUP

| | | | |
|---|---|---|---|
| 4 | ounces butter | 2 | tablespoons |
| 2 | cups yellow onion | | chopped fine fresh |
| 1¼ | tablespoons peeled | | tarragon |
| | garlic | ½ | teaspoon Tabasco |
| 1 | cup all-purpose | | sauce |
| | flour | 1⅓ | cups boneless |
| 2½ | quarts chicken | | skinless chicken |
| | stock | | breasts |
| 2½ | cups heavy cream | 1 | thinly sliced lemon |
| ¾ | cup lemon juice | | |

Melt butter in 5-quart sauce pan. Add the onions and garlic and sauté until transparent. Add the flour and mix well with a wire whip. Cook for 5 minutes. Add the stock a cup at a time to the flour mixture, whipping to make a smooth soup. Bring to a boil and simmer for 5 minutes. Add lemon juice, tarragon, Tabasco sauce and cream to the soup. Portion soup (12 ounces each) into bowls and garnish with lemon slices.

Yield: 1 gallon (10 to 12 portions)

## NEW ORLEANS CROISSANT BREAD PUDDING

| | | | |
|---|---|---|---|
| 6 | large eggs | ½ | cup melted salted |
| 2½ | cups sugar | | butter |
| 1 | tablespoon vanilla | ¼ | cup brandy |
| | extract | 1 | quart milk |
| 3 | teaspoons ground | 1 | cup toasted pecan |
| | nutmeg | | pieces |
| 3 | teaspoons ground | 1 | cup raisins |
| | cinnamon | 6 | day-old croissants |
| | | | cut in 1 inch cube |

In a mixing bowl, place the eggs, sugar, vanilla, spices, butter and brandy. Blend with a whisk until slightly thickened. Add the milk and blend another 2 minutes. Toss the raisins and pecans together. Place the cubes into a 9" x 13" baking pan. Toss the raisins and pecans with the cubes. Toss together. Let stand about 45 minutes or until all the liquid is absorbed. Place in a pre-heated 350 degree oven for 30 minutes or until pudding is well brown and puffy.

Yield: 9 portions

## CLAYTON-BLACKMON, INC., A BISTRO

### 4014 Hillsboro Circle
### Nashville, TN 37215

**Anne Clayton & Mary Blackmon**
**Owners**
*What started out to be a very successful take-out restaurant and catering business has turned into a full-service restaurant at their present location. The recipes listed below are a sampling of the incredible dishes offered at this bistro!*

## FRESH GREEN BEAN SALAD

2   pounds fresh or frozen haricots verts (baby green beans)
2   ounces thinly sliced red onion
1   small yellow pepper, thinly sliced

3   large ripe tomatoes, cut into wedges or 2 pints cherry tomatoes cut in half
4   ounces toasted pine nuts or almonds
6   ounces goat cheese or feta cheese

### DRESSING

4   ounces basil pesto
½   cup extra virgin olive oil
¼   cup red wine vinegar

Kosher salt and fresh ground pepper to taste

If using fresh green beans, blanch in boiling water for 1 minute to set color. Chill in ice water and drain. If using frozen beans, thaw under cool running water and drain. Mix beans with all other salad ingredients except cheese and nuts. Blend all dressing ingredients together and chill dress salad just before serving to preserve color of beans. Garnish with cheese, nuts and fresh basil leaves.

Serves 10 to 12.

## HERB ROASTED BEEF TENDERLOIN

Have butcher clean and trim 1 whole beef tenderloin. It should average 3 pounds after trimming.

Preheat oven to 400 degrees. Rub generous amount of garlic salt, dried basil and fresh ground black pepper and good olive oil over meat. Let meat come to room temperature. Roast in middle of 400 degree over for 30 minutes. Let meat sit for 20 minutes before slicing. Meat will be rare to medium rare. Wonderful hot or cold, served with a good horseradish sauce or a little basil pesto blended with a good brand of mayonnaise.

Serves 6 to 8 as a main course or 30 to 40 slices for small rolls.

## VIDALIA ONION SALAD

2   pounds assorted colorful bell peppers (we use red, yellow, orange, purple and green, thinly sliced
4   pounds Vidalia onions, thinly sliced

1   bunch green onions, tops only, chopped
1   bunch parsley chopped

Mix all together.

### DRESSING

¾   cup salad oil
½   cup white balsamic vinegar
2   heaping tablespoon Dijon mustard

2   tablespoons sugar
Salt and fresh black pepper to taste

Blend all dressing ingredients together and toss with salad. Chill (best if made one day in advance.) This actually gets better with age. Fantastic on roast meats or burgers!

Serves 15 to 20 if used as a condiment on sandwiches.

## COLD LEMON SOUFFLÉ

*A light & refreshing citrus dessert,*
*especially after a heavy or spicy meal.*

| | |
|---|---|
| 5 eggs separated (let whites come to room temperature) | 2 envelopes of unflavored gelatin, softened in ½ cup of water, heated to dissolve, let gelatin cool before adding to soufflé |
| 1¼ cups sugar | |
| ⅔ cup fresh lemon juice (do not use bottled juice) | 2 cups heavy cream, whipped |
| Grated zest of 3 lemons | ⅛ teaspoon cream of tartar |

Beat together egg yolks and sugar until light and pale yellow. Make sure all sugar is dissolved. Add lemon zest to egg yolks. Gradually beat in the lemon juice. Fold in the whipped cream. Beat the egg whites with the cream of tartar until stiff peaks form. Fold into lemon mixture. Spoon into pretty bowl and chill at least 3 hours. Serve garnished with lemon wheels and a little more grated lemon zest. Serve with seasonal berries alongside.

*We like to serve this in pretty wine glasses or at home in old fashioned champagne saucers topped with a few fresh blueberries or raspberries.*

Serves 8 to 10.

## OPRYLAND HOTEL

### 2800 Opryland Drive Nashville, TN 37214

*Opryland Hotel in Nashville, Tennessee is host to millions of visitors annually. Many attend business conventions while others are drawn here for the world-class amenities that this vacation property offers. Opryland Hotel opened in 1977 and offers luxurious accommodations (2,883 rooms) and first-class restaurants. It is one of the largest and most distinctive hotel convention centers in the nation (600,000 square feet of meeting and exhibit facilities).*

**Richard Gerst, Executive Chef**

*Richard Gerst joined Opryland Hotel in 1978 as a sous chef in the Old Hickory Restaurant. He was promoted to evening senior sous chef of the main kitchen in 1982, to executive sous chef in 1984, and to executive chef in 1988. His background includes positions with Princess Hotel in Hamilton, Bermuda; Sport Hotel Meierhof in Davos Dorf, Switzerland; Hotel Chaumont et Golf in Neuchatel, Switzerland and Residence and Edenwolff Hotel in Munich, West Germany. Chef Richard Gerst has won numerous awards in state, national, and international culinary competitions, including a gold medal in the 1981 National Restaurant Association Show.*

*All of the following recipes are from the Opryland Hotel's*
**A Taste of Tradition** *cookbook.*

## RACHEL'S KITCHEN

### 2800 Opryland Drive
### Nashville, TN 37214

*Rachel's Kitchen offers traditional family food. This restaurant is located near the Magnolia Lobby in the Galleria of shops. It features a large dining room & patio.*

## WHITE NAVY BEAN SOUP

| | | | |
|---|---|---|---|
| 14 | ounces dried navy beans | 1 | clove of garlic, crushed |
| 8 | ounces ham bones | ¼ | cup bacon grease |
| 4 | ounces salt pork, chopped | 14 | cups bouillon |
| 1 | cup chopped onions | 3 | medium potatoes, chopped |
| 1 | cup chopped leeks | 1 | (14-ounce) can tomatoes |
| 1 | cup chopped celery | | Salt & pepper to taste |

Rinse and sort the beans. Combine with water to cover in a bowl. Let stand for 8 hours. Drain the beans. Combine with the ham bones and salt pork in a large saucepan. Simmer until the beans are partially cooked. Cook the onions, leeks, celery and garlic in the bacon grease in a skillet over very low heat until tender. Add to the beans with the bouillon. Bring the soup to a boil. Add the potatoes. Cook for 1 hour or until the beans are tender. Add the tomatoes, salt and pepper. Cook until heated through. Garnish with parsley and croutons.

Yield: 16 servings

## CHICKEN SALAD

| | | | |
|---|---|---|---|
| 2½ | cups chopped cooked chicken | 2 | tablespoons lemon juice |
| ½ | stalk celery, chopped | ¼ | cup white vinegar |
| ½ | onion, diced | ½ | cup mayonnaise |
| 2 | hard-cooked eggs, chopped or sliced | | Salt & pepper to taste |
| 1½ | teaspoons Worcestershire sauce | | |

Combine the chicken, celery, onion, eggs, Worcestershire sauce, lemon juice, vinegar, mayonnaise, salt and pepper in a large bowl and mix gently; do not mix until all ingredients are in the bowl.

Yield: 8 to 10 servings

## HOT BROWN BUTLER

| | | | |
|---|---|---|---|
| ¼ | cup margarine | 4 | slices bread, crusts trimmed, toasted |
| ½ | cup flour | | |
| 2 | cups milk, scalded MSG, salt and white pepper to taste | 10 | ounces sliced turkey breast |
| | | 2 | tomatoes, sliced Paprika to taste |
| ½ | cup grated Parmesan cheese | 8 | slices bacon, crisp-fried |
| 2 | eggs | | |

Melt the margarine in a saucepan over very low heat. Stir in the flour. Whisk in the milk, MSG, salt, white pepper and 3 tablespoons of the cheese. Remove from the heat. Beat in the eggs. Place the toast in a baking pan. Arrange the turkey over the toast. Spoon the sauce over the top. Sprinkle with the remaining cheese. Place the tomato slices on top and sprinkle with paprika. Broil or bake at 425 degrees until golden brown. Arrange the bacon on top and serve immediately. You may substitute ham for the bacon, layering it under the turkey.

Yield: 4 servings

# THE CASCADES

## 2800 Opryland Drive
## Nashville, TN 37214

*The Cascades Restaurant is found in the heart of the Cascades. Opryland Hotel's breathtaking water garden offers dining in an unforgettable location. Without conventional walls, spectacular waterfalls define the restaurant on two sides. A one-acre glass roof stretches across the ceiling of the restaurant. The Hotel's award winning chefs feature a seafood menu at the Cascades Restaurant.*

# RED SNAPPER
# WITH BEURRE BLANC SAUCE

### BASIL BEURRE BLANC

| | | | |
|---|---|---|---|
| ½ | cup white wine | 8 | ounces unsalted |
| ½ | cup white vinegar | | butter, cubed |
| ¼ | cup chopped | 2 | tablespoons basil |
| | shallots | | Salt & pepper to |
| ½ | cup heavy cream | | taste |

### FISH

| | | | |
|---|---|---|---|
| 4 | (6-ounce) red snapper | | Clarified butter |
| | fillets | | for sautéing |
| | Flour | | |

For the basil beurre blanc, combine the wine, vinegar and shallots in a saucepan. Cook until reduced by ½. Add the cream. Cook until reduced by ½. Remove from the heat and whisk in the butter until melted. Strain the mixture into a saucepan. Season with the basil, salt and white pepper. Keep warm. Coat the fish lightly with flour. Sauté in clarified butter in a saucepan until golden brown. Serve with the sauce.

Serves 4.

# SEAFOOD GUMBO

| | | | |
|---|---|---|---|
| 1 | bay leaf | ⅓ | cup flour |
| ¼ | teaspoon thyme leaves, crumbled | ½ | teaspoon minced garlic |
| ⅛ | teaspoon oregano leaves, crumbled | 2¾ | cups seafood stock |
| 1 | teaspoon salt | 8 | ounces smoked sausage, cut into |
| ¼ | teaspoon each white, red and black pepper | | ½ inch pieces |
| | | 8 | ounces medium peeled shrimp |
| 1 | cup chopped onion | 6 | medium to large |
| 1¼ | cups chopped green bell pepper | | oysters in their liquid |
| ½ | cup chopped celery | 12 | ounces crab meat |
| 6 | tablespoons vegetable oil | | |

Combine the bay leaf, thyme, oregano, salt, white pepper, red pepper and black pepper in a small bowl and set aside. Mix the onion, green pepper and celery in a medium bowl and set aside. Heat the oil in a large heavy skillet for 5 minutes or just until it begins to smoke. Whisk in the flour. Cook for 2 to 4 minutes or until the roux is dark brown, whisking constantly. Add half the vegetable mixture. Cook for 1 minute, stirring constantly. Add the remaining vegetable mixture. Cook for 2 minutes, stirring constantly. Stir in the seasonings. Cook for 2 minutes, stirring frequently. Add the garlic. Cook for 1 minute. Bring the seafood stock to a boil in a 5½-quart stockpot. Add the roux mixture by spoonfuls, stirring well after each addition. Bring to a boil and add the sausage. Cook for 15 minutes, stirring occasionally. Reduce the heat and simmer for 10 minutes longer. Add the shrimp, undrained oysters and crab meat. Bring to a boil over high heat, stirring occasionally; discard the bay leaf. Serve over rice.

## PECAN PIE

| | | | |
|---|---|---|---|
| ½ | cup butter, softened | 1 | teaspoon vanilla extract |
| ½ | cup sugar | ⅛ | teaspoon salt |
| 3 | large eggs | 1½ | cups pecans |
| 1 | cup light corn syrup | 1 | unbaked (9-inch) pie shell |

Cream the butter and sugar in a large mixer bowl until light and fluffy. Beat in the eggs 1 at a time. Add the corn syrup, vanilla and salt. Stir in the pecans. Spoon into the pie shell. Bake at 450 degrees for 10 minutes. Reduce the oven temperature to 350 degrees. Bake for 30 minutes longer or until a knife inserted in the center comes out clean.

Serves 8.

# RISTORANTE VOLARE

## 2800 Opryland Drive
## Nashville, TN 37214

*Ristorante Volare offers wonderful Italian cuisine. It is located in the lush gardens of the Cascades Conservatory. The hotel's winning traditional Sunday Brunch is served here every Sunday. Located within Ristorante Volare is the Café Avanti Bar which features brick oven pizzas & calzones.*

## CRAB CAKES WITH FETTUCCINE & PEPPERCORN SAUCE

### CRAB CAKES

| | | | |
|---|---|---|---|
| 4 | ounces crab leg meat | 2 | tablespoons chopped onion |
| ½ | cup bread crumbs | 1 | egg |
| 2 | tablespoons chopped green or red bell pepper | | Black pepper and cayenne to taste |

### PEPPERCORN SAUCE

| | | | |
|---|---|---|---|
| 2 | tablespoons green peppercorns | | Salt & white pepper to taste |
| 3 | cups cream | 8 | ounces crayfish tail meat |
| 1 | tablespoon minced shallots | 2 | cups cooked fettuccini or linguini |
| 1 | tablespoon minced garlic | | |

For the crab cakes, mix the crab meat, bread crumbs, green pepper, onion, egg, salt, black pepper and cayenne in a bowl. Shape into patties. Sauté in a nonstick skillet until golden brown. For the peppercorn sauce, combine the peppercorns, cream, shallots and garlic in a saucepan. Cook until reduced by ½. Season with salt and white pepper. Add the crayfish meat. Toss this with the fettuccini. Serve with the crab cakes.

Serves 2.

**OPRYLAND**

## TOMATO BASIL SOUP

| | | | |
|---|---|---|---|
| 1 | cup chopped onion | 8 | cups chicken stock |
| 1 | cup chopped celery | | or water |
| 2 | tablespoons | 1 | tablespoon salt |
| | margarine | 1 | (6-ounce) can |
| 1 | clove of garlic, | | tomato paste |
| | crushed | ¼ | teaspoon crushed |
| 1½ | cups chopped | | dillweed or |
| | fresh basil | | tarragon |

Sauté the onion and celery in the margarine in a saucepan until tender. Add the garlic, basil, stock and salt. Simmer for 1½ hours. Stir in the tomato paste and dill. Cook until heated through.

Serves 8.

## VEAL SCALOPPINE

| | | | |
|---|---|---|---|
| 4 | (2 to 3 ounce) | ½ | cup heavy cream |
| | pieces of veal | 1 | cup unsalted |
| | Flour | | butter, cut into |
| | Clarified butter | | pieces |
| ½ | cup white vinegar | | Lemon juice to |
| ½ | cup white wine | | taste |
| 2 | tablespoons | | Salt and white |
| | chopped shallots | | pepper to taste |

Coat the veal lightly with flour. Sauté in clarified butter in a skillet; keep warm. Combine the vinegar, wine and shallots in a saucepan. Cook until the liquid is reduced by ½. Add the cream. Cook until reduced by ½. Remove from the heat. Whisk in the butter gradually. Strain through a sieve. Add the lemon juice, salt and pepper. Serve over the veal.

Serves 4.

## CATFISH PATÉ

| | | | |
|---|---|---|---|
| ½ | medium onion, chopped | 1 | teaspoon Tabasco sauce |
| 12 | ounces cream cheese, softened | 1 | pound hickory-smoked catfish, flaked |
| 2 to 3 | teaspoons chopped fresh dill | | |
| 2 | teaspoons (or more) freshly squeezed lemon juice | | |

Sauté the onion lightly in a nonstick skillet. Combine the onion, cream cheese, dill, lemon juice and Tabasco sauce in a food processor container. Process until mixed. Fold in the catfish. Serve on a bed of greens with basil vinaigrette and toast points.

Yield: 2 to 3 cups

## SOUTHWESTERN FILETS WITH BLACK BEAN & CORN SALSA & MAUI ONION RINGS

### RED PEPPER OIL

| | |
|---|---|
| 1 cup soybean oil | 1 cup chopped jalapeño peppers |

### ONION RINGS

| | |
|---|---|
| ¼ cup flour<br>Garlic powder, salt, cayenne and black pepper to taste | 3 onions, sliced into rings<br>Vegetable oil for frying |

### BEEF

| | |
|---|---|
| 5 (8-ounce) beef filets<br>Vegetable oil<br>Salt, pepper and garlic powder to taste | Black Bean & Corn Salsa (recipe follows) |

For the pepper oil, heat the soybean oil and jalapeños in a skillet until very hot. Let cool. Process in a blender until puréed. Let the oil rise to the top. Set aside. For the onion rings, mix the flour, garlic powder, salt, cayenne and black pepper in a bowl. Dredge the onion rings in the flour mixture. Heat oil to 350 degrees in a skillet. Add the onion rings. Fry until golden brown. Rub the filets with vegetable oil, salt, pepper and garlic powder. Cook by the method of your choice until done to taste. Spoon the salsa onto plates. Top with the filets. Top with generous portions of onion rings. Squirt the red pepper oil around the filets.

## BLACK BEAN & CORN SALSA

| | |
|---|---|
| ¼ cup olive oil | 1 cup cooked corn |
| ¼ cup chopped onion | ½ tablespoon chopped jalapeño |
| 1 tablespoon minced garlic | 1 tablespoon cumin |
| 2 cups cooked black beans | ½ cup white wine |
| ½ cup chopped tomato | ½ cup lime juice<br>Salt and pepper to taste |

Heat the olive oil in a sauté pan. Add the onion, garlic, beans, tomato, corn and jalapeño. Stir in the cumin, wine and lime juice. Season with salt and pepper. Keep warm until serving time.

Yield: 4 to 5 cups

## CRÈME BRÛLÉE

| | |
|---|---|
| 6 egg yolks | 2¼ cups heavy cream |
| 6 tablespoons sugar | 1 (1-inch) piece of vanilla bean |
| ⅛ teaspoon salt, or to taste | ½ cup sugar |

Combine the egg yolks, 6 tablespoons sugar and salt in a heavy enameled metal or stainless steel saucepan. Set aside. Combine the cream and vanilla bean in another saucepan. Bring to a boil, stirring occasionally to prevent scorching. Drizzle into the egg yolk mixture, stirring vigorously with a whisk or wooden spatula until mixed. Remove and discard the vanilla bean. Cook over medium heat for 3 minutes, stirring constantly. Strain into a 4-cup enameled metal heatproof glass or porcelain baking dish. Place the baking dish in a larger baking pan. Add enough water to the pan to reach halfway up the sides of the baking dish. Bake at 325 degrees for 35 minutes or just until the custard is set; do not overcook or allow the water in the baking pan to boil. Cool thoroughly or chill to desired temperature. Sift ½ cup sugar ¼ inch thick over the custard. Broil until the sugar caramelizes; the top should be hard and shiny and should sound hollow when tapped. Chill for several hours. Crack the crust when serving and serve a small amount of the crust with each portion of the custard. Serve with whipped cream if desired.

Yield: 4 to 6 servings

*Ryman Auditorium*

## ICHIBAN RESTAURANT & SUSHI BAR

### 108 2nd Street North
### Nashville, TN 37201

**Makoto Fujiwara, Chef/Owner**
*Ichiban's food, prepared to order by Chef Makoto Fujiwara and his team of Japanese-trained chefs includes such delicacies as nigiri, makimono, sashimi, nabermono, udon, ramen and soba dinners, donburi and close to twenty kinds of cooked seafood such as sawara saikyo, hotate tempura, ida maru yaki, kani karaage and karei karapon. Ichiban even offers sushi pizza!*

## EBI SHINJO

| | | | |
|---|---|---|---|
| 8 | jumbo shrimp, ground | 1 | teaspoon sake |
| | Green soybean, chopped | 1 | teaspoon light colored soy sauce |
| | Green onion, chopped | 1 | teaspoon (raw white of egg) |
| | Mountain potato yam, chopped & mashed (found in Japanese markets) | | Potato starch or cornstarch |

Mix all of the above ingredients with sauce (except potato starch) and make it into a small round ball and coat potato starch around the shrimp ball. Deep fry until it is done.

Yield: 2 servings

## GINDALA MIRIN BOSHI (BLACK COD)

| | | | |
|---|---|---|---|
| 2 | filets of black cod | 3 | teaspoons salt |
| 4 | ounces of mirin (sweet rice wine) | 1 | teaspoon soy sauce |

Marinate the filet with all the sauces for about 4 hours and hang them in the refrigerator overnight. Broil until golden brown.

Yield: 2 servings

## SASSO RESTAURANT

### 1400 Woodland Street
### Nashville, TN 37206

**Anita Hartel & Corey Griffith**
**Chef/Owners**
*Lockeland Springs, in East Nashville, is a neighborhood on the upswing, with Victorian and Craftsman houses being restored on nearly every block. Occupying one neatly renovated 1900s commercial building is Sasso, probably the nearest thing to a real neighborhood bistro you'll find in all of Tennessee. The **Nashville Scene**, **Food & Wine** Magazine and **The New York Times** have recognized the restaurant for its creative New South and fusion dishes! The chef/owner team of Anita Hartel and Corey Griffith share over 40 years' combined experience in the culinary arts.*

## PEANUT-CRUSTED SALMON

| | | | |
|---|---|---|---|
| 1 | cup peanuts | ½ | tablespoon Szechwan peppercorn (ground fine in coffee grinder) |
| ¼ | cup chopped cilantro | | |
| | | 1 | tablespoon flour |

Pour all into food processor; grind fine.

Coat salmon with tablespoon of oil. Coat in peanut crust. Pan sear and finish cooking in oven.

### SALMON SAUCE

| | | | |
|---|---|---|---|
| ½ | cup oyster sauce | 1½ | cups water |
| ½ | cup hoisin sauce | 4 | stalks lemongrass |
| ½ | cup soy | 1½ | tablespoons chili paste |
| 2 | tablespoons fresh ginger (chopped fine) | | |

Cook 10 minutes and strain. Stir-fry baby bok choy and sauce. Fry linguine noodles. Place sauce and choy on plate, add noodles and top with salmon.

Single serving

## SEA SCALLOPS IN FERMENTED BLACK BEAN SAUCE

| | | | |
|---|---|---|---|
| 16 | (20/30 count) scallops – cut in half | 8 | spring roll wrappers |
| 1 | tablespoon Thai chili paste | | Egg wash (1 egg beaten with 1 teaspoon water) |
| 1 | bunch cilantro, chopped fine | | Cornstarch |
| | | | Frying oil |

Mix first three ingredients. Let rest for one hour to marinate flavor. Place wrappers one at a time diagonally. On each put four scallop halves. Fold up the bottom corner, then each end to form envelope. Use egg wash to seal where necessary. Dust with cornstarch. Fry at 350 degrees until crispy. Drain. Place on shredded cabbage and surround with bean sauce (recipe below).

### FERMENTED BLACK BEAN SAUCE

| | | | |
|---|---|---|---|
| ¾ | cups fermented beans | 4 | tablespoons sugar |
| 3 | tablespoons minced garlic | 5 | tablespoons plus 1 teaspoon red chili paste |
| 5 | tablespoons plus 1 teaspoon rice wine vinegar | 5 | tablespoons plus 1 teaspoon vegetable oil |
| 5 | tablespoons plus 1 teaspoon light soy sauce | | |

Rinse beans to remove excess salt. Pat dry and chop fine. Sauté in oil and quickly add other ingredients. Bring to boil. Keep warm. Serves 4.

## CARAMELIZED BANANA WALNUT CHEESECAKE

### SUGARED NUTS

| | | | |
|---|---|---|---|
| 2 | cups walnuts | ½ | inch piece fresh ginger |
| ½ | cup sugar | | |
| 1 | vanilla bean | ½ | teaspoon coarse black pepper |
| 1 | teaspoon cinnamon | ¼ | cup egg whites |

Preheat oven to 325 degrees. Combine nuts and egg whites. Add sugar and spices. Toast 8 to 10 minutes till light brown. Reserve 1 cup of nuts to garnish each slice.

### CARAMELIZED BANANAS

| | | | |
|---|---|---|---|
| 4 | ripe bananas | 1 | vanilla bean |
| ¼ | cup butter | ½ | inch piece fresh ginger |
| ½ | cup light brown sugar | 1 | teaspoon cinnamon |

Melt butter in saucepan. Combine bananas, sugar and spices. Sauté in butter till bubbly and let cool.

### CRUST

| | | | |
|---|---|---|---|
| 1 | cup vanilla cookie crumbs | ¼ | cup melted butter |
| 1 | cup sugared walnuts | | |

Grind cookies and nuts in food processor and add butter. Press crumbs into pan; bake 8 to 10 minutes till light brown. Scoop bananas onto crust, reserve juices.

### CHEESECAKE

| | | | |
|---|---|---|---|
| 2 | pounds cream cheese at room temperature | ¼ | cup spiced rum |
| | | 3 | eggs |
| ¾ | cup sugar | ¼ | cup reserved banana juices |
| 1 | tablespoon vanilla | | |

In an electric mixer, cream together cheese, sugar, vanilla and rum till smooth. Add eggs 1 at a time. Fold in reserved banana juices. Bake 40 to 45 minutes till set, center 4 inches will be slightly wobbly. Wrap, chill 4 hours or overnight.

### SAUCE

| | | | |
|---|---|---|---|
| ½ | cup butter | 2 | tablespoons spiced rum |
| ½ | cup sugar | 1 | egg |

Melt butter in saucepan, whisk together sugar and egg, and add rum. Whisk into butter, whisking over heat till smooth and slightly thickened. Whisk in cocoa. Garnish with reserved nuts. Serves 16.

## THE MAD PLATTER RESTAURANT

### 1239 Sixth Avenue North Nashville, TN 37208

**Craig & Marcia Jervis, Owners**
*The Mad Platter Restaurant received the following Reader's Poll Awards from the 1999* **Nashville Scene**: *Best Dessert 2nd place, Most Romantic 3rd place, Best Catering 2nd place, Best Menu 3rd place and Best Restaurant 3rd place! The restaurant also received the Award of Excellence from* **Wine Spectator** *magazine.* **The New York Times** *described it, "An essential part of any trip to Nashville."*

## JICAMA, APPLE & BASIL SALAD WITH RED GRAPES

| | |
|---|---|
| 1 | jicama, peeled and julienned |
| 4 | apples (Granny Smith), julienned |
| 2 | cups red seedless grapes, cut in half |
| ¼ | cup fresh basil leaves, chopped |
| ½ | cup olive oil blend |
| ½ | cup lemon juice |

Combine oil and lemon juice, then marinate the remaining ingredients in this mixture for 2 to 24 hours. Serve well chilled.

Serves 6.

## MOUTARDE MIXTURE FOR RACK OF LAMB

| | | | |
|---|---|---|---|
| 4¾ | ounces dry bread crumbs | ⅔ | teaspoon minced garlic |
| ¼ | stick butter | 1⅔ | ounces Grey Poupon |
| ¼ | teaspoon basil | | |
| ¼ | teaspoon whole thyme | | |

Mix well in Cuisinart (should be able to shape the mixture at room temperature); then pat out into ¼ inch thick slab about the size of your palm and press onto the lamb racks just below the bones. Roast the racks at 350 degrees until the desired doneness is reached. Medium rare is best for lamb and should take about 15 to 20 minutes. (This will vary greatly depending on the oven, how full it is and how many times the door is opened).

Serves 6.

## RACK OF LAMB MOUTARDE – MARINADE

| | | |
|---|---|---|
| 2 | cups oil | Bay leaves |
| 2 | white wine | Rosemary |
| | Whole black pepper | Basil |

Mix all ingredients together and marinate.

## the MaD PLaTTeR

1239 sixth avenue north
2 4 2 . 2 5 6 3

## CHEF FREDDY BOOKER
## THE TRACE

*2000 Belcourt Avenue*
*Nashville, TN 37212*

## OSSO BUCCO

| | | | |
|---|---|---|---|
| 6 | to 8 veal shanks | 3 | bay leaves |
| | Salt & pepper to taste | ½ | cup chopped basil |
| | | 1 | cup chopped onion |
| 2 | cups flour | 1 | cup chopped celery |
| ½ | cup canola oil | 1 | cup diced carrots |
| 1½ | cups white wine | 1 | cup diced parsnips |
| 2 | cups veal stock | 2 | tablespoons |
| 4 | sprigs fresh thyme | | minced garlic |
| ½ | cup chopped Italian parsley | 16 | ounces canned diced tomatoes |

Heat the oil in a large Dutch oven. Salt and pepper the veal shanks. Dredge in flour, then brown well in the oil. Transfer finished shanks to a plate when finished. Pour off excess oil and deglaze the pot with white wine. (This is where the serious flavor is!) Add stock or broth and simmer for 4 to 5 minutes. Place thyme, parsley and bay leaves in a cheesecloth bag and add to broth. Return the veal shanks to pot. Add the onion, celery, parsnips, carrots, garlic and tomatoes to the pot. Cover pot and transfer to 350-degree oven for 2½ to 3 hours, check, occasionally and add more stock or white wine if needed. When meat is fork tender, put shanks on a warm serving platter. Put the Dutch oven on the stove and reduce the sauce slightly.

## BUTTERNUT SQUASH SPAETZLE

| | | | |
|---|---|---|---|
| 3 | pounds butternut squash (yields approximately 1 cup cooked purée) | ½ | teaspoon salt |
| | | ½ | teaspoon nutmeg |
| | | 3 | eggs, lightly beaten |
| | | ¾ | cup milk |
| | | | Butter to taste |
| 2 | cups (+) flour | 8 | cups water |

In a large saucepan, bring water to boil. In a large mixing bowl, combine squash purée, flour, salt and pepper. Stir in eggs and milk. Batter should be heavy. Place a spaetzle maker or colander over the boiling water and force the batter through the holes. The spaetzle will cook very quickly. As they rise to the surface, remove them with a slotted spoon and place in an ice bath immediately, and then drain. Repeat until the batter is gone. Sauté the spaetzle in butter until golden brown.

## GREMOLATA

| | | | |
|---|---|---|---|
| 4 | tablespoons minced Italian parsley | 1 | tablespoon minced garlic |
| 2 | tablespoons grated lemon rind | | |

Combine ingredients in a small bowl and mix well.

*The Hermitage*

## MARTHA STAMPS
### Chef/Author
### Nashville, TN

*My husband, John Reed, and I own our own catering and delivery business named **Food for Thought**, which was cited as the best new food service this year in **The Nashville Scene**. I have published three cookbooks and am a frequent contributor to many Nashville-based publications. My recipes have also been published in **Southern Living**. John and I live in Nashville with our two daughters, Moriah and Sadie.*

## CHEDDAR SPREAD WITH BACON & SCALLIONS

| | | | |
|---|---|---|---|
| 1 | pound sharp cheddar cheese, grated | 4 | slices bacon, cooked crisp, drained well and chopped |
| ½ | bunch scallions, sliced thinly | ½ | cup toasted sliced almonds |
| ½ | cup mayonnaise | ¼ | teaspoon cayenne pepper |
| ¼ | cup buttermilk | | |

Combine everything in a bowl and mix well. Pack into a crock or small bowl and serve at room temperature with crackers.

## SHRIMP & NOODLE SUMMER ROLL

| | | | |
|---|---|---|---|
| 6 | large cooked shrimp | | Juice of 1 lime |
| 1 | package cellophane noodles | 1 | package rice paper wrappers |
| 1 | tablespoon fish sauce | 1 | bunch fresh basil |
| 1 | teaspoon brown sugar | 1 | bunch fresh mint |
| | | 1 | tablespoon toasted sesame seeds |

Slice the shrimp in half, then set aside. Soak the cellophane noodles in hot water until soft. Drain and place in a bowl. Toss with the fish sauce, brown sugar and lime juice. Soak 1 rice paper wrapper in warm water until pliable, about 1 minute. Place on a clean dishtowel, then on a work surface. Place 2 shrimp halves on the lower third of the wrapper, then a bit of the noodles, topped with one or two basil leaves, a few mint leaves, then sprinkle with sesame seeds. Fold the sides of the wrapper in, then roll up like a spring roll. If you need to hold them, wrap in cellophane and refrigerate for up to three hours. Serve with dipping sauce (recipe follows).

### DIPPING SAUCE

| | | | |
|---|---|---|---|
| ⅓ | cup soy sauce | 1 | tablespoon grated carrot |
| ⅓ | cup water | 1 | tablespoon grated daikon |
| ⅓ | cup seasoned rice wine vinegar | 1 | tablespoon sliced scallions |
| 1 | tablespoon fish sauce | 1 | tablespoon grated ginger |
| 1 | tablespoon brown sugar | 1 | teaspoon toasted sesame seeds |
| | Juice of 2 limes | | |
| 1 | tablespoon sambal oelek | | |

Mix together well. Use as a dipping sauce for spring and summer rolls.

## HALIBUT IN
## TOMATO FENNEL BROTH

| | | | |
|---|---|---|---|
| 2 | tablespoons olive oil | 3 | tablespoons chopped tomatoes |
| 1 | bulb fennel, sliced thinly | 3 | tablespoons dry white wine |
| 1 | red onion, sliced thinly | 1 | cup fish or shrimp stock |
| 1 | stalk celery, sliced thinly | 4 | (6 ounce) halibut fillets |

First make the tomato fennel broth. Heat the olive oil in a sauté pan. Add the fennel, red onion and celery and sauté for about five minutes. Add the tomato and white wine and heat through and the stock and bring to a simmer. Taste for seasoning and reserve.

Preheat oven to 425. Season the halibut with salt and pepper. Heat an additional tablespoon of olive oil in a separate sauté pan. Sear the fish in the hot oil, coloring slightly. Turn and briefly cook, then add the broth. Bring to a simmer, then place in the hot oven for 5 minutes. Serve over arborio pancakes.

## ORANGE CAKE
## WITH GRAND MARNIER

| | | | |
|---|---|---|---|
| 3 | tablespoons unsalted butter, softened | | Grated zest of 1 orange |
| ⅓ | cup light olive oil | ½ | cup flour |
| ¾ | cup sugar | 1 | teaspoon baking powder |
| 1 | package almond paste, broken up | 3 | tablespoons Grand Marnier |
| 5 | eggs | | Confectioner's sugar |

Preheat oven to 325 degrees. Butter and flour a 9-inch cake pan. Line the bottom with parchment. Place the butter, olive oil and sugar in a mixing bowl and beat until fluffy. Add the almond paste and orange zest. Beat until smooth. Beat in the eggs, one at a time. Mix in the flour and baking powder. Pour into the prepared pan. Bake for 45 minutes. Remove from the oven and let cool in the pan. Invert the cake and place right side up on serving plate. Brush the liqueur over the cake. Sprinkle with confectioner's sugar and serve.

## PINEAPPLE ROOM
## RESTAURANT

### Cheekwood Museum & Botanical Gardens
### 1200 Forrest Park Drive
### Nashville, TN 37205

*Cheekwood, once the private home and estate of the Cheek family, is now a beautiful 55-acre property, providing visitors with a unique experience of art and gardens. Completed in 1932, Cheekwood first opened to the public in 1960.*

**Eddie Stewart, Executive Chef**

**Glenn McConnell, Asst. Food & Beverage Director, Executive Catering Chef**

*Chef Eddie has worked in the Nashville area for the last 15 years. He began his career as prep cook and worked his way from line cook, to Sous Chef, to Chef de Cuisine to his present position as Executive Chef. Chef Glenn has worked in the Tennessee area for the last 15 years. Chef Glenn holds a degree in Hospitality Management from Belmont University.*

## CREAM CHICKEN

| | | | |
|---|---|---|---|
| ½ | gallon béchamel sauce | 2 | cups portabella mushrooms |
| ¼ | case chicken | ½ | quart heavy cream |
| 1 | ounce butter | 1½ | tablespoons chicken base |
| 2 | cups carrots | | |
| 2 | cups celery | ½ | tablespoon salt |
| 1 | medium onion | ½ | tablespoon pepper |

Lay chicken out on sheet pan, season with salt and pepper and bake at 350 degrees for 15 minutes until cooked. While chicken is baking, cut all the vegetables into a large dice. Sauté vegetables in butter until tender. Heat béchamel in the top of the double boiler over simmering water. Add base and seasonings, stir well. Add vegetables and cream. Cut the fully cooked chicken into a large dice and add to the cream and vegetables. Allow to cook for another 10 minutes. Remove from heat and cool in an ice bath, stirring often. Store in a plastic cambro.

*Serving suggestion: Serve with favorite cornbread recipe.*

Yield: 1 gallon

## SMOKED GOUDA & ROASTED PEPPER SOUP

| | | | |
|---|---|---|---|
| 1½ | quarts heavy cream | 2 | cups chicken stock |
| 1½ | pounds smoked gouda cheese | ½ | cup fresh herb mixture of basil, thyme and parsley |
| 1 | bell pepper | | |
| 1 | medium-size onion | 2 | cloves fresh minced garlic |
| 1½ | cups celery | | |
| 1 | cup carrots | 1 | cup white roux |

Dice the onions, celery, carrots and bell peppers to a fine dice. Place in a one gallon saucepot with 2 ounces of butter and sweat. Add garlic and herbs. Add heavy cream. Cube cheese and add to soup. Add chicken stock. Bring to a boil, reduce to a simmer. Tighten with a white roux.

Yield: 1 gallon

## CREOLE BREAD PUDDING

| | | | |
|---|---|---|---|
| 2 | cups sugar | 2 | tablespoons vanilla |
| ½ | pound butter | ½ | cup raisins |
| 10 | eggs | 1 | loaf sliced French bread (about 1 inch thick) |
| 1 | quart heavy cream | | |
| ½ | teaspoon cinnamon | | |

In the mixer, cream together the sugar and butter. Add the eggs, cream, cinnamon, vanilla and raisins. Mix well. Lay the bread out in a 2-inch hotel pan and pour the cream over it. Let the bread soak for 5 minutes then turn it over and soak for 10 minutes more. Ladle 8 ounces into the serving dishes that have been greased and sugared. Bake in a water bath at 350 degrees for 20 minutes. When done, the custard should still be soft not firm. Serve with vanilla ice cream and Jack Daniel's caramel sauce (recipe follows).

Yield: 10 servings

## JACK DANIEL'S CARAMEL SAUCE

| | | | |
|---|---|---|---|
| 3 | ounces butter | 2 | teaspoons arrowroot |
| 3½ | ounces water | | |
| 7 | ounces sugar | 1 | ounce Jack Daniel's whiskey |
| 4 | ounces evaporated skim milk | | |

Cook butter, water and sugar to caramel color. Combine milk, starch and whiskey. Add carefully away from heat. Return sauce to heat and bring to a boil. Remove from heat and cool.

# TIN ANGEL RESTAURANT

## 3201 West End Avenue
## Nashville, TN, 37203

**Rick & Vicki Bolsom, Owners**
**Brooke Eubank, Manager**
*The Tin Angel opened in 1993 on West End Avenue in the Vanderbilt area of Nashville. The restaurant was started by Rick & Vicki Bolsom as a complement to their very successful Cakewalk Restaurant. The goal was to offer the area a locally oriented gathering place that featured excellent food and wine at reasonable prices, bistro style. The cuisine is far reaching, using ingredients and concepts both classic and creative and offering dishes that range from the comfort level of meatloaf and mashed potatoes to exotic fish dishes and interpretations of classics like Salad Niçoise, Lemon Veal, Chicken Schnitzel, among many offerings.*

## FRIED GREEN TOMATOES WITH HORSERADISH SAUCE

| | | | |
|---|---|---|---|
| 10 | green tomatoes – sliced ¼ inch thick | 2 | tablespoons garlic granules |
| 5 | eggs | ½ | tablespoon black pepper |
| 2 | cups flour | | |
| ½ | cup vegetable oil | 1½ | tablespoon celery salt |
| 4 | cups plain bread crumbs | | |
| | | 1 | tablespoon salt |
| 1½ | cups white cornmeal | 1 | tablespoon onion powder |

In one bowl place flour and set aside. In another bowl whisk eggs and set aside. In third bowl combine last seven ingredients and set aside. Heat oil in skillet over medium high heat. When oil is ready, first coat tomato with flour, second coat tomato with egg, third dredge tomato through cornmeal mixture. Place tomato in skillet and fry until golden brown.

### HORSERADISH SAUCE

| | | | |
|---|---|---|---|
| ½ | cup horseradish | ½ | teaspoon dry mustard |
| 2 | cups sour cream | | |
| 1 | cup mayonnaise | ½ | teaspoon sugar |
| | Juice from 1 lemon | ½ | teaspoon salt |
| 1 | tablespoon Worcestershire sauce | | |

Combine all ingredients and chill.

# VENETIAN FISH

| | | | |
|---|---|---|---|
| 1 | medium red onion, julienne | ¼ | cup white wine |
| | | | Juice of 2 lemons |
| 1 | green bell pepper, julienne | ¼ | cup honey or brown sugar |
| 1 | red bell pepper, julienne | ¼ | cup butter |
| | | | Salt and pepper to taste |
| ½ | cup dried fruit (your choice), hydrate with water | | |
| | | 4 | to 6 servings of light fish cooked as you wish – sautéed, broiled, etc.** |
| ¼ | cup toasted nuts (your choice), chopped or slivered* | | |

In large sauté pan with 2 tablespoons of oil, sauté onion and bell peppers until onion first becomes soft. Add fruit and nuts. Add honey or brown sugar. Sauté for 2 more minutes. Add wine and lemon juice. Reduce liquid by ½. Take off heat and melt butter in by swirling the pan. Pour this mixture over the cooked fish. Serve with cous cous or rice.

*The chef's preference is cranberries and almonds.*
**The chef's preference is trout.*

# SHRIMP BISQUE

| | | | |
|---|---|---|---|
| 2 | pounds shrimp with shells | 2 | cups whole cream |
| | | 6 | ounces can tomato paste |
| 1 | medium onion | | |
| 2 | medium carrots | 1 | cup dry sherry |
| 4 | ribs celery | 2 | tablespoons vegetable oil |
| 3 | cloves garlic | | |
| 1 | teaspoon salt | ½ | cup butter |
| 1 | teaspoon white pepper | ½ | cup all-purpose flour |

Peel shrimp. To make shrimp stock, place shells in small saucepan, cover with water and simmer for 40 minutes. Strain and discard shells. In food processor, finely chop the following items separately – onion, carrots, celery and garlic. Place 8-quart stockpot on stove on medium heat. Add 2 tablespoons vegetable oil and processed vegetables and garlic. Simmer until vegetables are tender. While vegetables are simmering, finely chop (by hand) the shrimp and any other shellfish you want to add. Make a roux: in a small pan melt ½ cup butter and whisk in ½ cup flour. Cook for 5 minutes then set aside. Add white wine, dry sherry, cream and tomato paste to shrimp stock. Heat while stirring until tomato paste is dissolved. Add shrimp and bring to a boil. Add roux, whisking in thoroughly. Bring to hard simmer for 10 minutes. Enjoy your shrimp bisque!

### NICK OF THYME
#### GOURMET TO GO & CAFÉ

*4910 Thoroughbred Lane
Brentwood, TN 37027*

**Cathy Lewis, Chef/Owner**

## SPANIKOPITA

| | | | |
|---|---|---|---|
| 1 | pound filo dough | ¼ | cup freshly grated Parmesan |
| 2 | cups clarified butter | | Pinch of freshly grated nutmeg |
| 1 | small onion, minced | ¼ | teaspoon dried rosemary |
| 1 | tablespoon olive oil or butter | ¼ | teaspoon oregano |
| 4 | ounces feta cheese | 1 | beaten egg |
| 10 | ounces spinach, blanched, drained or chopped (or 1 package of 10 ounce frozen spinach, thawed, squeezed dry and chopped | | Salt, preferably sea salt (remember cheeses are very salty) Freshly ground pepper |

Sauté the onion in the olive oil until tender. In a medium-sized mixing bowl, beat the egg and crumble in the feta cheese. Add remaining ingredients and stir together. Preheat oven to 375 degrees. Remove filo dough from package and carefully unfold. Remove sheet of dough and brush with clarified butter. Lay another sheet on this and another sheet on the second one. Butter the third sheet and add 2 more sheets. Butter the fifth sheet and add two more. Now cut this seven-layer sheet into equal-sized squares, the size of which will depend on the size triangle you want and the number of them. Remember that you will be placing filling on each square and folding it in half like a triangle and that the sheets are delicate, so you will need a certain amount of surface area to play with. Butter the top sheet of filo and place a spoonful or two of filling in the center of each square. Butter the edges or brush with egg. Fold the square over on the diagonal to make a triangle and press the edges together. Brush the edges of the seal with butter or egg. Place on a buttered baking sheet and bake for 30 minutes or until golden.

Yield: 3 dozen

## AEGEAN GRILLED SHRIMP

| | | | |
|---|---|---|---|
| 2 | pounds shrimp – shell on | 3 | tablespoons fresh chopped dill |
| 1 | cup extra virgin olive oil | | Salt & pepper to taste |
| ⅓ | cup fresh squeezed lemon juice (fresh only) | 2 | cups mixed Greek/Italian olives |
| 2 | teaspoons fresh minced garlic | 1 | cup sheep's milk feta cheese, crumbled |
| 1 | large ripened tomato, seeded & peeled, then diced into ½ x ½ inch square dice | | |

Rinse shrimp in water and pat dry. Preheat grill or make a moderately sized fire. Coat shrimp with 1 tablespoon of oil and season with salt & pepper. Take all of the remaining ingredients and whisk together in a bowl to make a marinade. When fire or grill is ready, grill shrimp 3 minutes, flip over and grill 2 more minutes. Once all grilled remove shrimp from shell, devein them and drop warm shrimp into marinade. Let marinate overnight in the refrigerator.

**To serve**, place shrimp around the platter, sprinkle with crumbled feta and place olives in the middle of the platter. Season with additional salt and pepper if needed and drizzle a little olive oil over the top.

Serves 4 to 6.

## LEMON SCENTED ASPARAGUS

| | | |
|---|---|---|
| 2 | pounds asparagus | Salt & pepper to taste |
| 3 | tablespoons olive oil | Zest of 3 lemons |

Bring water to boil. Trim ends of asparagus if necessary, then drop in boiling water. Have a bowl of ice water ready so that you can shock the asparagus when it is done. Blanch asparagus for 3 minutes, then remove into ice bath. Remove from ice bath when cooled and dry with a towel. Heat pan with oil. When hot, zest in pan and briefly sauté. Add asparagus and coat with oil, zest and toss around. Add salt and pepper to taste.

Serves 6.

## QUAILS RESTAURANT

### 4936 Thoroughbred Lane
### Brentwood, TN 37027

**Mathew Igwonobe, Owner/Executive Chef**
*Quails was voted by the **Nashville Scene** Reader's Poll as "The Best Restaurant in Brentwood."*

## ENGLISH CUCUMBER & FRUIT GAZPACHO

| | | | |
|---|---|---|---|
| 4 | English cucumbers or (seedless cucumbers) peeled & chopped | 6 | ounces seedless grapes |
| 16 | ounces non-fat plain yogurt | 2 | tablespoons Jamaican curry powder |
| 1 | tablespoon ground cumin | 1 | cup extra virgin olive oil |
| 4 | ounces fine diced honeydew melon | | Kosher salt as needed |
| 4 | ounces fine diced cantaloupe | | Fresh ground black pepper as needed |
| 4 | ounces fine diced Fuji apples | | Fresh oysters (optional) |

In a bar blender or food processor, purée the cucumbers, yogurt and cumin until very smooth. Keep cold. In a separate bowl, combine all the diced fruit and chill. Heat a sauce pan or sauté pan on low heat with the olive oil and curry powder for about 10 to 15 minutes. Set aside and let cool. After it has cooled, strain through cheesecloth or coffee filter.

**To serve:** Season the puréed cucumber and yogurt with kosher salt and pepper. Taste and add seasoning and cumin as needed. In each serving bowl, place the diced fruit (and oysters) in the center and surround with the cucumber mixture. Drizzle with the curry infused olive oil.

Yield: 6 servings

## PERUVIAN POTATO & CRAB & LOBSTER SALAD

| | | | |
|---|---|---|---|
| 6 | medium purple potatoes or 4 medium Yukon potatoes peeled and sliced | 2 | ounces chopped fresh tarragon |
| | | 4 | tablespoons white truffle oil |
| 3 | ounces lump crab meat | 2 | ounces white balsamic vinegar |
| 8 | ounces Maine lobster meat, cooked and chopped | 1 | ounce minced shallots |
| | | 4 | ounces each of baby arugula and watercress* |
| 8 | each garlic cloves, slow roasted | | Kosher salt |
| 2 | cups heavy cream | | Fresh ground black pepper |

Cook the potatoes in boiling water until they are done, but do not overcook. Roast garlic cloves in oven to golden. Remove from oven. Transfer drained potatoes into a mixing bowl, blend roasted garlic with cream and add to potatoes. Also add butter, 1 ounce chopped tarragon, 2 ounces of truffle oil and crab meat. Whip until smooth and has not potato lumps. Salt and pepper to taste. Make a vinaigrette with the balsamic vinegar, minced shallots, 2 ounces of truffle oil, 1 ounce of chopped fresh tarragon and salt and pepper.

**To serve:** Pipe the potato mousse on center of plate, surround with lobster meat and dressed greens. Sprinkle some of the vinaigrette on the lobster meat. Serve.

*Mesclun greens may be substituted for watercress and arugula.*

Yield: 6 portions

## QUAILS
RESTAURANT

### MISS MARY BOBO'S BOARDING HOUSE

#### Lynchburg, TN 37352

**Lynne Tolley, Proprietress**
*Lynne is the great-grandniece of Jack Daniel.
The recipes listed below are from **Miss Mary Bobo's Boarding House Cookbook**.*

## JACK DANIEL'S PECAN PIE

| | | | |
|---|---|---|---|
| 3 | extra-large eggs, slightly beaten | ¼ | cup Jack Daniel's whiskey |
| 1 | cup sugar | ½ | cup semisweet chocolate chips |
| 2 | tablespoons butter, melted | 1 | cup pecan halves |
| 1 | cup dark corn syrup | 1 | unbaked 10-inch pie shell |
| 1 | teaspoon vanilla extract | | |

In a medium bowl combine the eggs, sugar, butter, syrup, vanilla and Jack Daniel's whiskey. Mix well. Sprinkle the chocolate chips over the bottom of the unbaked pie shell and add the pecans. Pour the filling over the chips and pecans. Bake at 375 degrees for 35 to 40 minutes, or until a knife inserted about halfway between the center and the edge comes out clean. Set aside to cool.

Yield: 6 to 8 servings.

## TENDERLOIN TIPS

| | | | |
|---|---|---|---|
| ¼ | cup butter | ½ | cup burgundy wine |
| 2 | pounds beef tenderloin tips, thinly sliced | ½ | cup Jack Daniel's whiskey |
| 2 | teaspoons salt | 1 | cup canned tomatoes, crushed |
| 1 | cup mushrooms, slice | 2 | cubes beef bouillon |
| ¼ | cup onion, chopped | 2 | teaspoons sugar Mashed potatoes |
| 1 | clove garlic, minced | | |

In a large skillet melt the butter and sauté the meat quickly, half at a time, until browned. Add the salt, mushrooms, onion and garlic and simmer for several minutes, adding extra butter if needed. Add the wine, Jack Daniel's whiskey, tomatoes, bouillon cubes and sugar. Simmer for 30 minutes or until tender. Serve on a platter with mashed potatoes.

Yield: 4 servings

*Jack Daniel's Distillery*

## OLD NATCHEZ COUNTRY CLUB

### 1323 Sneed Road West Franklin, TN 37069

*Old Natchez Country Club is ten minutes from Green Hills and a world apart. Take the short drive down Hillsboro Road and you'll find a site of unsurpassed natural beauty, a challenging golf course and a great place to relax! Founded more than a century ago as the Standard Club and located on Woodmont Boulevard, Old Natchez is the area's oldest country club in continual existence.*

### Jeff Lunsford, Food & Beverage Director

*Chef Lunsford, a Nashville native, is a specialist in Classical French and Cajun/Creole cuisine. Prior to joining Old Natchez Country Club as Food and Beverage Director, Jeff held many prestigious culinary positions such as Executive Chef at Sunset Grill and Sous Chef at Bayona in New Orleans. Other restaurants in his resume include Peristyle in New Orleans, Bottega and Highlands Bar & Grill in Birmingham, Alabama and The Orangery in Knoxville.*

## ARUGULA & ORGANIC TOMATO SALAD WITH GRILLED RED ONIONS, ASIAGO CHEESE & A BASIL VINAIGRETTE

### FOR THE VINAIGRETTE

| | | | |
|---|---|---|---|
| 2 | tablespoons red wine vinegar | 6 | tablespoons olive oil |
| 1 | tablespoon shallots, minced | | Fresh basil, chopped |
| | Salt and pepper to taste | | |

In a small mixing bowl combine the shallots, vinegar, salt and pepper. Whisk in the olive oil and then add basil to your taste.

| | | | |
|---|---|---|---|
| 4 | ounces of arugula Assorted tomatoes | 4 | ounces asiago cheese, a good quality Parmesan may be substituted |
| 2 | red onions | | |

Slice assorted yellow, red and green organic tomatoes ¼ inch thick and reserve. Slice the onions ¼ inch thick, brush them with oil and season with salt and pepper. Grill the onions until tender and reserve the rings. Slice the asiago cheese with a vegetable peeler to get nice ribbons and reserve. On chilled plates arrange the arugula in small bunches, stems pointed toward the middle of the plate. Arrange slices of the tomatoes in the middle of the plate and then garnish with the grilled onions, asiago cheese and drizzle the salad with the vinaigrette.

Serves 6.

## SWEET POTATO SOUP SHIITAKE MUSHROOMS

| | | | |
|---|---|---|---|
| 4 | pounds sweet potatoes | 2 | tablespoons flour |
| 1 | cup onion, diced | 8 | cups vegetable or chicken stock |
| 1 | cup celery, diced | ½ | cup heavy cream (optional) |
| 1 | cup carrot, diced | | |
| 2 | tablespoons vegetable oil | 12 | shiitake mushrooms |

Roast the whole sweet potatoes, skin on, at 350 degrees for an hour or until tender. While roasting the potatoes place a heavy soup pot on medium heat with the oil. Add the onion, celery and carrots and cook until tender and translucent. Add the flour and stir so the flour does not stick to the bottom of the pan. Deglaze with the stock and bring to a simmer, stirring often. Peel the warm potatoes and add the pulp to the simmering soup. Allow the soup to come back to a simmer and season with salt and pepper. Purée the mixture in a blender, strain it and return it to a fresh pot. Slowly warm the soup and add the cream if desired and re-season. Brush the shiitake mushrooms with oil and roast until tender. Slice the mushrooms. Place the soup in warm serving bowls and garnish with the mushroom slivers.

Serves 6.

## BLACKENED MAHI MAHI ON WILTED GARLIC-SPINACH WITH A BLACK-EYED PEA RELISH & SMOKED CORN

| | | | |
|---|---|---|---|
| 4 | cups uncooked black eyed peas | ½ | cup balsamic vinegar |
| | Water | 1 | tablespoon salt |
| 1 | bay leaf | 1 | tablespoon red wine vinegar |
| 10 | thyme sprigs | | |
| 10 | black peppercorns | 2 | tablespoons olive oil |
| 5 | parsley sprigs | | |
| 2 | cloves garlic | 1 | small red onion, diced |
| 3 | ounces, bacon (optional) | 1 | teaspoon sage, chopped |

In a heavy saucepan place the peas and enough water to cover, then over high heat bring the peas to a boil. Turn the heat off and allow to sit for 1 hour. Wrap and tie the next six ingredients in cheesecloth to form a sachet and place it in with the peas as well as the balsamic vinegar. Bring to a simmer and cook until the peas are just tender. Turn off the heat, add the salt and let stand for fifteen minutes. Drain the peas, discarding the sachet. In a mixing bowl whisk the oil, vinegar, red onion and sage together. While the peas are still warm toss them in the sage vinaigrette and reserve at room temperature.

**For the corn:** While cooking the peas place three ears of corn brushed with oil and seasoned with salt and pepper in a smoker or on a grill. After smoking slice the corn off the cob and reserve.

Serves 6.

### MAHI-MAHI

| | | |
|---|---|---|
| 6 | (6 ounce) mahi fillets | Olive oil |
| | Blackening spice | Salt |
| | Spinach | Red chili flakes |
| | Garlic, chopped | Clarified butter |

Place a cast iron skillet on high heat until the pan starts to smoke. Dredge the mahi fillets in clarified butter, allow to drain, and then dredge in the blackening spice. For less heat dredge one side, for more excitement dredge both sides. Place the fillets, spice side down, then reduce the heat to medium. Allow to blacken, keeping in mind that this will produce an ample amount of smoke. Turn the fillets and finish cooking to desired temperature.

While the fish cooks, warm a sauté pan over low heat and add the olive oil. When the oil is warm add the garlic and red chili flakes allowing the oil to be infused with their flavors. Add the spinach and allow it to wilt in the infused oil. Season the spinach with salt.

**To serve:** Place the spinach in the middle of a warm plate and top it with the blackened mahi. Place two tablespoons of pea relish on the fish. Spoon some of the vinaigrette on the plate as well, then garnish with the smoked corn kernels.

## INDIVIDUAL CUSTARDS FLAVORED WITH STRONG BLACK COFFEE

| | | | |
|---|---|---|---|
| 8 | egg yolks | 2 | cups heavy cream |
| ½ | cup sugar | 6 | 5-ounce ovenproof ramekins |
| 4 | cups black coffee | | |

In a saucepan reduce the coffee to one cup. Remove from the heat and whisk the heavy cream into the coffee and allow to cool to room temperature. In a mixing bowl whisk the egg yolks and sugar to ribbon stage. Whisk the coffee mixture into the egg and refrigerate the custard base until cool. Skim off any surface air bubbles that appear. Preheat the oven to 300 degrees. Pour the custard base into the ramekins and place them in an ovenproof pan. Fill the pan with enough warm water so that it comes half way up the side of the ramekins. Cover the pan with aluminum foil and bake them for 30 minutes. Check to see if the custard has set by gently shaking, they should be set around the edges yet have an area in the middle that jiggles. Refrigerate the custards overnight. To serve place in the middle of a dessert plate and garnish with chocolate covered espresso beans.

Serves 6.

*Belle Meade Mansion*

## 4TH & MAIN RESTAURANT

### 108 4th Avenue South Franklin, TN 37064

**Ed Butler, Executive Chef**
*4th & Main Restaurant is located in a 100-year-old building in historic downtown Franklin. The beautifully restored building features rotating artwork from a nearby gallery.*

## HERB ENCRUSTED HALIBUT WITH ROASTED RED PEPPER CREAM SAUCE & GARLIC MASHED POTATOES

### HERB ENCRUSTED HALIBUT

| | | | |
|---|---|---|---|
| 6 | ounces portion of halibut (per serving) | ¼ | cup fresh fine chopped thyme and rosemary |
| ½ | cup herbed olive oil | | |
| 3 | cups Japanese bread crumbs | | |

### ROASTED RED PEPPER CREAM SAUCE

| | | | |
|---|---|---|---|
| 1 | quart heavy whipping cream | ½ | tablespoon chopped garlic |
| ½ | quart chicken stock | | Cornstarch and water |
| 3 | tablespoons puréed roasted red pepper | | |

### GARLIC MASHED POTATOES

| | | | |
|---|---|---|---|
| 5 | pounds washed new potatoes | 1 | tablespoon garlic |
| ½ | pound butter | | Salt and ground black pepper to taste |
| 1 | cup half & half | | |

## SPINACH SALAD WITH CITRUS DRESSING

### SPINACH SALAD

| | | | |
|---|---|---|---|
| 4 | ounces spinach, picked and washed | ¼ | cup toasted sunflower seeds |
| ¼ | cup mandarin oranges | 3 | ounces citrus dressing |
| ¼ | cup chopped smoked bacon | | |

### CITRUS DRESSING

| | | | |
|---|---|---|---|
| 1 | cup balsamic vinegar | ½ | cup orange juice |
| ½ | cup Triple Sec (non-alcoholic) | ½ | cup pineapple juice |
| | | ½ | quart olive oil |

## CRAW CAKES WITH CREOLE MUSTARD LOBSTER DRESSING

### CRAW CAKES

| | | | |
|---|---|---|---|
| 2 | pounds crawfish meat | 1 | red pepper (minced) |
| 1 | quart Japanese bread crumbs | 2 | celery stalks (minced) |
| 3 | eggs | 2 | parsley sprigs (finely chopped) |
| ½ | red onion (minced) | 3 | ounces lobster base |
| 2 | scallions (finely | | |

Combine eggs and lobster base in a large stainless steel mixing bowl. Mix thoroughly with a wire whisk. Add onions, peppers, celery and parsley. Blend by hand. Fold in crawfish meat. Blend thoroughly by hand. Mix in bread crumbs and let set for 1 hour.

### CREOLE MUSTARD LOBSTER DRESSING

| | | | |
|---|---|---|---|
| 1 | cup ranch dressing | 1 | teaspoon lobster base |
| 2 | teaspoons Creole mustard | | |

Serves 6.

## VIKING CULINARY ARTS CENTER

### c/o The Factory At Franklin
### 230 Franklin Road
### Franklin, TN 37064

**Mary Stodola, Cooking School Director**
*Viking Range Corporation, the originator of commercial-style appliances for the home, has launched a new concept in culinary adventures — the Viking Culinary Arts Center, a combination world-class teaching kitchen, state-of-the-art theatre demonstration kitchen and retail shop offering professional caliber cooking tools. The Franklin location opened in November, 1999.*

## PASTA ALLA PUTTANESCA

| | | | |
|---|---|---|---|
| 3 | tablespoons olive oil | ¼ | cup black olives, pitted & chopped |
| 3 | cloves garlic, minced | 2 | tablespoons capers |
| ¼ | cup onion, chopped | ½ | teaspoon crushed red pepper |
| | Bacon | 3 | tablespoons basil, fresh, chopped |
| 1¾ | pound canned Italian diced tomatoes | 1 | teaspoon salt |
| | | ½ | teaspoon sugar |
| | | ½ | cup dry white wine |

Heat oil in large skillet; add onion and garlic and sauté over low heat, stirring until just golden. Add bacon and cook till done and light brown. At this point you can absorb some of the oil with paper towel if you want to lower the fat but you will also be removing flavor. Add the rest of the ingredients and simmer for 20 minutes longer. Cook linguine; drain and toss with the sauce and Parmesan cheese. Sprinkle chopped Italian parsley on top and serve.

*Now for some history: translated, Spaghetti alla Puttanesca is spaghetti in the style of the prostitute. The ladies would attract their clients with the enticing aroma of this flavorful and gutsy dish. Also it's quick preparation made it popular as a fast snack between clients.*

Yield: 4 servings

## ARROZ CON POLLO

| | | | |
|---|---|---|---|
| 1⅛ | cup rice, converted | 1½ | large tomatoes, canned, diced |
| 9 | chicken breast halves without skin | 4½ | tablespoons parsley, fresh |
| 4½ | cloves garlic, minced | 4½ | tablespoons oregano, fresh |
| 1½ | large onions, chopped | 3 | bay leaves |
| 1½ | green bell pepper, chopped | 3 | cups chicken stock, as needed |
| 1½ | red bell pepper, chopped | ¾ | cup green peas, frozen, petite |
| 1½ | small carrot, grated | | |
| 4½ | pieces Italian sausage, sweet or hot | | |

Sauté garlic, onion, peppers and sliced Italian sausage together. Cut chicken breast into large chunks or just quartered and add to sauté mixture. Cook for 5 minutes, add drained tomatoes, carrot, bay leaves and fresh herbs. Simmer for 15 minutes. Use the juice from tomatoes and chicken broth to make 2½ cups of liquid and add to mixture. In separate fry pan heat butter and sauté rice till coated and just beginning to turn brown. Add to chicken mixture, stir well, cover with foil and bake in a 375 degree oven for 25 to 35 minutes till rice is just done and most of the liquid is absorbed. Remove from oven and add the petite peas and a little kosher salt and fresh pepper if needed.

*Serving Idea: Garden salad with red wine vinaigrette*

Yield: 6 servings

## BAKED STUFFED ZUCCHINI

| | | | |
|---|---|---|---|
| 12 | zucchini (½ pound each) | 12 | eggs |
| ⅜ | cup margarine | ⅜ | cup fresh parsley, minced |
| 6 | scallions, chopped | 3 | tablespoons fresh basil, chopped |
| 1½ | pounds mushrooms, chopped | ½ | cup grated Parmesan cheese |
| 1½ | cups walnuts | | Salt & black pepper to taste |
| 3 | cups soft bread crumbs | | |

Scrub zucchini and cut in half lengthwise. Scoop out and reserve pulp, leaving shells ¼ inch thick. Drop shells into boiling water and boil for 5 minutes. Chop pulp and sauté in margarine. Add scallion or green onions and mushrooms; sauté 3 minutes longer. Add nuts and remove from heat. Beat eggs with parsley, basil, salt and pepper to taste. Add egg mixture and fresh bread crumbs to pulp mixture. Spoon into zucchini shells that have been drained. Top with grated cheese. Use your choice of cheese; Parmesan is only one suggestion. Place into a baking dish that has been greased with margarine. Add ½ inch of water and bake, uncovered, in preheated 350-degree oven for about 30 minutes. Let stand 5 minutes, then serve.

Yield: 12 servings

## MAGNOLIAS RESTAURANT

### 230 Franklin Road Franklin, TN 37064

*Magnolias is a four diamond AAA restaurant. The restaurant has been recognized in **People's Magazine**, **Southern Living**, **Cigar Aficionado**, **Celebrity Dish**, **TV Guide** and **Country Life** for its culinary accomplishments. Magnolias received the Reader's Poll Award from **Nashville Scene** as "the best restaurant in Franklin."*

**Richard Hamilton, Chef/Owner**
*Chef Hamilton is a James Beard recognized chef. He trained at the Le Cordon Bleu in Paris.*

## BANANA BREAD

| | | | |
|---|---|---|---|
| ½ | cup sugar | ¼ | teaspoon salt |
| ½ | cup light brown sugar | ¼ | teaspoon nutmeg |
| ½ | cup solid vegetable shortening | ¼ | teaspoon cinnamon |
| 1 | cup mashed over ripe bananas | ¼ | teaspoon vanilla |
| | | 1¼ | cups flour |
| 1 | teaspoon baking soda | 2 | eggs |
| | | ½ | cup walnuts |

Blend shortening and sugar till creamy. Add eggs one at a time while mixing. Add bananas. Add remaining ingredients. Pour into greased loaf pan and place in a 350 preheated oven. Cook till golden and pulls from sides slightly. Remove from pan and place on a cooling rack.

Yield: 1 loaf

## VELVETY PUMPKIN SOUP

| | | | |
|---|---|---|---|
| 2 | pounds trimmed pumpkin, cubed | 3 | tablespoons water |
| 1 | quart chicken stock (substitute canned if unavailable but fresh is preferred) | 1½ | cups heavy cream |
| | | 6 | tablespoons chilled unsalted butter cubed |
| 2 | tablespoons chopped onion | 1 | teaspoon cinnamon |
| 1 | tablespoon chopped celery | 1 | teaspoon nutmeg |
| | | 1 | teaspoon powdered ginger |
| 2 | teaspoons sugar | | Salt and white pepper to taste |
| 2 | tablespoons cornstarch | | |

In pot place pumpkin, onion, celery, stock and sugar. Bring to boil and then simmer medium for 20 minutes. Cook pumpkin till done and place in a food processor and purée till smooth. Strain through coarse strainer to remove threads from celery or unprocessed pumpkin and onions. In a small bowl dissolve cornstarch and water. Place soup on oven in pot and bring to soft boil. Add cornstarch and whisk quickly as to not form lumps and allowing starch to blend well. Add cream and seasoning except salt and white pepper. Simmer for 10 minutes stirring not to allow to scorch or stick. Remove from heat and whisk in butter stirring not to allow to separate. Once incorporated add salt and pepper to taste. Serve immediately.

## MONKFISH WRAPPED WITH BLACK PEPPER & BACON ON CREAMY CABBAGE & LEEKS

| | | | |
|---|---|---|---|
| 4 | portions monkfish (about 6 ounces a piece) | 2 | leeks (whites only) cut in half and washed well |
| 8 | pieces thick cut smoked bacon | 2 | cups heavy cream |
| ¼ | cup coarse black pepper | | Juice of one lemon |
| | | | Pinch of nutmeg |
| 8 | cups Savoy cabbage, cleaned and cored | | Salt and pepper to taste |
| | | 2 | tablespoons olive oil |

Take monk portions and salt each piece well making sure all membranes and skin are removed from fish. Wrap each piece with 2 pieces of bacon encasing completely. Tie with a string to hold bacon in place. Roll the filets in the pepper making sure to press well to hold as much of the pepper on. In a very hot skillet sear the bacon and monk on all sides. Remove and place on a pan and cook in 375 degree oven till done through. Approximately 15 minutes; depending on sear time and thickness of the fish. Make sure not to burn bacon. In another skillet heat oil and add sliced leeks. Sauté till they begin to soften slightly. Make sure leeks are sliced fairly thin. Add cabbage. Toss with leeks to blend. Add cream and lemon. Reduce cream by slightly more than half and is slightly thick. Add nutmeg and season to taste. Place cabbage and leek mixture in the center of plate. Remove string from fish and slice one time at an angle from top to bottom. Stand up making a point on cabbage.

Serves 4.

# THE BEECHWOOD

## 673 Charles Golden Road
## Sparta, TN 38583

*Dine in the rich ambiance of the Old South and experience the splendor of an 1820 middle Tennessee plantation mansion. The Beechwood offers private dining rooms for luncheons and dinner parties for groups of ten or more.*

### Dave & Carolyn Hamer, Chef/Owners

*Executive Chef Dave attended the prestigious Culinary Institute of America, now located in Hyde Park, New York. Following his extensive training in culinary arts, Dave was employed as the head chef in a New York restaurant. Shortly after their marriage Dave and Carolyn began traveling with their teaching ministry. For ten years they traveled nine months per year ministering two hundred times annually. Dave and Carolyn continued developing their culinary skills working each summer in the beautiful Adirondack Mountains of New York. Carolyn and Dave purchased Beechwood in 1997.*

## CRAB STUFFED SHIITAKES

|       |                          |       |                |
|-------|--------------------------|-------|----------------|
|       | Clarified butter         | ½     | cup cheddar    |
| ½     | cup diced onion          |       | cheese         |
| ½     | cup fresh crab           |       | About 8 to 10  |
|       | meat                     |       | shiitake       |
| 1     | cup medium white         |       | mushrooms      |
|       | sauce flavored with      |       |                |
|       | lobster stock or         |       |                |
|       | chicken bouillon         |       |                |

Brown diced onion in clarified butter. Add ½ cup fresh crab meat. Mix together. Add 1 cup of medium white sauce flavored with lobster stock or chicken bouillon. This is to bind the mixture together. Add ½ cup cheddar cheese and let it melt a bit before topping your prepared shiitake mushrooms with mixture. To prepare mushrooms: Quickly sauté the mushrooms in clarified butter just blanching them. Place in an oven-ready pan and bake in 350 degree oven for about 15 minutes.

## SHIITAKE ROCKEFELLER

|       |                          |       |                      |
|-------|--------------------------|-------|----------------------|
| ½     | pound bacon, diced fine  | 1     | cup medium white cream sauce enriched with chicken bouillon or chicken base |
| ½     | cup shallots, diced fine |       |                      |
| 1     | bag fresh spinach or 1 pound flaky frozen spinach | ¼ | cup fresh grated Romano cheese |
| ¼     | cup seasoned bread crumbs | 8    | to 10 shiitake mushrooms |

Cook diced bacon and diced shallots until done. Drain off bacon fat. Add 1 bag of fresh spinach or 1 pound frozen spinach (if fresh is not available) and cook until soft. Add ¼ cup bread crumbs and ¼ cup Romano cheese. In the meantime, quickly sauté your shiitake mushrooms in clarified butter just blanching them on both sides. Prepare pan for oven. Top each shiitake with a couple of tablespoons of Rockefeller mixture. Bake in 350 degree oven for about 15 minutes. Serve as an appetizer.

## FILET MIGNON-TOPPED SHIITAKE MUSHROOMS

|       |                          |       |                      |
|-------|--------------------------|-------|----------------------|
|       | Salt and pepper to taste | 6     | shiitake mushrooms   |
| 6     | ½" thick filets that will fit on mushrooms | 6 | morel mushrooms (fresh or reconstituted from dry) |
|       | Clarified butter         |       |                      |

Season filets with salt and pepper. Quickly cook filets in clarified butter and sauté lightly. Remove from heat and place a filet on each shiitake that has already been blanched briefly in clarified butter. Top each filet with a morel mushroom. These are ready to serve but can be placed in a warming oven to hold.

*The Beechwood*

CHATTANOOGA is a beautiful river city surrounded by scenic Appalachian mountains and the Cumberland plateau. It is also known for its family attractions, historic Civil War battlefields, cultural and educational museums, shopping, and outstanding restaurants. It has been hailed as one of the top ten family vacation cities in America. Chattanooga calls itself the "Environmental City" because of a massive effort that has taken place over the last twenty years to make it one of the cleanest cities in America. *Family Fun* magazine named Chattanooga as the American city with the "Best Friendly Spirit."

GATLINBURG is located at the northern entrance to the Great Smoky Mountains National Park. It is often referred to as the "honeymoon capital of the South" because thousands of newlyweds visit here annually. It was voted the favorite mountain getaway by *Southern Living's* Readers Choice Awards. Gatlinburg is known for its variety of accommodations – lodges, hotels and bed & breakfast homes for vacationers. In addition to arts and crafts, Gatlinburg has many Alpine-decorated specialty shops to entice the tourists.

THE GREAT SMOKY MOUNTAIN NATIONAL PARK is the most visited park in the United States with more than 10,000,000 visitors annually. It is part of the larger Appalachian Mountain chain. There are sixteen peaks in the park higher than 6,000 feet. Clingman's Dome is the second highest peak in the eastern United States at 6,643 feet. Cades Cove is the most visited area in the national park. The scenic cove is a limestone basin one mile wide and four miles long, ringed by mountains. Picturesque log cabins, a grist mill, two churches and several old cantilevered barns have been restored.

PIGEON FORGE is in Sevier County, joining Gatlinburg to the north. It is best known as a shopping mecca because of the many outlet malls in the area. It was voted the favorite shopping spot in the South in *Southern Living's* Readers Choice Poll. Pigeon Forge is also the home of the Dollywood Theme Park.

SEVIERVILLE was named for the first governor of Tennessee, John Sevier. Sevierville, along with Gatlinburg and Pigeon Forge, host the annual WinterFest. Sevier County is the home of Dolly Parton. The eighteen-hundred-seat Lee Greenwood Theater is located in Sevierville.

NEWPORT is the county seat of Cocke County. Newport was established in 1799 near a ford on the French Broad River. Today, Cocke County is the largest producer of apples in Tennessee. The Cherokee National Forest has three recreation areas in Cocke County. The Appalachian Trail runs from the northeastern edge of the Great Smoky Mountains National Park along the southern edge of the county.

OAKRIDGE was the site of a top-secret facility for the development of the atomic bomb during World War II. In 1942, the facilities at Oakridge were built under the direction of the Manhattan Corps of Engineers to oversee the development of atomic energy. The finest engineers and scientists from across the United States were recruited for this massive undertaking. Today, the Oakridge National Laboratory of the Department of Energy is based here and is now known throughout the world for its scientific research and development. The American Museum of Science and Energy is open to visitors.

KNOXVILLE is located northwest of the Great Smoky Mountains on the Tennessee River. In the fall of 1791, the city was officially founded and named for General Henry Knox, President Washington's Secretary of War. The Tennessee Valley Authority (TVA) arrived in the 1930s and brought hydroelectric power to the area. The availability of hydroelectric power was important for developing atomic energy at nearby Oak Ridge. Knoxville was the host of the 1982 World's Fair with the theme "Energy Turns the World." Knoxville is the home of the University of Tennessee, the largest university in the state. The University of Tennessee Vols won the 1999 National College Football Championship. The University of Tennessee football stadium is the second largest in the country. The UT women's basketball team has been a perennial winner of the women's national basketball championship. The Women's Basketball Hall of Fame is located next to Volunteer Landing.

GREENEVILLE is the second oldest town in Tennessee and the home of the seventeenth President of the United States, Andrew Johnson. Greeneville was the capital of the Lost State of Franklin from 1785 to 1787. The Andrew Johnson Presidential Library is located on the campus of

Tusculum College a few miles east of Greeneville. Davy Crockett's birthplace is only 10 miles away.

JONESBOROUGH is over two hundred years old and the oldest town in Tennessee. It is listed on the National Registry of Historic Places. Andrew Jackson practiced law here in 1788. Jonesborough is the host of the National Storytelling Festival and has become known as the birthplace of the American storytelling revival.

JOHNSON CITY is the largest city in the Tri-Cities area. After three name changes it became Johnson City in 1869. During the Civil War, the town was called Haynesville in honor of Landon Carter Haynes. This estate, now known as the Tipton-Haynes Historic Site, is owned by the Tennessee Historical Commission and is open to the public. East Tennessee State University and The Quillen College of Medicine at ETSU are located here.

ELIZABETHTON is located in Carter County on the site of a Cherokee village called the Watauga Old Fields near shoals in the Watauga River known as Sycamore Shoals. In 1772, four years before the Declaration of Independence was signed, "Overmountain" men travelling westward across the Appalachian Mountains established the Watauga Association, thought to be the first constitution written by native-born Americans. Roan Mountain is located near here.

KINGSPORT is the second largest city in the Tri-Cities area. It is located just 60 miles from the geographic center of the eastern United States and within a day's drive of over half the nation's population. More than 200 years ago, an important route westward called The Great Stage Road wound its way through these Southern foothills. Follow the path and you will find the roots of Tennessee – and some of the most significant sites in our nation's history.

BRISTOL has the distinction of being divided by the state line of Tennessee and Virginia. The twin cities have been designated as the "Official Birthplace of Country Music" by the U.S. Congress in 1998. The Bristol Motor Speedway is located here. It is NASCAR's fastest half-mile track.

# ADAMS HILBORNE MANSION INN & RESTAURANT

## 801 Vine Street
## Chattanooga, TN 37403

*European-style hotel with twelve exquisitely decorated guest rooms, private baths, fireplaces, and complimentary breakfast. The Adams Hilborne Mansion has a ballroom, meeting and reception areas and private dining rooms. It is located only minutes from Chattanooga museums, fine shopping, the aquarium, UTC arena and other cultural events and attractions. Call 1 (423) 265-5000 for reservations.*

**David & Wendy Adams, Innkeepers
Eric Wood, Chef**

*Mrs. Adams serves as Executive Chef and is a graduate of the prestigious Culinary Institute of America in Hyde Park, New York. Chef Adams completed two accelerated CIA courses available to professional chefs with at least three years previous training in the culinary arts.*

## BANANA-RASPBERRY BISQUE

| | |
|---|---|
| 1 | cup fresh raspberries |
| 4½ | cups half-and-half, divided |
| ½ | cup whipping cream |
| 3 | tablespoons powdered sugar |
| 4 | ripe bananas, peeled, sliced and frozen |

Combine raspberries, ½ cup half-and-half, whipping cream and powdered sugar in container of an electric blender; process until smooth, stopping once to scrape down sides. Pour through a wire mesh strainer into a large bowl, discarding seed. Cover and refrigerate. Just before serving, combine half of bananas and 2 cups half-and-half in container of an electric blender; process until smooth. Pour banana mixture into a large bowl and repeat procedure with remaining 2 bananas and 2 cups half-and-half. Pour banana mixture into small bowls. Using a squirt bottle, carefully drizzle raspberry mixture over banana mixture.

## SUNBURST CHICKEN & WALNUT SALAD

| | | | |
|---|---|---|---|
| 1½ | cups water | 1½ | tablespoons vegetable oil |
| 1 | stalk celery | ½ | teaspoon dried tarragon |
| 4 | black peppercorns | | |
| 4 | 4-ounce skinless, boneless chicken breast halves | ½ | teaspoon orange rind, grated |
| 2 | tablespoons cider vinegar | 2 | oranges, peeled and sectioned |
| 2 | teaspoons honey | 8 | lettuce leaves |
| ½ | teaspoon dry mustard | 2 | tablespoons walnuts, chopped and toasted |

Combine first 3 ingredients in large skillet and bring to a boil. Cover, reduce heat, simmer 10 minutes. Place chicken in skillet; cover and simmer 10 minutes or until tender. Remove chicken, let cool. (Discard vegetables and reserve broth for another use.) Cut chicken into strips. Combine vinegar and next five ingredients, stirring with wire whisk. Add orange sections. Line each plate with 2 lettuce leaves. Remove orange sections from dressing, divide evenly among plates. Place chicken strips in dressing and toss. Divide strips evenly among plates. Drizzle remaining dressing evenly over salads. Sprinkle with ½ tablespoon walnuts.

Serves 4.

## Adams Hilborne Mansion
### INN AND RESTAURANT
### 1889

## SOUTHSIDE GRILL

### 1400 Cowart Street
### Chattanooga, TN 37408

**Nathan Winowich, Executive Chef**
**Jeremy Riemer, Chef de Cuisine**

*Chef Winowich is an Ohio native. He joined Southside Grill in 1994. Chef Winowich has set a goal to make Southside a destination restaurant to spotlight Southern cuisine. He has done this by finding his own unique cooking style which combines regional influence, innovation and impeccable ingredients from all over the world. The restaurant has obtained a wonderful following from all over the South and has received many accolades, such as the **Wine Spectator** Award of Excellence, **Cityscope** "Best Restaurant" and features in **Southern Living** and **The Atlanta Constitution**.*

## GINGERED-PEACH CRÈME BRÛLÉE WITH SHORTBREAD COOKIES

| | | | |
|---|---|---|---|
| 3 | cups heavy cream | ½ | cup granulated sugar |
| 8 | egg yolks | | |
| ½ | cup granulated sugar | 2 | teaspoons pure vanilla extract |
| 2 | to 3 inch piece of fresh ginger root, peeled and minced | ½ | cup granulated sugar |
| 4 | ripe peaches | | Propane torch for burning tops |

Preheat oven to 300 degrees. If using a convection oven, preheat to 250 degrees. Wash peaches, then remove seed and dice large. Place in non-aluminum pot for best results, cover with second sugar measure and minced ginger and place over medium heat with lid, simmer until peaches become very soft and tender. Remove from heat, reserve. Purée this mixture in a food processor as soon as it becomes cool enough to manage. Place cream in a pot on medium-high heat. At the same time place a pot, half full of water over heat and bring to a boil. Place egg yolks in a bowl large enough to fit all listed ingredients. Add first sugar measure and vanilla, and

combine with a whisk. Place bowl atop boiling water and continue mixing with whip until mixture becomes very warm, not too hot as this will cause the mixture to "break" or separate. Remove from heat and after cream has come to a boil, remove it from the heat. Add ginger peach purée to cream and mix well, net, slowly pour hot cream mixture into warm egg mixture whipping constantly. When completely combined, strain this mixture through a very fine sieve or cheesecloth. Place ramekins inside deep baking pan as they are baked in a water bath. Fill 4 to 6 ramekins, depending on which size is being used, with brûlée custard and place pan in oven then fill halfway with hot water (water should reach half of the ramekins. Bake custards for 2 to 3 hours in conventional over or 1½ hours in convection oven. Custards should be just slightly wobbly in the center and firm around edges when done. Turn oven off and let custards rest for 30 minutes before removing them from the oven. Remove from water bath and chill in refrigerator for at least 2 to 3 hours before serving. When completely cool, sprinkle sugar in even thin layer all over tops and burn with propane torch. Sugar should not turn black, but an amber-brown caramel tone.

Serves 4 to 6.

### SHORTBREADS

| | | | |
|---|---|---|---|
| 4 | ounces unsalted butter, room temperature | ½ | teaspoon ground ginger |
| ½ | cup granulated sugar | ½ | teaspoon baking powder |
| 1 | egg | 1 | egg white |
| 1 | teaspoon pure vanilla extract | ½ | cup granulated sugar |
| 1½ | cups all-purpose flour | | |

Preheat oven to 375 degrees (conventional) 325 degrees (convection). Sift flour, ginger and baking powder together, reserve. Cream butter in a mixing bowl slightly, add sugar and blend well, do not mix fluffy. Add egg, blend well again, do not overmix. Mixture should look smooth and combined. Add dry ingredients at once and mix by hand to avoid overmixing. Mix only to combine, any overmixing will result in a tough cookie. Roll dough on floured surface to about ¼ inch thick and cut with cutter to desired shape, brush with egg white and sprinkle tops with sugar. Bake on parchment paper-lined pan for about 8 minutes or until golden brown.

## RARE SEARED TUNA WITH FOIE GRAS GRITS, ROASTED PORTOBELLA MUSHROOMS WITH RED WINE REDUCTION

| | | | |
|---|---|---|---|
| 4 | 4-ounce #1 quality tuna steaks | 2 | cups quick-cook grits |
| 4 | ounces A grade foie gras | 2 | portobella mushrooms |
| 3 | cups milk | 2 | teaspoons minced garlic |
| 1 | cup cream | ½ | cup olive oil |
| 1 | yellow onion | | Salt & pepper to taste and S & P for the grits |
| ½ | cup fresh Parmesan cheese | | |
| 2 | tablespoons butter | | |

Julienne and sauté the onion in butter. Season foie gras with salt and pepper, sear both sides in pan with the onions, then remove the foie gras from the pan, slice and reserve on paper towel. Add cream and milk to onions and bring to a boil then slowly whisk in the grits, Parmesan, salt and pepper to taste then you can fold in the foie gras. When the grits are finished they should be smooth and creamy.

### FOR THE PORTOBELLA MUSHROOM

Place the mushrooms gill side up and coat well with olive oil, garlic and salt & pepper. Roast in the oven at 350 degrees for 8 minutes and julienne when finished.

### RED WINE REDUCTION INGREDIENTS

| | | | |
|---|---|---|---|
| 3 | cups Pinot Noir | 1 | tablespoon honey |
| 1 | cup balsamic vinegar | | |

Reduce above ingredients over medium heat until thick (like syrup) and reserve. This can be done well in advance and kept in the refrigerator for up to a week, but should be slightly warmed before serving.

### TUNA

Heat a sauté pan to a high heat then season the tuna steaks with salt & pepper, add olive oil to the pan and quickly sear both sides until well browned.

**To plate the dish:** Spoon grits on to the center of the plate and place tuna directly on top. Top tuna with julienne mushrooms and drizzle lightly with wine reduction.

Serves 4.

## MAPLE ROASTED SWEET POTATO PURÉE WITH APPLEWOOD SMOKED BACON & CARAMELIZED VIDALIA ONIONS

| | | | |
|---|---|---|---|
| 4 | medium sweet potatoes (peeled and chopped small) | ½ | pound slab applewood smoked bacon diced |
| 3 | Vidalia onions, diced | ¼ | cup and 2 tablespoons olive oil |
| 2 | stalks celery, diced | | Salt & pepper to taste |
| 2 | medium carrots, diced | ¼ | cup finely chopped chives |
| 4 | cups chicken stock | | |
| ½ | cup and 2 tablespoons maple syrup | | |

Preheat oven to 350 degrees; place sweet potatoes, 1 Vidalia onion, celery, carrots, maple syrup, olive oil and 2 teaspoons salt and 2 teaspoons pepper in a large mixing bowl. Toss until everything is evenly coated, place in a roasting pan and roast for 30 to 40 minutes (until sweet potatoes are soft). While vegetables are roasting, heat chicken stock (medium heat) in a large pot. Heat two separate sauté pans, in one (medium-high heat) sauté remaining Vidalia onions with 2 tablespoons olive oil until lightly brown, add 2 tablespoons of maple syrup, 1 teaspoon pepper and 1 teaspoon salt and set aside. With the other pan cook bacon crispy, drain and set aside. Once sweet potato mix is soft, add to chicken stock and simmer for 20 minutes. Purée with blender or food processor until completely smooth. Return to pot and add Vidalia onions. Adjust salt and pepper as needed and serve in a large soup bowl with crispy bacon and chopped chives as garnish.

## CHATTANOOGA CHOO CHOO – HOLIDAY INN

### 1400 Market Street Chattanooga, TN 37402

*On December 1, 1909, a crowd of several hundred gathered in the 1400 block of Market Street for the dedication of Chattanooga's "Gateway" – Terminal Station. Almost 61 years after the opening, the grand old building was closed to the public when the last train stopped on August 11, 1970. In 1973, beautiful Terminal Station once again opened its doors to welcome visitors to Chattanooga – this time as a unique vacation complex! The Chattanooga Choo Choo, famous in history and song, is now a magnificently restored structure for all to enjoy.*

**Jim Wynn, Food & Beverage Director**

*The restaurant facilities include the following: The Gardens, a family style restaurant. The Station House, a casual restaurant serving steak, seafood and ribs; Dinner in the Diner, a small gourmet restaurant and Café Espresso which serves deli selections, gourmet coffees and desserts.*

## CHATTANOOGA CHOO CHOO CORN FRITTERS

| | | | |
|---|---|---|---|
| 3 | cups flour | 1 | tablespoon vegetable oil |
| 2 | tablespoons baking powder | 3 | eggs, beaten |
| 1½ | teaspoons sugar | 1 | cup whole kernel corn, drained |
| 1½ | teaspoons salt | | Deep fat for frying |
| ¾ | cup milk | | Powdered sugar |

Sift first four ingredients. Mix eggs and milk and add to dry mixture; add oil and corn and beat until blended. Drop heaping tablespoons into 350-degree deep fat and fry 2 to 3 minutes, or until golden brown. Drain on absorbent paper. Keep warm and serve with powdered sugar.

## BUTTERMILK PECAN CHICKEN WITH ORANGE BLOSSOM HONEY BUTTER SAUCE

| | | | |
|---|---|---|---|
| 6 | 8-ounce boneless chicken breasts | 2 | cups Japanese bread crumbs (or coarse bread crumbs) |
| 1 | quart buttermilk | | |
| 2 | cups pecans (medium dice) | ½ | cup vegetable oil |

Remove any sinew (skin) from the chicken breasts. Place between two pieces of plastic wrap and gently flatten with a meat mallet or heavy flat object. Marinate in buttermilk for one hour. Combine pecans and bread crumbs. Remove chicken one at a time from buttermilk and dredge in pecan bread crumb mixture coating evenly on both sides. Heat oil in a cast iron skillet to 325 degrees and sauté until lightly brown on both sides. Remove and drain on paper towels. Yield: 6 servings

### ORANGE BLOSSOM HONEY BUTTER SAUCE

| | | | |
|---|---|---|---|
| 2 | cups honey (Orange Blossom preferred but others will do) | 3 | tablespoons cornstarch |
| 2 | cups chicken stock (or water with chicken bouillon cubes) | ½ | pound unsalted butter (cubed and chilled) |

In a saucepan, bring chicken stock to a slight boil. Mix 2 tablespoons of cold water with cornstarch to create a slurry mixing thoroughly. Slowly add to chicken stock and stir with wire whip until slight boil returns then remove from heat. Slowly stir in honey mixing well then swirl in cold butter. Glaze chicken breast just before serving.

Yield: 6 servings

*Chattanooga Choo Choo*

## LOBSTER BISQUE

*(from **Dinner in the Diner**)*

| | | | |
|---|---|---|---|
| 3 | cloves garlic, minced | 2 | tablespoons lobster base |
| 2 | shallots, diced | 8 | ounces lobster meat, diced |
| 1 | tablespoon olive oil | | |
| ½ | cup celery, diced | 20 | ounces heavy cream |
| ½ | cup carrots, diced | | |
| ⅓ | cup brandy | 1 | teaspoon cayenne |
| ⅓ | cup white wine | 1 | tablespoon paprika |
| ⅓ | cup sherry | | |

Sauté garlic and shallots in olive oil. Add carrots and celery and sauté for 2 minutes then add brandy, sherry and white wine and reduce to half the volume on low heat. Add lobster base, cayenne and paprika then lobster meat and heavy cream. Reduce on low heat for 45 minutes and serve.

Yield: 4 servings

## CHATTANOOGA CHOO CHOO PEANUT BUTTER PIE

| | | | |
|---|---|---|---|
| 1 | 9-inch graham cracker pie crust | 1¼ | cups powdered sugar |
| | Heaping ½ cup peanut butter | 2½ | cups heavy cream |
| | Scant 4 ounces cream cheese | ½ | cup toasted almonds |

Cream peanut butter with cream cheese until blended. Add powdered sugar and mix well. Whip cream until light and stiff, being careful not to whip into butter. Reserve some of cream for garnish; blend remaining cream into peanut butter mixture, with about ⅔ of almonds. Spread filling in crust, pipe or spoon remaining cream on top and sprinkle with remaining almonds. Chill before serving.

Serves 8.

## PECAN DIAMONDS

### CRUST

| | | | |
|---|---|---|---|
| 10 | tablespoons unsalted butter | 3 | cups all-purpose flour |
| 9 | tablespoons sugar | 1 | tablespoon baking powder |
| 6 | tablespoons shortening | ½ | teaspoon salt |
| 1 | egg | | |
| 2 | teaspoons vanilla extract | | |

Soften butter and cream in mixer with the sugar and shortening on medium speed for 4 minutes. Add egg, vanilla, flour, baking powder and salt. Gently mix on low until just blended. Form into a ball and wrap in plastic then let rest for four hours or overnight. Roll out dough between two sheets of plastic wrap the size of a 17¾" x 12⅞" sheet pan. Remove one sheet of the plastic wrap and place dough side down into the buttered sheet pan. Using a toothpick gently dock the dough (prick with holes) through the plastic wrap. Remove plastic and blind bake (without filling) until just lightly brown being careful not to overbake.

### FILLING

| | | | |
|---|---|---|---|
| 2 | cups unsalted butter (or 1 pound) | 2½ | cups light brown sugar (or 1 pound) |
| 1⅛ | cup honey | 8 | cups pecan halves |
| ½ | cup sugar | ½ | cup heavy cream |

Preheat oven to 350 degrees. Mix butter, honey, sugar and brown sugar in a deep pot and bring to boil for three minutes on medium-high heat. Do not stir. Remove from heat. Fold in pecans and heavy cream. Pour and spread filling over crust. Place on top rack of oven and line bottom rack with aluminum foil for over-boil and bake for 30 minutes. Cool a couple of hours and cut with a sharp knife ¼ inch from the sides of the sheet pan. Then cut lengthwise two inch strip bars. Angle cut the bars forming triangles for the diamonds.

## THE LOFT

### 328 Cherokee Boulevard
### Chattanooga, TN 37405

*Year in and year out this restaurant is rated as one of the best restaurants for fine dining in Chattanooga according to the **City Scope** Reader's Poll. The Loft received the 1997 award from **City Scope** Reader's Poll for "Best Steak." According to a Reader's Poll from **Southern Living**, The Loft was voted one of the "Top Ten Privately Owned Restaurants" in the country. The Loft's menu features steaks, seafood, prime rib, chicken and veal as well as other popular items.*

**Hamid Andalib, Owner**
**Maurice Weddington, Executive Chef**
**Earnest Crutcher, Jr., Executive Sous Chef**

## ROASTED PRIME RIB

| | | | | |
|---|---|---|---|---|
| 1 | 12 to 13 pound rib | | 1 | teaspoon coarse |
| 1 | cup red wine | | | black pepper |
| ½ | cup chopped garlic | | 2 | carrots, chopped |
| | | | 1 | onion, chopped |

Place one 12 to 13 pound rib on a roasting pan with 1 cup of red wine. Rub down with chopped garlic (½ cup). Place 1 teaspoon of coarse black pepper, 2 chopped carrots and 1 chopped onion over rib roast and bake for 4½ hours at 200 degrees. Cover with foil while in oven.

Yield: 10 servings

## CHICKEN PICCATA

| | | | | |
|---|---|---|---|---|
| 1 | 8-ounce chicken breast | | | Salt & pepper to taste |
| | Egg wash (1 egg mixed with ½ cup milk) | | ½ | cup heavy cream |
| | | | ¼ | cup white wine |
| | Flour | | ¼ | cup lemon (squeezed) |
| 1 | tablespoon capers | | | |

Dip the chicken into egg wash, then flour and pan fry until golden brown. Strain off oil from pan, add 1 tablespoon of capers, salt and pepper, ½ cup cream, ¼ cup white wine, ¼ cup squeezed lemon and let simmer for 2 to 3 minutes, then serve.

Yield: One single serving

# BLUFF VIEW ART DISTRICT

## 412 East Second Street Chattanooga, TN 37403

*At the turn of the century as the Tennessee River and Chattanooga continued to attract wealth and industry, many of the families on the forefront of those ambitions built their lives and raised their children in a neighborhood known as Bluff View. Today, while their families' legacies live on in other Chattanooga landmarks, the neighborhood they once called home thrives as the Bluff View Art District. Fueled by the same entrepreneurial spirit of the original resident "cliff dwellers," the Art District's cornerstone was established in 1991, when Dr. Charles and Mary Portera bought the former Newell House on the corner of High Street and East Second Street. The first of many investments the couple has made in the area, the District has become an award-winning example of sustainable urban renewal and preservation excellence – a place where the past meets the present to create a lively, sophisticated ambience perfect for meeting, dining, an overnight getaway or enjoying the fine arts.*

*Applauded year-round for inventive menus, elaborate culinary salutes, and signature specialty pastas, breads, French pastries and chocolates, the Bluff View Art District has evolved into a cutting-edge culinary district as well. There are four unique restaurants in the Art District: Back Inn Café, Rembrandt's Coffee House, Tony's Pasta Shop & Trattoria and Renaissance Commons.*

**Mary Barnett, Marketing Director**

# BACK INN CAFÉ

**Tim Benton, Chef**

## SALMON CAKES

| | | | |
|---|---|---|---|
| 2 | pounds salmon, skinned | 2 | cups Ritz brand crackers, crushed |
| ½ | cup butter | 2 | tablespoons Dijon mustard |
| 1 | medium red onion, chopped | 1 | teaspoon Old Bay seasoning |
| 2 | tablespoons garlic, chopped | | Salt & pepper to taste |
| 2 | eggs, beaten | | Olive oil |
| ¼ | cup basil, chopped | | |

Preheat oven to 350 degrees F. Bake the salmon on a baking sheet until ¾ done, about 15 minutes. Do not overbake salmon. Set aside to cool. Meanwhile, melt butter over medium heat in a medium sized skillet. Add onion and garlic and sauté for 5 minutes. Do not overcook. Set aside to cool. Flake the cooled salmon into medium sized pieces and in a large bowl mix the salmon, onion and garlic mixture, and remaining ingredients until well blended. Allow mixture to sit for about an hour. Shape into 3-inch patties. The mixture will make a dozen cakes. Heat a thin layer of olive oil in a medium sized skillet. Add cakes and cook over medium heat until cakes are golden brown, about 3 or 4 minutes on each side. Remove cakes from skillet and drain them on paper towels.

### DILL AIOLI

| | | | |
|---|---|---|---|
| 3 | egg yolks | 3 | dashes dry dill |
| ¼ | cup cider vinegar | 1 | cup extra virgin olive oil |
| 1 | tablespoon Dijon mustard | | Salt & pepper to taste |
| 1 | clove garlic | | |

Using a food processor, mix for 30 seconds on high speed the egg yolks, vinegar, mustard, garlic and dill for 30 seconds on high speed. Slowly add the oil until the mixture reaches desired consistency. Add the salt and pepper to taste. Do not over-mix.

Note: You may use a ½ cup to a full cup of olive oil depending on the consistency you desire.

### HORSERADISH SLAW

| | | | |
|---|---|---|---|
| 1½ | pounds cabbage, shredded | 2 | tablespoons Dijon mustard |
| 1 | small red onion, chopped | ¼ | cup honey |
| 1 | medium carrot, shredded | 2 | tablespoons horseradish |
| ½ | cup mayonnaise | | Pinch fresh parsley |
| ½ | cup red wine vinegar | | Salt & pepper to taste |

Toss cabbage, carrots and onion. In a separate bowl, combine the mayonnaise, vinegar, Dijon, honey horseradish and parsley to prepare the slaw dressing. Add the dressing to the cabbage mixture, season with salt and pepper and mix thoroughly. Store in an airtight container and refrigerate several hours before serving. Spoon horseradish slaw over hot salmon cakes, then drizzle with dill aioli.

Serves 4.

## BLACKBERRY GLAZED CHICKEN WITH GNOCCHI

### BLACKBERRY SAUCE

| | | | |
|---|---|---|---|
| 1½ | tablespoons olive oil | 1 | cup frozen blackberries |
| ¼ | cup shallots, peeled and diced | ¼ | cup balsamic vinegar |
| 2 | tablespoons garlic, chopped | 2 | cups chicken stock |
| 1 | sprig fresh rosemary | | Salt & pepper to taste |

In a skillet, over medium heat, sauté shallots in olive oil until translucent. Add garlic, rosemary and blackberries. Cook until mixture turns to liquid, about 5 minutes. Add the balsamic vinegar and chicken stock, then simmer for 45 minutes, stirring occasionally. Force through a fine strainer and season with salt and pepper.

### CHICKEN

| | | | |
|---|---|---|---|
| 4 | chicken breasts | ½ | cup blackberry sauce |
| 1 | tablespoon olive oil | | |

Remove fat from chicken. Place chicken on a cutting board and cover with 2 layers of plastic wrap. Beat chicken with a meat hammer (mallet) until tender. Do not over-beat the chicken. Mix a tablespoon of olive oil with ½ cup of blackberry sauce to make the marinade. Coat chicken thoroughly with marinade and place in a shallow pan. Place in a refrigerator to marinate for several hours.

### POTATO GNOCCHI

| | | | |
|---|---|---|---|
| 1 | pound mashed potatoes | 1 | teaspoon garlic, chopped |
| 1 | pound ricotta cheese | 2 | cups flour |
| 2 | eggs | | Salt & pepper |

In a large bowl, mix potatoes, ricotta, eggs and garlic. Gradually add the flour, then salt and pepper to taste. Knead well on a floured board until mixture is firm. Next, bring a large pot of water to a boil. Meanwhile, shape the potato mixture into inch-long rolls about the thickness of a finger. Drop gnocchi rolls in boiling water and boil until gnocchi floats to the top. Remove gnocchi, strain and toss with cold water. Coat with enough olive oil to prevent gnocchi from sticking together. Set to the side.

Heat a thin layer of olive oil in a large skillet over medium heat. Carefully place chicken and blackberry marinade in the skillet and cook on each side for 4 minutes. Reduce heat and add the remaining blackberry sauce. Simmer for 5 to 10 minutes, until chicken is done. If sauce is thin, remove chicken and then simmer sauce until it reaches desired thickness. In the meantime, heat a thin layer of oil in a separate skillet. Add gnocchi and sauté until golden brown. Season with salt and pepper. To serve, divide chicken breasts among 4 plates. Top with gnocchi and finish with blackberry sauce.

Serves 4.

Back Inn Café
an Italian Bistro

## RENAISSANCE COMMONS

**Brad Grafton, Chef**

### PROSCIUTTO & GOAT CHEESE BISCUITS

| | |
|---|---|
| ¼ | pound prosciutto, sliced paper-thin (cut into 40 pieces 1 inches by 2 inches) |
| ½ | pound goat cheese |
| 2 | teaspoons fresh sage, minced |
| 2 | teaspoons fresh rosemary, minced |
| 2 | teaspoons fresh thyme, minced |
| 10 | biscuit doughs, quartered |
| 1 | egg, whipped Salt & pepper to taste |

Preheat oven to 350 degrees. Mix fresh herbs with goat cheese. Season well with salt and pepper. Evenly spread a thin layer of cheese mixture on a piece of prosciutto and roll it up. Repeat process 40 times. With a rolling pin, roll out biscuit dough into 40 small triangles. Place prosciutto and cheese mixture on the dough and roll into the shape of a croissant. Place on baking sheet and brush tops with whipped egg. Bake until golden brown, approximately 12 to 15 minutes. Makes 40 pieces. The rolls can be prepared ahead of time and stored, uncooked, in a freezer until needed.

Renaissance Commons
*a place to gather*

## MIA'S ASIAN CHICKEN SALAD

### SALAD

| | | | |
|---|---|---|---|
| 6 | boneless , skinless chicken breasts | 1 | large carrot, shredded |
| 1 | head bok choy, clean & thinly sliced | 1 | pound rice noodles or angel hair, cooked and chilled |
| 1 | bunch green onion, minced | 2½ | cups Mia's Asian Dressing |

Using 1 cup Mia's Asian Dressing (see recipe below), marinate chicken for 4 hours. Grill chicken until thoroughly cooked. Allow chicken to cool, then slice on bias into strips. Toss chicken strips and vegetables with ¾ cup Mia's Asian Dressing. In a separate bowl, toss remaining ¾ cup of dressing with noodles. To serve, remove chicken strips from vegetables. Place vegetables onto 4 plates. Place a layer of noodles on top of vegetables and then finish with chicken strips.

Makes 4 entrée salads

### DRESSING & MARINADE

| | | | |
|---|---|---|---|
| 1 | cup rice wine vinegar | 1 | tablespoon garlic, minced |
| 1 | cup soy sauce | 2 | tablespoons fresh ginger, minced |
| 1 | bunch green onions, chopped | ½ | cup brown sugar, light or dark |
| 1 | bunch cilantro, chopped | 1 | tablespoon sesame oil |
| 3 | limes, juiced | | |

Blend all ingredients until smooth. This is also great as a marinade or as a dipping sauce for hors d'oeuvres. For marinating, drizzle over the meat and let sit for several hours. This sauce goes great on all types of meat.

Makes 3 cups

## REMBRANDT'S COFFEE HOUSE

### David Padial, Chef

## ORANGE ALMOND TUILE WITH FRESH FRUIT IN A GRAND MARNIER SABAYON SAUCE

### ORANGE ALMOND TUILE

| | | | |
|---|---|---|---|
| ½ | stick butter, melted | 2 | tablespoons orange |
| ½ | cup sugar | | zest |
| 2 | eggs | 1 | teaspoon vanilla |
| ¼ | cup all-purpose flour | 1 | cup almonds, sliced & blanched |

Preheat oven to 350 degrees. Melt butter and set aside. In a separate bowl, mix sugar and eggs. Add the flour, orange zest and vanilla and mix thoroughly. Slowly blend in the melted butter and add almonds. Place two heaping tablespoons on a greased baking pan and spread into a 5 to 6 inch circle. Bake until edges are a light golden brown, about 5 minutes. Using a spatula, remove the tuile from the pan and immediately place the tuile cookie over the bottom of a cup to form the tuile cup.

### GRAND MARNIER SABAYON

| | | | |
|---|---|---|---|
| 1¼ | cups heavy whipping cream | 4 | ounces sugar |
| 12 | egg yolks | 2 | tablespoons Grand Marnier |

Using an electric mixer, beat the heavy cream over medium speed until cream begins to stiffen. Without heat, combine the egg yolks and sugar in the top of a double-boiler. Scrape the sides of the double boiler with a spatula then place over very gently simmering water. Remove from heat and place egg and sugar mixture in a separate bowl. With an electric mixer, whip on medium speed for five minutes. Whisking constantly, slowly add the Grand Marnier and whisk for another five minutes. Fold this mixture into the whipped cream. Place in refrigerator until sabayon is completely cooled. Place tuile basket on plate, spoon fresh fruit into tuile basket and top with sabayon.

Yield: 12 servings

## CRÈME DE CARAMEL

### CARAMEL SUGAR

| | | | |
|---|---|---|---|
| 2 | cups granulated sugar | ¼ | cup water |

Place sugar and water in a small, heavy saucepan. Heat over medium heat, stirring occasionally, until a clear syrup forms. Increase heat to high and, using a candy thermometer, boil to 320 degrees. Quickly remove from the heat and submerse bottom of saucepan into ice bath. Immediately pour caramelized sugar, about ¼ inch into six 8-ounce ramekins.

### FLAN

| | | | |
|---|---|---|---|
| 8 | whole eggs | ½ | cup sugar |
| 4 | egg yolks | 1 | quart milk |
| 2 | tablespoons vanilla | | |

Preheat oven to 350 degrees. Mix together eggs, egg yolks, vanilla and sugar. Meanwhile, scald the milk. Remove from heat and gradually whisk the egg and sugar mixture. Pour the flan into six 8-ounce ramekins. Place ramekins in a water bath and bake for 40 minutes or until a knife inserted into the ramekins comes out clean. Remove flan from oven and refrigerate to cool. To unmold, briefly dip the ramekins into hot water and gently loosen with a knife. Turn ramekin upside-down to invert onto individual plates.

Yield: 6 8-ounce servings

Rembrandt's
*coffee house*

# 212 MARKET RESTAURANT

## 212 Market Street
## Chattanooga, TN 37402

**Maggie Moses, Registered Dietitian/Owner**
**Sally Moses, Manager/Owner**
**Susan Moses, Chef/Owner**

*Chef Susan Moses graduated from the Culinary Institute of American in 1986. She was chosen to represent Tennessee & Chattanooga at the James Beard House for Tennessee's Bicentennial. 212 Market Restaurant has won numerous awards including Mobile & Fodor's 3 Diamond Rating (and favored restaurant in Chattanooga) and winner of **Wine Spectator** Magazine Award of Excellence. **City Scope** Magazine awarded 212 best: Wine List, Most Romantic, Best Restaurant, and Best Appetizers. 212 Market Restaurant will be featured in a fall 2001 **Southern Living** edition.*

## RACK OF LAMB WITH PEACH CHUTNEY & PEANUT CRUST

### MARINADE

| | | | |
|---|---|---|---|
| 1 | cup canola oil | 1 | tablespoon fresh rosemary, minced |
| 4 | garlic cloves, minced | 1 | tablespoon ground black pepper |
| 2 | shallots, minced | | |

For the marinade, combine everything.

### PEANUT CRUST

| | | | |
|---|---|---|---|
| 4 | tablespoons roasted peanuts, chopped | 1 | cup fresh bread crumbs |
| 4 | tablespoons parsley, chopped | | Salt & pepper to taste |

For the peanut crust, combine everything.

### PEACH CHUTNEY

| | | | |
|---|---|---|---|
| 6 | fresh peaches, medium dice | | Pinch of red pepper flakes |
| ½ | of a red onion, fine dice | 2 | ounces peach liquor |
| | Crystallized ginger, fine dice | | Salt & pepper to taste |
| 1 | tablespoon cider vinegar | | |

For the chutney, sauté first 5 ingredients in butter. Flambé with peach liquor and check seasonings.

Take 4 "frenched" lamb racks. These need 2 inches of clean bone. Marinate the racks for 15 to 20 minutes. Sear or grill the whole racks for 2 minutes on first side, 1 minute on second side. Coat with chutney mixture. Dust with peanut crust. Transfer to shallow roasting pan. Roast at 375 degrees for 10 minutes for rare (115 degrees).

Serves 4.

## CORN CHOWDER

| | | | |
|---|---|---|---|
| 1 | tablespoon oil | 1 | cup chicken broth |
| ⅓ | cup diced onion | 1 | cup skim milk |
| 1 | carrot, sliced thin | 1 | cup fresh corn kernels |
| 1 | rib celery, sliced thin | | Cayenne to taste |
| 1 | bay leaf | | Salt & pepper to taste |
| 1 | teaspoon basil, chopped | | Large baking potato |
| 1 | teaspoon tarragon | | |
| ¼ | cup parsley | | |

In large heavy saucepan, heat the oil and add the onion, carrot, celery, bay leaf, salt and black pepper to taste. Cook 5 to 10 minutes until vegetables are crisp tender. Add the potato, ⅓ inch diced) and the broth. Bring mixture to a boil and simmer for 10 to 15 minutes or until potato is tender. Add the milk and corn and simmer for about 3 minutes or until corn is tender. Discard the bay leaf. Transfer about 1 cup of the mixture to blender and purée. Add the purée to the pan with the cayenne, basil, tarragon, parsley and stir the chowder until it is combined well. Divide the chowder into bowls and top with a dollop of low fat yogurt and parsley or other topping as desired. Makes two large bowls of chowder.

## CEDAR PLANKED TROUT WITH MUSTARD SAUCE

Soak planks in water for about 20 minutes. Put on top of grill to char. When the wood smolders and becomes fragrant, the plank is ready. Season trout fillet with salt and fresh pepper. Sprinkle with dry mustard. Shave a thin slice of butter on top of fillet. Put trout fillet on smoldering plank and roast in oven or inside the closed grill until just done.

### MUSTARD SAUCE

| | | | |
|---|---|---|---|
| 1 | tablespoon chopped shallots | 2 | tablespoons smooth Dijon mustard |
| 1 | tablespoon chopped parsley | 1 | cup chicken stock |
| 1 | tablespoon chopped tarragon | 1 | cup cream |
| 2 | ounces Grand Marnier | 1 | cup ripe tomato, diced |
| | | | Salt & pepper to taste |

Sauté first three ingredients in butter. Add liquor and flambé. Add mustard and stock and reduce by half. Add cream and reduce by half. Add diced tomatoes. Adjust seasonings.

## WARM PEAR & PECAN CREAM TART

| | | | |
|---|---|---|---|
| 7 | ounces puff pastry dough | 1 | large egg |
| 6 | tablespoons butter | 2 | to 3 pears, peeled and cut into thin wedges |
| 3 | tablespoons sugar | | |
| 4 | tablespoons pecans, finely ground | 2 | tablespoons honey |

Roll out puff dough to ⅛ inch thick and a 5½ inch diameter. Refrigerate. Take half of the butter and cream it well with the 3 tablespoons sugar. Add pecans and egg. Spread some on pastry circle to ½ inch of edge. Arrange pears in concentric circles on this. Dot with rest of butter. Drizzle with honey. Bake 20 to 25 minutes. Serve warm with Armagnac cream (whipped cream with sugar and Armagnac), or caramel sauce or cream fraiche.

---

## ADAMS EDGEWORTH INN

### Monteagle Assembly Monteagle, TN 37356

*One hundred-year-old inn boasts English country cottage décor, fine antiques, original artwork, and elegant gourmet dining. Twelve rooms with private baths. Inn has been featured as one of the top 54 historic inns in America by **National Geographic Traveller**. 1 (931) 924-4000*

**David & Wendy Adams, Innkeepers Jenny Rollins, Chef**

*Mrs. Adams serves as Executive Chef and is a graduate of the prestigious Culinary Institute of America in Hyde Park, New York. Chef Adams completed two accelerated CIA courses available to professional chefs with at least three years previous training in the culinary arts.*

## OLD FASHIONED EDGEWORTH CHESS CAKE

| | | | |
|---|---|---|---|
| 1 | box butter cake mix | 1 | box powdered sugar |
| ½ | cup butter | 8 | ounces cream cheese |
| 1 | egg | 3 | eggs |

Combine cake mix, butter and 1 egg. Mix well. Pat into a 3x9x2-inch pan. Mix together powdered sugar, cream cheese and 3 eggs. Pour this mixture over cake mix. Bake at 350 degrees for 45 minutes. Can be served with fresh peaches marinated in sugar and a liqueur.

## STUFFED BASS

1 whole sea bass, 4 to 4½ pounds, dressed (leave head and tail on)
1 cup fresh lump crab meat
8 saltine crackers
½ cup butter, melted
3 tablespoons lemon juice
Salt & pepper to taste

¼ cup scallions, chopped (use 2 inches of green stem)
2 tablespoons red or yellow peppers, chopped
½ teaspoon Dijon mustard
½ cup dry white wine Italian parsley, chopped

Wash fish well with cold water and pat dry. Pick through crab meat and remove cartilage and shells. Crush crackers into coarse crumbs and stir in ¼ cup melted butter, 2 tablespoons lemon juice, 1 teaspoon salt, 1½ teaspoons pepper, celery, onions, parsley and mustard. Add crab meat and mix. In separate bowl, mix wine with 4 tablespoons butter. Rub fish with remaining lemon juice. Sprinkle with salt and pepper. Fill fish with crab mixture. Pour wine butter over fish. Bake for 30 minutes at 400 degrees. Baste several times while baking. Serve with baked polenta.

Serves 4 to 6.

# Adams Edgeworth Inn

## "A Spa For The Spirit"

## BLACKBERRY FARM
### 1471 W. Millers Cove Road Walland, TN 37886

*Blackberry Farm is a tranquil resort nestled in the foothills of the Smokies about 30 miles southeast of Knoxville. In addition to luxurious accommodations, the inn has 4 tennis courts on the property as well as an outdoor swimming pool. There are ponds and streams scattered over the 1100 acre property offering an abundance of bream, bass and trout. Fly-fishing is a popular pastime here. Hiking is another.*

**John Fleer, Executive Chef**

*Chef Fleer is a native of North Carolina. He attended undergraduate school at Duke University. While in undergraduate school, John spent six months in Venice and became hooked on "the culture of food." His master's thesis even reflected his new love for food. After working in an Italian restaurant in the Chapel Hill area as a pastry chef, John turned his career plans toward professional cooking. He enrolled in The Culinary Institute of America in Hyde Park, New York, and after completing its two-year program, he stayed on for an additional year-long fellowship at St. Andrew's Café, one of the institute's restaurants. His creative talents at the CIA caught the attention of Kreis and Sandy Beall, owners of Blackberry Farm. John became Executive Chef at Blackberry Farm in 1992.*

## ASPARAGUS SOUP WITH CRAYFISH TAILS

| | | | |
|---|---|---|---|
| 1¾ | pounds asparagus, middle sections, reserve tips | 1 | quart chicken stock |
| ½ | ounce olive oil | ½ | ounce lemon juice |
| 2½ | ounces celery, chopped | ¾ | teaspoon lemon zest |
| 2 | ounces leeks, wash well, chopped | ¾ | teaspoon salt |
| 2½ | ounces onions, chopped | ¼ | teaspoon black pepper |
| | | ½ | ounce blond roux |
| | | ½ | cup half and half |

### GARNISH

| | | | |
|---|---|---|---|
| ¼ | pound crayfish tails | 40 | each asparagus tips |

### LEMON CRÈME FRAICHE

| | | | |
|---|---|---|---|
| ½ | cup crème fraiche | ¾ | tablespoon lemon zest, minced |
| ½ | tablespoon lemon juice | | |

Trim asparagus, reserving tips for garnish; throw away woody ends. Sauté onions, leeks and celery in olive oil until translucent. Add asparagus middles and sauté for 10-15 minutes until most of the liquid is released from asparagus. Add stock, salt, pepper, lemon juice and lemon zest. Bring to a boil. Whisk in roux and simmer for 10 minutes. Remove from heat; purée and strain through china cup (not chinois). Temper half and half and stir into purée. Test seasoning.

For garnish: Sauté crayfish tails in a little clarified butter, deglaze with white wine. Blanch asparagus tips in salted boiling water until tender. Prepare lemon crème fraiche by heating lemon juice and zest together and then stirring into crème fraiche; keep chilled. Line soup bowls with crayfish tails and asparagus tips; garnish with lemon crème fraiche on top of soup.

**BLACKBERRY**

A COUNTRY HOUSE HOTEL
AND MOUNTAIN CLUB

## SHEEPSMILK CHEESECAKE

### CRUST

| | | | |
|---|---|---|---|
| 3 | tablespoons melted butter | ¼ | cup chopped pistachio nuts |
| ¾ | cup toasted bread crumbs | ¼ | cup grated dry jack cheese |

### FILLING

| | | | |
|---|---|---|---|
| 1 | pound cream cheese | ¼ | teaspoon cracked black pepper |
| 1½ | pounds Old Chatham Cheese (fresh sheep's cheese) | ¼ | cup chopped chives |
| 4 | eggs | 1 | tablespoon chopped parsley |
| ¼ | cup heavy cream | 1 | teaspoon salt |

Combine crust ingredients. Line springform pan with ¾ of the crust. Cream cream cheese. Add eggs, cream, sheep's cheese and beat until smooth. Stir in herbs and seasoning. Pour into springform pan. Sprinkle top of cake with remaining ¼ of the crust prior to baking. Bake for 1½ hours at 325 degrees. Turn oven off and allow to sit for 30 minutes. Let cool.

Serves 16

## WHITE CHOCOLATE BROWNIE

| | | | |
|---|---|---|---|
| ½ | pound white chocolate | 1½ | cups all-purpose flour |
| ½ | pound butter | ¼ | teaspoon salt |
| 1½ | cups granulated white sugar | 5 | ounces chocolate chips |
| 6 | eggs | ¼ | pound pistachio nuts |
| ⅛ | cup dark rum | | |
| 1½ | teaspoons vanilla | | |

Melt white chocolate and butter over water bath (or you can melt chocolate over a water bath and melt butter in microwave). Pour into mixing bowl, add in the following order: sugar, flour eggs, rum, vanilla, salt and pistachios. Mix with paddle on first speed, increasing to second briefly at the end. Do not overwork or they will become chewy and the top crust will flake off. Pour butter into greased and parchment-lined 9x13-inch pan. Sprinkle chocolate chips over top. Use the side of the rubber spatula to pat them down. Bake at 350 degrees for 60+ minutes. Rotate every 30 minutes top to bottom and give a half turn. When done, top will be golden and the center will spring back. If center sinks upon removal from oven, return it to the oven ASAP and continue to bake. The brownies can be salvaged.

## QUAIL IN WINE

| | | | |
|---|---|---|---|
| 6 | to 8 quail – split in half | ½ | cup mushrooms |
| | Salt & pepper to taste | 2 | tablespoons bell pepper, chopped |
| 1 | stick butter | 1 | tablespoon flour |
| 1 | carrot, diced | 1 | cup chicken stock |
| 1 | small onion, chopped | ½ | cup white wine |

Salt and pepper birds. In skillet, lightly brown birds in butter. Remove to buttered casserole dish. In same skillet, sauté vegetables for 5 minutes. Stir in flour and gradually add stock or broth. Simmer 10 minutes. While sauce is simmering, pour wine over birds. Cover and bake 1½ hours at 350 degrees.

Serves 3 to 4.

## LOWFAT APPLE RAISIN PIE

| | | | |
|---|---|---|---|
| 2 | egg whites | 1¼ | cups diced, peeled Macintosh apples |
| ½ | cup sugar | | |
| 1 | teaspoon baking powder | ¼ | cup raisins |
| 1 | teaspoon vanilla | ¼ | cup pecans, chopped |
| ½ | cup unbleached flour | 4 | sheets phyllo dough |
| | Butter flavored nonstick cooking spray | | |

In medium bowl, whisk the egg whites, sugar, baking powder and vanilla. Whisk in the flour until smooth. Stir in the apples, raisins and pecans. Set aside. Coat a 9-inch pie plate with nonstick spray. Working quickly to avoid letting it dry out, fold 1 phyllo sheet in half crosswise. Gently press the folded sheet into the pie plate with the ends of the sheet extending over the edge of the plate on either side. Spray the folded sheet with the nonstick spray. Repeat with the remaining 3 phyllo sheets, staggering the ends so that the corners of the sheets are evenly spaced around the rim of the plate. Spoon the apple mixture into the pie shell. Fold the ends of phyllo toward the apples to form a rim of dough around the edge of the pie plate. Set the pie on a baking sheet. Bake at 350 degrees until the filling is puffed and lightly browned – about 30 minutes.

# WOODLAWN BED & BREAKFAST

## 110 Keith Lane
## Athens, TN 37303

### Susan & Barry Willis, Innkeepers

*A beautifully preserved antebellum home located in historic downtown Athens, Woodlawn was formerly the Keith Mansion, built by Alexander Keith in 1858. **The Tennessean** called Woodlawn "A Classic B&B," filled with gorgeous antiques and furnishings. The house was a hospital during the Civil War. Reservations: 1-800-745-8213*

## BAKED APPLE FRENCH TOAST

| | | | |
|---|---|---|---|
| 1 | 12-ounce package of frozen escalloped apples | 3 | eggs |
| | | 1 | cup milk |
| ⅓ | cup brown sugar | ½ | teaspoon vanilla |
| 2 | tablespoons butter, melted | 6 | to 7 slices bread (1 inch thick) |

Preheat oven to 350 degrees F. Combine defrosted apples, brown sugar and butter in 9x13 inch pan. In medium bowl, whisk eggs, milk, and vanilla until well combined. Dip bread into egg mixture. Place bread on top of apple mixture. Spoon any remaining egg mixture on top of bread. Bake 35 to 40 minutes.

Yield: 6 to 7 pieces

*Woodlawn Bed & Breakfast*

# LG's ON THE RIVER RESTAURANT

## 2530 Winfield Dunn Parkway
*(Adjacent to Lee Greenwood Theater at River Bluff Landing)*
## Sevierville, TN 37764

*Situated high on a rocky bluff overlooking the scenic French Broad River you'll enjoy some of the most spectacular views of the Smokies anywhere at Lee Greenwood's new restaurant. Enjoy a delicious meal in their 428-seat dining room complete with magnificent stack stone fireplaces for that rustic, cozy atmosphere.*

## STUFFED FLOUNDER

| | | | |
|---|---|---|---|
| ¼ | pound of butter | 3 | bay leaves chopped up fine |
| ½ | pound chopped celery (chopped into ¼ inch pieces) | ½ | pound small cooked shrimp |
| ½ | pound yellow onion (chopped into ¼ inch pieces) | 2 | ounces seafood base |
| 1 | tablespoon chopped garlic | 2 | pounds snow crab meat |
| 1 | tablespoon coarse ground black pepper | 1 | pint unseasoned croutons |
| 1 | tablespoon cayenne pepper | 1 | cup unseasoned bread crumbs |
| 1 | tablespoon dry dill weed | 6 | to 8 flounder fillets |

Melt butter in small pot, cook celery, onions and garlic until translucent. Add spices, dill, bay leaves and seafood base. Add shrimp, crab meat and cook for 5 to 10 minutes on low heat. Add croutons and pour onto sheet pan. Add bread crumbs and let cool for 30 minutes to 1 hour. After it has cooled, ball up into 4 ounce portions and wrap flounder fillets around it.

Yield: 6 to 8 servings

### INGREDIENTS FOR FLOUNDER TOPPING (TARRAGON SHALLOT SAUCE)

| | | | |
|---|---|---|---|
| 2 | diced shallots | 1 | teaspoon white pepper |
| ½ | cup white wine | 1 | teaspoon salt |
| 1 | quart heavy whipping cream | ¼ | cup of cornstarch and water (roux) |
| ½ | cup dry tarragon leaves | | |

In saucepan, cook shallots in white wine till translucent. Add whipping cream, spice and tarragon. Bring to boil then add roux to thicken.

Place stuffed flounder on pan. Butter each and add salt, pepper and fresh dill weed on top of flounder. Place flounder in oven on 350 degrees for 12 to 16 minutes and top with 2 ounces of tarragon shallot sauce after it is done.

*Scenic Barn*
*Sweetwater, Tennessee*

## BLACK BEAN SOUP

| | | | |
|---|---|---|---|
| 4 | cups black beans | ½ | tablespoon salt |
| 1 | gallon water | 1 | tablespoon cumin |
| 1 | ham hock | 1 | tablespoon garlic in oil |
| 1 | cup diced red onion | 1 | tablespoon Tabasco sauce |
| ½ | tablespoon ground black pepper | | |

Place one gallon of water and add black beans. Trim meat from hocks and dice. Place meat and hock in stockpot. Add remaining ingredients. Cook on high heat stirring frequently for two hours. Add ½ gallon of water and cook until beans are soft. Remove hock bone and stir with a wire whip.

Yield: 1 gallon

## GREEN ONION HOUSE DRESSING

*(Available at all Stokely Restaurants)*

| | | | |
|---|---|---|---|
| 1 | cup mayonnaise | ½ | teaspoon lemon juice |
| ½ | cup sour cream | 4 | ounces buttermilk |
| 3 | to 4 green onions (chopped) | | Salt (to taste) |
| ½ | teaspoon Worcestershire sauce | | Lawrey Season Salt (to taste) Garlic (to taste) |

Combine ingredients in bowl and mix thoroughly. Chill one hour before serving.

Yield: 2 cups

## HONEY MUSTARD DRESSING

*(Available at all Stokely Restaurants)*

| | | | |
|---|---|---|---|
| ½ | gallon mayonnaise | 3 | tablespoons paprika |
| 2 | cups honey | | |
| ¾ | cup mustard | | |

Warm honey (140 degrees). Blend warm honey and paprika. Add remaining ingredients.

## APPLEWOOD GRILL

### Apple Valley Road off U.S. 441 Sevierville, TN 37862

*The Applewood Farmhouse Grill overlooks the Little Pigeon River nestled in an orchard of apple trees. The Grill makes its own Apple Julep, Apple Fritters and Homemade Apple Butter and serves them with every Applewood Farmhouse Grill meal.*

## APPLEWOOD JULEP

*(Available at Applewood Grill & Applewood Farmhouse)*

| | | | |
|---|---|---|---|
| 1 | quart apple juice | 1 | cup orange juice |
| 1 | cup pineapple juice | ¼ | cup lemon juice |

Mix and serve over ice.

Serves 6.

## APPLE FRITTERS

*(Available at Applewood Grill & Applewood Farmhouse)*

| | | | |
|---|---|---|---|
| ½ | cup milk | 1 | teaspoon vanilla |
| 1 | egg | 1½ | cups cake flour |
| 2 | tablespoons melted butter | ¼ | teaspoon salt |
| 1 | tablespoon orange peel | 1 | tablespoon baking powder |
| ½ | cup chopped apples (skin on) | ½ | cup sugar |

Blend all wet ingredients. Fold in orange peel, salt and baking powder. Fold in flour. Fold in chopped apples. Do not over mix. Drop spoonfuls of batter in 325 degree oil and fry until golden brown.

## BURNING BUSH RESTAURANT

### At the Entrance to the National Park Gatlinburg, TN

*Elegant dining in the rich splendor of polished woods, pewter and candlelight, overlooking the wonderland of the National Park from a spacious glass dining room. The Burning Bush Restaurant adds its special flair to classic cuisine. Voted "Best Breakfast & Dinner" by* **Blue Ridge Country** *Magazine. The Burning Bush Restaurant has served visitors to the Smoky Mountains since 1975.*

## LECONTE SUNRISE JUICE

| | | | |
|---|---|---|---|
| 2 | cups orange juice | 1 | cup capped strawberries |
| 2 | cups apple juice | | |
| ½ | cup chopped pineapple | 3 | bananas |

Blend all ingredients in food processor; place in freezer until almost completely frozen. Re-blend and serve.

Serves 6.

## STUFFED POTATO IN GREEN PEPPER

| | | | |
|---|---|---|---|
| 6 | medium size potatoes | 2 | ounces bacon bits |
| 1 | tablespoon chopped chives | 2 | ounces Parmesan cheese |
| ½ | cup sour cream | | Salt & pepper to taste |

Preheat oven to 450 degrees. Wash, pat dry and place potatoes in oven on baking sheet. Bake at 450 degrees for 45 minutes or until done. Cut potatoes in half and scoop out pulp. In mixing bowl, combine potato pulp, chives, sour cream and bacon bits. Mix thoroughly. Fill the pepper shells with potato mixture. If desired, sprinkle the potato tops with Parmesan cheese. Broil under low heat until cheese is melted or until potatoes are hot if cheese is used. Salt and pepper to taste.

Serves 6.

## BRASS LANTERN RESTAURANT
### 710 Parkway Gatlinburg, TN

*The Brass Lantern Restaurant has served visitors to the Smoky Mountains since 1968. In a lively, casual atmosphere you'll find a wide variety of great food and friendly service. The Brass Lantern serves a mixture of all-time favorites, as well as light and vegetarian cuisine. A diverse selection of appetizers, succulent ribeyes and Smoky Mountain trout are offered.*

## SPINACH GUSTO

| | | | |
|---|---|---|---|
| 1 | pound frozen chopped spinach | 1 | teaspoon cracked red pepper |
| 1 | quart cheddar cheese sauce | ½ | cup bread crumbs |
| 4 | eggs | ½ | cup Parmesan cheese |

Thaw spinach completely and squeeze out all excess water. Fold in eggs and cheese sauce. Top with bread crumbs and Parmesan cheese mixture. Bake covered at 350 degrees for 15 minutes. Uncover and bake 15 additional minutes.

# THE OLDE ENGLISH TUDOR INN

## 135 West Hollyridge Road Gatlinburg, TN 37738

**Steve & Linda Pickel, Innkeepers**
*Located in Gatlinburg, half a mile from the National Park entrance and walking distance from Gatlinburg's restaurants and other attractions. Seven attractive guestrooms have private baths, cable TV/HBO.*
*The inn has a large common room with fireplace and secluded patio overlooking Gatlinburg.*
*Reservations: 1 800 541-3798*

## OLDE ENGLISH TUDOR INN SWEET SCONES

| | | | |
|---|---|---|---|
| 1 | cup water | 1 | cup all-purpose |
| ½ | cup butter | | flour |
| ¼ | teaspoon salt | ½ | cup sugar |
| | | 4 | eggs |

Bring water, butter and salt to boil. Remove from heat and stir in sugar and flour. Beat over low heat until mixture leaves sides of pan. Remove from heat. Beat in eggs, one at a time. Beat until shiny and satiny and broken in strands. Drop into Pam-coated scone cups. Bake at 375 degrees for 35 to 40 minutes. Will sound hollow when tapped. Keep from drafts.

Serving Size: 12

Preparation Time 30 to 40 minutes.

## SMOKY MOUNTAIN FRENCH TOAST

| | | | |
|---|---|---|---|
| 8 | ounces cream cheese | 1 | loaf bread (sandwich sliced) |
| 4 | ounces of your favorite jam | 5 | eggs |
| | | ¼ | cup canned eggnog |

Mix cream cheese and jam together with fork in a medium mixing bowl until smooth. Spread mix onto bread making sandwiches, place finished sandwiches back into bag (will hold for four to five days in refrigerator). When ready to make toast, heat griddle to highest temperature. Whisk eggs and canned eggnog together. Pour into pie pan and dip sandwiches both sides and place directly on griddle. Cool both sides to golden brown, sprinkle powered sugar on top and serve hot.

Serving Size: 10 (2 pound loaf)

Preparation time: 20 to 30 minutes

*John Cable Mill*
*Cades Cove, Tennessee*

# THE PEDDLER RESTAURANT

## 820 River Road
## Gatlinburg, TN 37738

**Geoffrey A. Wolpert, Owner**

*Geoff Wolpert has been setting the standard for dining excellence in the Smokies for more than 20 years. That experience and expertise has been recognized by **Southern Living** Magazine and is evident in everything about his restaurants, from the buildings themselves to preparation, presentation and service.*

*Built around the historic C. Earl Ogle log homestead, The Peddler exudes rustic charm. Custom-cut steaks presented at your table by the "peddler" are hickory grilled to perfection. From unique appetizers to grilled chicken, seafood entrées or your favorite wine or cocktail as you relax by the river, The Peddler promises the perfect end to your day in the Smokies.*

## MARINATED CHICKEN

| 1 | can pineapple juice | ½ | cup cooking sherry |
| ½ | cup soy sauce | 1 | cup sugar |

Combine above ingredients for marinade. Marinate 4 to 6 chicken breasts for 24 hours in refrigerator. Bake until done.

## TOM'S CHOCOLATE FUDGE CAKE

| 1 | cup water | 2 | eggs |
| ¼ | cup cocoa | 1 | teaspoon vanilla |
| ½ | pound butter | 1 | teaspoon baking |
| 2 | cups flour | | soda |
| ½ | cup buttermilk | | |

Bring water, cocoa and butter to a boil. Sift flour and sugar together. Combine butter, milk, eggs, vanilla and soda together. Pour boiling liquid over dry ingredients (add slowly). Whisk in liquids (eggs). Bake at 400 degrees for 20 minutes.

Yield: 1 cake

## CRAB STUFFED MUSHROOMS

| 1 | pound crab meat | 2 | tablespoons chopped parsley |
| 2 | whole eggs | | |
| 1 | cup mayonnaise | 2 | tablespoons lemon juice |
| 1 | cup bread crumbs | | |
| 1 | teaspoon Cajun seasoning | ½ | red pepper (minced) |
| 1 | pinch thyme | ½ | green pepper (minced) |
| 1 | pinch red pepper flakes | ½ | cup minced scallions |

Combine all ingredients and stuff in silver dollar mushrooms. Brush bottom of mushrooms with butter. Bake at 400 degrees for 6 minutes.

### CRAB STUFFED MUSHROOM SAUCE

| 1 | can chicken broth | ½ | cup lemon juice |
| 1 | teaspoon white pepper | 8 | dashes Tabasco sauce |

Bring ingredients to boiling point

Combine ½ cup butter and 1 cup of flour and whisk into liquid until thick paste. Add half and half to thin.

*Tipton Place
Cades Cove, Tennessee*

# THE PARK GRILL

## 1110 Parkway
## Gatlinburg, TN 37738

**Geoffrey A. Wolpert, Owner**
*Opened in 1995 and located only 200 yards from the entrance to the Great Smoky Mountains National Park, The Park Grill is a hospitable blend of majestic mountain lodge, casual elegance and faultless dining. From the sweeping stone porch with massive pillars of Idaho spruce and an outdoor fireplace to the diversified menu of beef, pork or chicken prepared on the wood burning hickory grill, to fresh mountain trout and pasta and award-winning desserts made fresh daily by their own pastry chef, The Park Grill transports diners back to a less harried era.*

## PARK GRILL P-KAN CHICKEN

| | | | |
|---|---|---|---|
| 4 | pieces (6 ounces each) boneless skinless chicken breasts | 3 | eggs |
| 1 | cup plain yogurt | ½ | cup milk |
| 1 | cup fat-free Italian dressing | ½ | ounce Jack Daniel's whiskey |
| | Salt and ground white pepper to taste | 1 | cup Captain Crunch cereal |
| | Nutmeg to taste | 1 | cup Japanese or dry coarse bread crumbs |
| ½ | cup flour | ½ | cup toasted pecan pieces; almost crushed |

Blend yogurt with Italian dressing. Immerse breasts into mixture and refrigerate covered overnight; blanch breasts in pre-heated oven (350 degrees) 10 minutes for not quite cooked all the way and very moist; cool to room temperature; combine toasted pecans, cereal and bread crumbs, hold nearby. Season flour with salt, pepper and nutmeg, then dredge both sides of breasts; whisk eggs, milk and ½ ounce Jack Daniel's whiskey together and soak floured breasts in this for 4 to 5 minutes. Remove and press both sides of all breasts into the breading mixture until thoroughly coated. It may be necessary to repeat this process; deep fry 350 degrees until golden brown for 3 to 4 minutes.

Yield: 4 (6-ounce) chicken breasts

## SAUCE FOR PARK GRILL P-KAN CHICKEN

| | | | |
|---|---|---|---|
| ½ | pound soft butter | 3 | ounces Jack Daniel's whiskey |
| ½ | cup toasted pecan pieces | 6 | ounces heavy cream |

Slowly melt ¼ pound of butter in sauce pot. Add pecans and Jack Daniel's and simmer on low heat to avoid flare up from liquor for 3 to 4 minutes. Add heavy cream and bring to brief boil. Remove from heat and stir. Place back on medium-low heat for 7 to 8 minutes until cream reduces and sauce becomes of medium consistency. Whip in other ¼ pound of butter until thoroughly incorporated. Hold in warm spot until needed.

## ABRAM'S CREEK PAN FRIED RAINBOW TROUT

*Fresh, local boneless trout with a caper lemon butter sauce served with wild rice*

| | | | |
|---|---|---|---|
| 2 | fillets boneless trout | ½ | ounce neutral stock or wine |
| ½ | cup hot fry flour | ½ | ounce whole soft butter |
| 1 | ounce clarified butter | 1 | teaspoon chopped Italian parsley |
| ½ | ounce minced shallots | | Sea salt and ground white pepper to taste |
| ½ | ounce capers | | |
| ½ | ounce fresh lemon juice | ⅙ | lemon wedge |
| | | ⅙ | chopped herb |

Season flesh of trout with salt and pepper; dredge both sides in semolina, add oil to preheated skillet and cook trout skin side up first for 1-2 minutes, carefully turn over with spatula and add shallots, capers and lemon juice; place in oven approximately 3 to 4 minutes at 400 degrees. Remove and place trout (flesh side up) on oval platter. Over trout fillets ladle 2 ounces of piccata sauce, garnish with lemon wedge and chopped herb.

## RASPBERRY LEMONADE

| | | | |
|---|---|---|---|
| 2 | (½ gal. size) lemonade concentrate | 1 | (5 pound) bag I.Q.F. raspberry |
| | | 1 | (2 qt.) jar Smuckers strawberry preserves |

Divide raspberries in ½ in blender, fill with water and purée. Pour into 22-quart square Lexan tub. Do the same with strawberry preserves. Add concentrate and fill with cold water to about 4 inches from top. Add ice to 1 inch from top and whisk vigorously. Serve with extra ice in glass, lemon slice and fresh mint sprig.

# MAXWELL'S BEEF & SEAFOOD RESTAURANT

## 1103 Parkway
## Gatlinburg, TN 37738

**Charlynn Maxwell Porter, Owner**

*Mrs. Porter has been a restaurateur since 1984. She owns and operates Legend's By Max & Copper Kettle as well as Maxwell's Catering Company in the Gatlinburg area. Mrs. Porter has a BA degree from Bryan College and attended the Masters Program at the University of Tennessee. She is currently serving as a commissioner for the City of Gatlinburg for the 1999 to 2003 term. Charlynn is the Past President of the Gatlinburg Rotary Club and has served as Chairperson for the United Way for 3 years. She is a distance runner who has competed in 15 marathons.*

## SOY VINAIGRETTE

| | | | |
|---|---|---|---|
| 3 | ounces soy sauce | 2 | ounces distilled |
| 5 | egg yolks | | white vinegar |
| | Pinch of salt & pepper | 2 | cups vegetable oil |

Separate egg yolks and place yolks in stainless steel bowl. Add all ingredients except oil. Stirring with a wire whip drizzle oil into egg mixture slowly. If mix becomes too thick, it can be thinned with white wine. Great sauce for seafood.

*Becky Cable House*
*Cades Cove, Tennessee*

## CAESAR'S SALAD FOR TWO

| | | | |
|---|---|---|---|
| 1 | tablespoon minced garlic | 1 | coddled*egg yolk |
| 2 | tablespoons olive oil | 1 | tablespoon red wine vinegar |
| 11 | capers | ¼ | cup grated Parmesan or Romano cheese |
| 4 | anchovy fillets | | |
| 1 | teaspoon Worcestershire sauce | ½ | cup croutons |
| | | 1 | head of romaine lettuce |
| | Juice of ½ lemon | | Fresh ground peppercorns |
| ¼ | teaspoon dry mustard | | |

In a large wooden salad bowl mix the garlic, olive oil, capers and anchovy fillets into a paste. Add the coddled egg, Worcestershire sauce, lemon, vinegar and mustard. Blend well. If too dry add more olive oil and blend. Add the grated cheese and blend well. Add the romaine lettuce and croutons and toss until the lettuce leaves are coated. Serve on chilled plates. Top with more Parmesan cheese and fresh ground pepper.

*\*Note to coddle an egg yolk: Place an egg in a container of very hot water for a few moments. Separate the egg white and the egg yolk.*

*Also note: Adjust ingredients to your own taste. For a spicy taste add more garlic, anchovies and capers. Be careful when adding more dry mustard, it can make the salad very hot.*

## LEMON & DILL VINAIGRETTE

| | | | |
|---|---|---|---|
| 2 | lemons | 4 | ounces distilled white vinegar |
| ¼ | cup chopped fresh dill | | |
| 5 | egg yolks | | Pinch of salt and black pepper |
| | | 2 | cups vegetable oil |

Separate egg yolks and place yolks in stainless steel bowl. Squeeze lemon juice into a container and then strain. Add all ingredients to egg mixture except the oil and stir. While stirring with wire whip, drizzle vegetable oil into mixture with 2 ounce ladle. If mixture becomes too thick it may be thinned with white wine.

## DOLLYWOOD

### 1020 Dollywood Lane
### Pigeon Forge, TN 37863-4101

*Southern Living's Reader's Choice Poll has named Dollywood one of the top five theme parks in the Southeast! Dollywood offers the best value on live concerts by artists like Lorrie Morgan, Michael English and Chubby Checker. Dollywood offers rides that'll thrill the entire family and crafts, attractions and live music. It also offers some of the best food in the Smoky Mountains!*

**Scott Thurman, Food Manager/Purchaser**
**Pat Gleason, Chef**

*Chef Gleason was born in North Carolina and raised in Pennsylvania. He attended Indiana University and the Pennsylvania Academy of Culinary Arts. Pat has worked in various restaurants in the Pennsylvania area. After culinary school, Pat came to work as a chef at Dollywood. He has worked at the Backstage Restaurant for 5 years. Patrick is the personal chef to Dolly Parton when she is at Dollywood.*

## SMOKED TURKEY BREASTS

| | | | |
|---|---|---|---|
| 6 | turkey breasts, boneless and skinless, thawed | 2 | cups water |
| 2 | cups honey | 2 | cups brown sugar |
| | | 1 | teaspoon mesquite seasoning |

Combine all ingredients except turkey in a hotel pan. Place turkey breasts into marinade and let sit in the refrigerator for 24 hours. Place the turkey breasts in a smoker and cook until they have reached an internal temperature of 165 degrees. Baste every 30 minutes until done. Remove turkey breasts from smoker and serve.

Yield: 6 servings

## MEATLOAF

| | | | |
|---|---|---|---|
| 2½ | pounds ground beef | ½ | teaspoon black pepper |
| 2 | ounces yellow onion, diced small | 8 | eggs, beaten |
| 2 | ounces green pepper, diced small | 1½ | teaspoons granulated garlic |
| 2 | ounces Worcestershire sauce | 6 | ounces oatmeal |
| 1½ | teaspoons salt | 4 | ounces tomato sauce |
| | | 2 | ounces ketchup |

Combine all ingredients into mixer with a paddle attachment and mix until all ingredients are combined equally. Form meatloaf onto a pan and bake at 350 degrees until it has reached an internal temperature of 165 degrees. Remove from oven and place a thin layer of ketchup on top of the meatloaf. Slice into 8 ounce portions and serve.

Yield: 8 servings

## FRIED GREEN TOMATOES

*Dolly has this dish every time she visits the park!*

| | | | |
|---|---|---|---|
| 6 | each green tomatoes, sliced | 1 | dozen eggs, beaten |
| 1 | pound bread crumbs, seasoned | 1 | tablespoon salt and pepper |
| 1 | pound flour | 2 | pints vegetable oil |

Combine salt and pepper with the flour. Place the flour, eggs and bread crumbs in separate pans. Coat the tomato slices with the flour then place them into the eggwash. After coated with the eggwash place them in the bread crumbs and coat completely. Place the slices onto a pan and place in the refrigerator for 5 minutes. Place the vegetable oil into a skillet so the oil is about ½ inch thick. Place the tomato slices into the oil and cook both sides until they are golden brown. Serve immediately.

Yield: 6 servings

## SMOKED BEAN SOUP

| | | | |
|---|---|---|---|
| 2 | pounds great northern beans, soaked overnight | ⅛ | cup fresh basil, chopped |
| 1½ | gallons water | ¼ | teaspoon white pepper |
| 1¼ | pounds smoked pork, diced small | ¼ | teaspoon black pepper |
| 1¼ | pounds carrots, diced small | ¼ | tablespoon fresh garlic, chopped |
| ½ | pound celery, diced small | 3 | ounces ham-flavored concentrate |
| ½ | pound yellow onion, diced small | ¾ | each bay leaf, whole |
| ¼ | cup fresh parsley, chopped | | |

Place the beans in a bowl and add enough water to cover the beans. Let them soak overnight. Sauté the celery, onion and garlic till transparent. Add the carrots and sauté 5 minutes. Add the pork and sauté 5 more minutes. Add the water and base and bring to a simmer. Add the beans and seasonings and simmer 1 to 1½ hours until the beans are soft. Remove the bay leaves and serve hot.

Yield: 48 servings or 3 gallons

# THE ORANGERY
## 5412 Kingston Pike
## Knoxville, TN 37919

*The Orangery is considered one of the top 4-star restaurants in Tennessee for fine dining. It has received the coveted DiRoNa Award (Distinguished Restaurants of North America Award). This is the only award resulting from independent anonymous restaurant inspections. This inspection examines the total dining experience from reservation to departure, but emphasizes the quality of food and its presentation. Only six restaurants in Tennessee have received this award.*

### David Pinckney, Executive Chef/Owner

*Chef David Hume Pinckney is a native of Chapel Hill, North Carolina. David is a graduate of The University of Tennessee in Business. Chef Pinckney has been the Executive Chef at the Orangery restaurant for 14 years. He attended the Cordon Bleu in London and has appeared on the TV Food Network. Live at Five, Good Morning Tennessee, WBIR Morning and Noon shows and NOONDAY with Walter Lambert. Chef Pinckney's recipes have appeared in* **Gourmet, Southern Living** *and the Knoxville News-Sentinel. Chef Pinckney was also invited to prepare the "Taste of Tennessee" dinner at the James Beard Foundation in New York City.*

## LOBSTER CREPES

| | | | |
|---|---|---|---|
| 6 | ounces lobster meat | 1 | tablespoon chopped parsley |
| 1 | cup mushrooms | 1 | cup heavy cream |
| 1 | tablespoon butter | ½ | shot Grand Marnier |
| 1 | tablespoon chervil | | |

Sauté lobster meat and mushrooms in butter. Add parsley and chervil. Flame with Grand Marnier. Pour off the liquid into a sauté pan and add heavy cream. Reduce the sauce until thick. Put lobster and mushrooms back in the sauce and heat up. Spoon lobster and mushrooms into 6-inch crepes and roll up. Pour the remaining sauce over the top of the crepes.

# PHEASANT MOUSSE

| | | | |
|---|---|---|---|
| 10 | ounces pheasant (breast meat only) | 1 | teaspoon fresh marjoram or thyme |
| 8 | ounces heavy cream | | Chilled food processor bowl and blade |
| 1 | egg | | |
| | Salt & pepper to taste | 4 | ounces chopped morels |
| ½ | teaspoon shallots | 4 | ounces chopped pistachios |

Purée the meat, add the cream, egg, shallots, salt, pepper and fresh marjoram. Remove the mix from the food processor; place in a mixing bowl and fold in the pistachios and the morels. Roll out puff pastry, form pheasant mousse at one end of the pastry long ways. Egg wash the other end and roll up, fold ends under. Bake at 400 degrees for 20 minutes, and let chill.

## SAUCE

| | | | |
|---|---|---|---|
| 1 | cup heavy cream | 1 | ounce Dijon mustard |
| 2 | ounces champagne | | |
| | Salt & white pepper | | |

Flame the champagne and reduce, then add the cream and reduce till thick, then add the Dijon.

**To serve:** Slice two thin slices, brush with butter, warm for 5 minutes at 425 degrees then serve on the sauce. Garnish with red peppers and fresh herbs.

# SALMON WELLINGTON

| | | | |
|---|---|---|---|
| 2 | ounces chopped spinach | 2 | egg whites |
| 1 | cup heavy cream | | Salt & pepper to taste |

Wilt spinach in 2 tablespoons of water. Add salt and pepper. Reduce heavy cream by ⅓ volume and add to the spinach. Mix well. Allow to cool. Fold in the 2 egg whites beaten to stiff peaks. Add salt and pepper to taste. Spread on top of the salmon fillets and wrap in puff pastry. Bake at 400 degrees for 20 minutes. Serve with Tomato Chervil Sauce (recipe follows). Serves 6.

# TOMATO CHERVIL SAUCE

| | | | |
|---|---|---|---|
| 1 | cup heavy cream | 2 | tablespoons white wine |
| 1 | tablespoon chervil | | |
| 2 | tablespoons tomato juice | | Salt & pepper |

Reduce all ingredients until thick.

# CHOCOLATE GANACHE

### FOR CRUST

| | | | |
|---|---|---|---|
| 1½ | cups pecans | ¾ | cup sugar |
| ¾ | cup light brown sugar | 3 | ounces melted butter |

Grind all ingredients except butter up in a food processor, then slowly add butter. Press the crust into a 9 inch springform pan that has been sprayed with a non-stick cooking spray. Bake for 15 minutes at 350 degrees or until light brown.

### FOR FILLING

| | | | |
|---|---|---|---|
| 2 | cups heavy cream | 1 | pound semi-sweet chocolate |

Boil the cream. Take off of heat and add the chocolate and mix together. Pour the chocolate filling into the crust and put in the cooler. Serve with caramel sauce, whipped cream and pecans.

## WHITE CHOCOLATE CHEESECAKE

| | | | |
|---|---|---|---|
| 3 | tablespoons unsalted butter, softened | 3 | 8-ounce packages cream cheese, softened |
| 1 | cup finely chopped walnuts | 1 | cup sugar |
| 24 | ounces fine quality white chocolate, chopped | ¼ | cup all-purpose flour |
| ¼ | cup heavy cream | 4 | large eggs at room temperature |
| | | 1 | tablespoon vanilla |

Coat the bottom and side of a 10-inch springform pan with the butter, coat them with the walnuts and chill the pan in the freezer for 15 minutes. In the top of a double boiler set over barely simmering water melt the chocolate partially, add the cream, scalded, whisking, and heat the mixture, whisking, until it is smooth. Remove the top of the double boiler from the heat. In a large bowl with an electric mixer cream the cream cheese, beat in the sugar, and beat the mixture until it is smooth. Beat in the flour and beat in the chocolate mixture. Beat in the eggs, 1 at a time, beating well after each addition and beat in the vanilla. Pour the mixture into the prepared pan and bake the cheesecake in the middle of a preheated 425 degree oven for 20 minutes. Reduce the heat to 300 degrees and bake the cheesecake for 45 to 55 minutes more, or until it is firm in the center and a tester comes out clean. Turn the oven off and let the cheesecake cool in the oven for 30 minutes. Transfer the cheesecake to a rack and let it cool completely in the pan. Chill the cheesecake, covered, for at least 6 hours and up to 24 hours. Run a thin knife around the edge of the pan, remove the side, and with the knife dipped in hot water cut the cheesecake.

Yield: 1 cheesecake

## BAKER-PETERS JAZZ CLUB LOBSTER BISQUE

| | | | |
|---|---|---|---|
| 1 | pound butter | ½ | pound lobster base |
| 2½ | pounds lobster meat | ¼ | pound beef base |
| 1 | cup diced shallots | 1 | gallon water |
| 1¼ | pounds celery | 2 | cups tomato paste |
| 1 | cup cooking sherry | 1 | teaspoon pepper |
| ½ | cup white wine | 1 | cup flour |
| 4 | bay leaves | ½ | cup butter |
| | | 1 | quart heavy cream |

In butter, sauté lobster, shallots, celery until soft. Deglaze pan with sherry and white wine. Add ingredients from bay leaves through pepper and simmer two hours. Strain and purée in food processor. Cook butter and flour into a roux and add to sauce. Finish with heavy cream.

Yield: 2 gallons

## FRESH AUSTRALIAN LAMB LOIN

| | | | |
|---|---|---|---|
| 9 | ounces lamb loin, trimmed | | reconstituted cranberries |
| 2 | ounces marinade | 3 | pieces toast |
| 2 | ounces vodka | 4 | eggplants |
| 1 | ounce vermouth | | Salt and pepper |
| 1 | teaspoon garlic | | Marinated roasted |
| 1 | ounce olive oil | | peppers |
| 1 | ounce | | |

Season lamb with salt and pepper and sear to desired temperature.

**To make sauce:** sauté garlic and cranberries in olive oil. Deglaze with vodka, vermouth glace and add pancetta (Italian bacon).

## CHICKEN BEL PAESE

| | | | |
|---|---|---|---|
| 1 | 8 ounce chicken breast | 2 | ounces brandy |
| 2 | ounces Bel Paese cheese | 1 | tablespoon olive oil |
| 1 | ounce thinly sliced prosciutto ham or pancetta | | Seasoned flour |

### MUSHROOM FILLING

| | | | |
|---|---|---|---|
| 1 | pound sliced mushrooms | | Salt and pepper to taste |
| 4 | ounces butter | 5 | dashes Tabasco |
| 2 | ounces olive oil | | sauce |
| 2 | tablespoons Worcestershire sauce | | |

Dust chicken in seasoned flour. Add olive oil to hot sauté pan. Cook until one side is golden brown. Turn chicken over and top with mushroom, ham and cheese mix. Deglaze with brandy. Add 2 ounces of white wine and place in 450 degree oven. Cook 8 minutes or till golden brown. Serve with sautéed spinach and sundried tomatoes.

Single serving

## BRUCE BOGARTZ

*Corporate Chef*
*Home & Garden Television*
*9701 Madison Avenue*
*Knoxville, TN 37922*

*Chef Bogartz is a 1989 graduate of the Philadelphia Restaurant School. He also earned a degree in economics from Emory University in Atlanta. Bogartz spent six years as executive chef of the Warner Brothers resort in Aspen, CO, introducing his version of Southern cooking to entertainment executives and entertainers alike. He returned to his Knoxville roots in 1995 to open the Gettysvue Golf & Country Club. Chef Bogartz opened his first restaurant, Southbound at the L & N in Knoxville in 1996. Bogartz caught the eye of the James Beard Foundation and was invited to provide dinner to members of the foundation in New York in conjunction with Jack Daniel's Distillery. Following 18 months of independent operation, Bogartz closed Southbound to join forces with a well-known restaurant family. Regas Brothers, Inc., to open Harry's by Regas. Bogartz now acts as Corporate Chef for Home & Garden Television. He also is a consultant for Copper Cellar Restaurants and Fairbanks Roasting Room where he guides menu development and periodically acts as guest chef.*

## PASTRAMI CURED BREAST OF DUCKLING, SWEET POTATO BREAD PUDDING & PLUM PRESERVES

| | | | |
|---|---|---|---|
| 6 | skin-on, 10 ounce breasts | 1 | tablespoon fennel seeds |
| 1 | cup kosher salt | ½ | cup mustard seeds |
| 1 | cup sugar | 8 | bay leaves |
| ½ | cup cardamom | ½ | cup pepper melange |
| 2 | tablespoons whole cloves | 2 | teaspoons allspice |
| 2 | tablespoons star anise | | |

Combine all spices in spice mill and grind to a medium coarse grind to make cure. In non-reactive pan, stack breasts. First coat skin side with cure. Place breasts skin side down and then sprinkle cure over flesh. Repeat process until all duck is stacked in pan. Top with weights – 10 pound can work well – and allow to cure 24 to 48 hours. Drain liquids that have collected in pan at the end of the cure time. Shake off excess cure. In a hot, dry skillet, sear breast skin side down until brown and crisp – approximately 3 minutes. Turn over and sear flesh side down for another 3 minutes. Remove duck from skillet. Place in a pan and place in a 180-degree oven for approximately 2 hours so that fat may render. At this point you can chill the duckling and reheat for service later or serve immediately.

**To serve:** Slice on a bias, fan over bread pudding and finish with plum preserves.

Serves 6.

### SWEET POTATO BREAD PUDDING

| | | | |
|---|---|---|---|
| | Large sweet potato roasted with skin on | 1 | cup orange juice |
| 3 | cups brioche (egg bread), cubed | 1 | tablespoon ground cinnamon |
| 3 | egg yolks | 2 | cups milk |
| 1 | cup wildflower honey | | Salt & pepper to taste |

Peel sweet potato and mash. Beat eggs into chilled sweet potato. Add remaining ingredients excluding brioche. Mix until homogenous. Pour mixture over brioche and fold until evenly mixed. Turn into greased baking pan. Bake at 325 degrees for 30 minutes until pudding is just set.

### PLUM PRESERVES

| | | | |
|---|---|---|---|
| 6 | cups fresh plums, chopped with skins intact | ½ | cup minced ginger |
| | | 4 | cups sugar |
| | | 1 | cup cider |

In heavy gauged saucepan, combine first two ingredients. Top with sugar and cider. Cook over low heat approximately 1½ hours. Do not stir and do not scrape the bottom. Remove from heat and chill.

## OYSTER FRICASSEE

| | | | |
|---|---|---|---|
| 1 | pound Benton's smoked bacon, diced | ½ | cup all-purpose flour |
| 2 | cups onion, diced | 3 | cups shucked oysters |
| 2 | cups celery, diced | 2 | cups oyster liquid |
| 1 | stick or ¼ cup butter | 2 | cups chicken stock |
| 3 | cups portabello mushroom caps, chopped | 2 | cups heavy cream |
| | | 1 | cup bourbon |
| | | 1 | cup veal demi-glaze (optional) |
| 2 | cups leeks (white part only), julienne | ¼ | cup ground sage |
| | | | Salt & white pepper to taste |

Melt butter over medium heat. Add diced bacon until light brown and crisp. Add celery, onion, leeks and mushrooms. Sauté until fragrant. Stir in flour until thoroughly mixed and no flour clumps appear. Add warm chicken stock and simmer. When mixture begins to boil, add bourbon and cream. Simmer until reduced by a third. Stir in oysters and sage. Adjust flavor with salt and white pepper. If using, add demi-glaze and cook until just dissolved. Be careful not to overcook oysters.

Serves 6.

## CARAMELIZED PEAR TART WITH MUSCADINE WINE SORBET

| | | | |
|---|---|---|---|
| 6 | firm pears (red, peeled, sliced to ⅛ inch) | ¼ | cup butter |
| 3 | cups sugar | 1 | 10 x 12 inch puff pastry sheet |

Toss pear slices in sugar to completely coat. Simultaneously melt butter over medium heat in cast iron skillet. When butter is completely melted, remove from heat. Add pear slices in concentric circles until 3 layers are complete. Place pan back on medium heat and cook until mixture begins to bubble an amber color and caramel smell is released. Remove pan from heat. Top with sheet of puff pastry. Form a seal all around pan. Place in a preheated 400 degree oven. Bake until pastry rises and is golden brown, approximately 10 minutes. Remove from oven. Invert onto platter while still hot. If tart cools too much, it will not release from the pan.

Serves 6.

### MUSCADINE WINE SORBET

| | | | |
|---|---|---|---|
| 4 | cups muscadine wine | 1 | teaspoon ground cinnamon |
| 2 | cups sugar | 1 | teaspoon ground ginger |
| 1 | cup lemon juice | | |
| 1 | tablespoon vanilla extract | | |

Combine wine and sugar in heavy saucepan. Stir to dissolve. Cook over medium heat 15 minutes. Remove from heat. Stir in the other ingredients and chill. Pour into ice cream maker and follow instructions.

**To serve:** Serve tart at room temperature. Garnish with a small scoop of sorbet.

## REGAS RESTAURANT*

### 318 North Gay Street Knoxville, TN 37917

*Regas Restaurant has been a Knoxville tradition for over 80 years. Operating out of the original location on Gay Street, Regas has made several expansions through the years to better serve its guests. Daily specials include tender USDA choice and prime steaks, mouth-watering fresh seafood or delicious, marinated pork tenderloin.*

*\*After 81 years in business, the original Regas has closed. Knoxville remains proud of the Regas family.*

## REGAS CRAB CAKES

| | | | |
|---|---|---|---|
| 1 | pound lump crab meat | 1 | teaspoon salt |
| ½ | cup sour cream | ¼ | teaspoon cayenne pepper |
| 1 | egg | ¼ | teaspoon granulated garlic |
| 1 | tablespoon Gulden's brand mustard | ¼ | teaspoon Tabasco brand sauce |
| 3 | tablespoons finely diced celery | ½ | teaspoon lemon juice |
| 3 | tablespoons finely diced green onion | 1 | cup bread crumbs Additional bread crumbs for coating |
| 3 | tablespoons finely diced red onion | | |

Combine all ingredients and reserve extra bread crumbs for coating. Form into 3-ounce balls. Flatten each ball into a cake shape, about 2 inches wide and ½ inch thick. Coat each side with extra bread crumbs. Place on wax paper until ready to cook. Sauté crab cakes in butter until nicely browned on both sides.

Makes 6 to 8 cakes.

## RED VELVET CAKE

| | | | |
|---|---|---|---|
| 2½ | cups self-rising flour | 1 | teaspoon cocoa |
| 1 | cup buttermilk | 1 | teaspoon white vinegar |
| 1½ | cups vegetable oil | 1 | teaspoon baking soda |
| 1½ | cups sugar | 1 | teaspoon vanilla |
| 2 | large eggs | | |
| 1 | one-ounce bottle red food coloring | | |

Preheat oven to 350 degrees. Sift the flour, baking soda and cocoa together. Cream the sugar and oil in a large mixing bowl until well blended. Add the eggs one at a time, beating well after each addition. Add the flour mixture gradually along with the buttermilk, beating well after each addition and scraping the sides of the bowl occasionally. Add the white vinegar. After beating well, add the red food coloring and vanilla. Spoon the batter into 3 greased and floured 9-inch cake pans. Bake at 350 degrees for 25 to 30 minutes or until the cake tests done. Cool in the pans for several minutes, remove to a wire rack to completely cool. Spread the icing between layers and cover the top and side of the cake.

### RED VELVET ICING

| | | | |
|---|---|---|---|
| 1⅓ | sticks of butter (softened) | 1 | box confectionery sugar |
| 10 | ounces of cream cheese (softened) | 1 | tablespoon vanilla |

Cream the butter and cream cheese together. Add the confectionery sugar and beat until light and fluffy. Add the vanilla.

Yield: 12 servings

## AMERICAN RED ONION SOUP

| | | | |
|---|---|---|---|
| 2 | ounces butter | 3 | cups veal stock |
| 2 | quarts red onion julienned | 2 | teaspoons salt |
| 2 | tablespoons flour | 1 | teaspoon ground black pepper |
| 1 | teaspoon brown sugar | | Toasted baguette croutons |
| 1 | bottle brown beer | 16 | ounces Gruyère Swiss cheese |
| 3 | cups chicken stock | | |

### SACHET BAG OF

| | | | |
|---|---|---|---|
| 2 | parsley stems | 1 | teaspoon black peppercorns |
| 1 | bay leaf | | |
| 1 | teaspoon dry thyme | | |

Sauté onions with butter over medium heat in a 4-quart pot. Sprinkle in flour and brown sugar and pour in brown beer. Pour in both chicken and veal stock. Add sachet bag. Simmer on low heat for 45 minutes and let flavor develop. Season with salt and pepper.

**To Serve:** Pour hot soup into 8 to 10 ounce soup bowls. Place fresh approximately 8 croutons on top of soup and sprinkle with Swiss cheese. Melt in broiler and serve.

Serves 8.

## CRÈME BRÛLÉE

| | | | |
|---|---|---|---|
| 2 | cups of heavy cream | ½ | cup sugar |
| 1 | vanilla bean | 3 | eggs |

Cut vanilla bean in half and combine with heavy cream and half the sugar. Bring mixture to a boil. Combine egg yolks and remaining sugar. Beat egg yolks. Slowly ladle some of the hot cream mixture to temper eggs and add yolks to cream. Cook until thick enough to coat the back of a spoon. Strain through a fine sieve. Split vanilla in half and scrape the vanilla beans. Add to custard. Fill individual oven-proof dishes a quarter inch from the top. Place in water bath approximately 1 inch up on side of dish. Place in a 325-degree oven and cook for approximately 45 minutes. Place in refrigerator and allow to set overnight. Before serving, cover the surface with sugar and caramelize the sugar until a golden brown.

Yield: 3 to 4

## RIVERSIDE TAVERN BY REGAS

### 950 Volunteer Landing Lane Knoxville, TN 37915

*Riverside Tavern is the newest addition to Knoxville's riverfront dining experience. Located at Volunteer Landing, Riverside Tavern is the new gathering place for the downtown lunch and dinner crowd. Featured menu items from the wood-fired rotisserie and grill include herb-roasted rotisserie lamb, chicken, pork tenderloin, fresh grilled salmon and legendary grilled USDA choice and prime steaks.*

## CHICKEN CORN CHOWDER

| | | | |
|---|---|---|---|
| 1 | slice Applewood bacon | 4 | ounces potatoes (unpeeled and diced) |
| 2 | ounces celery | 4 | ounces corn |
| 2 | ounces onions | 10½ | ounces chicken* (diced ½ inch) |
| 2 | ounces carrots | | |
| ⅓ | cup garlic | ⅓ | cup fresh thyme |
| 1 | tablespoon butter | 4 | ounces heavy cream |
| ⅓ | cup salt Dash pepper | | |
| 1 | tablespoon flour | 6 | teaspoons Tabasco brand sauce |
| 1 | pint chicken stock | | |

*Sauté chicken in a little olive oil, salt and pepper before adding to soup. Dice chicken ¼ inch before cooking.*

Dice bacon into ¼ inch pieces. Cook until fat turns clear. Add celery, onions and carrots. Sauté until tender. Add garlic and cook for 2 minutes more. Add butter and melt. Add flour, salt, pepper and cook for 3 minutes. Add chicken stock and bring to a boil. Add potatoes and corn kernels. Cook until potatoes are tender. Add the chicken and chopped thyme, heavy cream, Tabasco sauce and simmer. Check seasoning.

Yield: 10 servings

## CHOCOLATE MELTDOWN

| | | | |
|---|---|---|---|
| 1½ | pounds bittersweet chocolate | 13 | egg yolks |
| 1½ | pounds butter, no salt | 1 | pound granulated sugar |
| 13 | eggs | 7 | ounces all-purpose flour |

Melt chocolate and butter in a double boiler. In a mixer, whip eggs, egg yolks and sugar together. Fold the flour into the egg mixture and whisk in the melted chocolate and butter. Spray molds with non-stick coating and line the bottom with a round piece of parchment paper. Fill the molds ½ way with the cake mixture. Place a chocolate truffle ball* in the center of the mold and fill up the remainder with the cake mixture. Bake in a 325 degree oven on a sheet tray until ¾ cooked, about 18 minutes.

*Note: Chocolate truffles must be made and allowed to chill before starting recipe. (Recipe follows)

### CHOCOLATE MELTDOWN TRUFFLES
*Yield: 8x8 pan 1" thick*

**Ingredients in order of mixing:**

| | | | |
|---|---|---|---|
| 1 | pound Calbaut Chocolate | ¼ | cup brandy |
| | | ⅔ | cup heavy cream |
| 3¼ | ounces butter, no salt | 2 | ounces light corn syrup |

Chop up chocolate into small pieces and combine it with cubed butter. Melt both in a double boiler. In a small saucepan, heat the brandy, heavy cream and corn syrup together. Once the brandy is heated, pour the hot brandy mixture over the chocolate/ butter mixture. Stir slowly until incorporated and all chocolate/butter mixture. Stir slowly until incorporated and all chocolate is melted. Pour into 8x8 pan. Let the mixture cool. Place in the freezer and let it set. With a small melon baller, scoop out 1-ounce balls and roll in the palm of your hand to form a ball.

### CHOCOLATE SAUCE

| | | | |
|---|---|---|---|
| 2½ | ounces bittersweet chocolate | 4 | ounces light corn syrup |
| 5 | ounces granulated sugar | 1 | cup water |
| | | 4 | ounces cocoa powder |

Melt chocolate in a double boiler. In a heavy saucepan, combine sugar, water and corn syrup. Bring mixture to a boil. Sift cocoa powder into sugar and mix well with a whisk. Add melted chocolate and mix well with whisk. Refrigerate in a sealed container. (Shelf life: 72 hours) Yield: 1 pint

## 1000 ISLAND DRESSING

| | | | |
|---|---|---|---|
| ½ | pint sweet relish (drained) | 2 | quarts mayonnaise |
| 1 | pint celery, finely chopped | 1½ | pints chili sauce |
| ½ | cup onions, finely chopped | ½ | cup sugar |
| ½ | pint green peppers, finely chopped | ¼ | cup Worcestershire sauce |
| ½ | pint sour cream | 1/12 | cup white pepper |
| | | 1/12 | cup garlic (granulated) |
| | | 1/16 | cup lemon pepper |

Drain relish in china cap and press out extra juice. Chop celery, onions and peppers in the buffalo chopper until diced very small. Press out all extra juice through china cap. Mix all ingredients together until thoroughly incorporated.

Yield: 1¼ gallons

## BLACK BEAN SOUP

| | | | |
|---|---|---|---|
| ½ | pound slab bacon (¼" diced) | ½ | tablespoon chicken base |
| ½ | cup carrots (peeled and diced small) | 1 | tablespoon chili powder |
| ¾ | cup celery (diced small) | ¾ | tablespoon cumin |
| 1½ | cups onions (diced small) | 1 | teaspoon black pepper |
| 1 | large bay leaf | 1½ | #10 cans black beans (approximately 18 cups) |
| 1 | tablespoon minced garlic | | |
| ¾ | gallon cold water | ¼ | cup cornstarch |
| 1½ | tablespoon ham base | ¼ | cup cold water |

Sauté bacon in large skillet until bacon turns brown and fat renders out. Add vegetables to bacon and fat. Sauté until soft, about 5 to 10 minutes. Add ingredients to the bacon and vegetables. Bring to a boil on medium high heat, then simmer for 5 minutes. Drain black beans and rinse in cold water. Add black beans and simmer for 35 more minutes, stirring occasionally. Dissolve cornstarch in water and add to soup, then simmer for 5 more minutes. Remove from heat and cool. Remove bay leaf and refrigerate.

Yield: 1½ gallon

## CHOPS GRILL
### 1612 Downtown West Blvd. Knoxville, TN

## CRAB CAKES

| | | | |
|---|---|---|---|
| 1¼ | cups red pepper (dice fine) | 1 | tablespoon salt |
| 1¼ | cups celery (dice fine) | ½ | teaspoon cayenne pepper |
| 1¼ | cups green onion (dice fine) | 2½ | teaspoons granulated garlic |
| 1¼ | cups red onion (dice fine) | 2½ | teaspoons Tabasco brand sauce |
| 5 | pounds blue crab meat | 5 | cups Progresso bread crumbs |
| 2½ | cups sour cream | 1 | cup + 1½ tablespoons eggs |
| ¼ | cup + 1 tablespoon mustard | | Japanese bread crumbs as needed |

Mix all ingredients together thoroughly. Portion into 4 ounce balls. Flatten each ball into cakes. Coat each side of cake with Japanese bread crumbs. Place cakes on a lined sheet pan and cover with plastic wrap. Pan fry until golden brown.

Yield: 35 to 40 cakes

## COLE SLAW

| | | | |
|---|---|---|---|
| 5 | lbs. cabbage, shredded | 2 | cups sugar |
| 2 | green peppers (½ inch diced) | 1⅓ | cups cider vinegar |
| | Salt to taste | | Black pepper to taste |
| ¾ | pound yellow onions (½ inch diced) | 1⅓ | pints mayonnaise |

Run the green peppers, onion and carrots through the ⁵⁄₁₆ inch slicing attachment. Mix all the vegetables together in a lexan. In a mixing bowl combine all the other ingredients and whip together thoroughly. Pour sauce over the vegetables and mix well.

Yield: 1 gallon

## NASCAR CAFÉ

### 1425 Hurley Drive
### Sevierville, TN 37862-6904

### PIMIENTO CHEESE

| | | | |
|---|---|---|---|
| 5 | pounds Velveeta brand cheese | ½ | cup sugar |
| 1½ | 14-ounce cans pimientos, drained and chopped fine | ½ | gallon mayonnaise |

Drain and chop the pimientos in the food processor. Combine all ingredients in a lexan. Mix well until the Velveeta cheese is in small pieces (approximately ¼ inch to ½ inch chunks)

Yield: 1¼ gallons

### THUNDER ROAD BURGER

#### TOP

| | | | |
|---|---|---|---|
| | Bun (toasted) | 1 | slice tomato (sliced ⅜ inch) |
| ¾ | cup lettuce (shredded) | | |

#### BOTTOM

| | | | |
|---|---|---|---|
| | Bun (toasted) | ⅓ | cup sautéed onions |
| 1 | 8-ounce burger patty | 1 | jalapeño |
| | Scoop pimiento cheese | 7 | ounces French fries |

Grill burger to requested temperature. Baste bun with margarine and toast. When burger is done, top it with a scoop of pimiento cheese and melt in the steamer. Assemble buns as listed along one side of a dinner plate. Place fries on opposite side of plate.

## COPPER CELLAR CORPORATION

### P. O. Box 50370
### Knoxville, TN 37950

**Curt Gibson, Director of Operations**
**Paul Rentachler, Corporate Chef**
*The Copper Cellar Corporation owns and operates The Copper Cellar Restaurants, Calhoun's, Cappuccino's, Chesapeake's and Smoky Mountain Brewery.*

### FRESH MARYLAND CRAB CAKES

*(Recipe used at Chesapeake's & Copper Cellar)*

| | | | |
|---|---|---|---|
| 1½ | tablespoons chopped parsley | ½ | tablespoons lemon juice |
| 1⅛ | teaspoon cayenne pepper | ¾ | cup mayonnaise |
| 1 | teaspoon ground mustard | 1 | egg |
| ¼ | teaspoon baking powder | 1 | pound blue crab meat |
| ¼ | teaspoon Worcestershire sauce | | Bread crumbs as needed |

Place all ingredients except crab and bread crumbs in a mixing bowl. Mix with a whisk until completely blended. Pick shells from crab meat and add to mixing bowl. Gently mix with a large spoon so that the crab meat will not break apart excessively. Form 2½ ounce (net weight) – approximately ⅜ cup of crab mixture – in a ball. Bread in medium coarse fresh bread crumbs. Flatten out to approximately 1 inch thick crab cake. Heat 6 ounces of clarified butter in a 10 inch sauté pan with medium high heat. When butter is hot, place 3 or 4 crab cakes at a time in sauté pan. Brown each side for 3 minutes (internal temperature should be 165 degrees). Be careful not to burn the bread crumbs. Remove from sauté pan and place on a serving plate. Serve with tartar sauce.

Yield: 6 to 8 servings

## SPINACH MARIA

*(Available at Calhoun's, Chesapeake's*
*& Copper Cellar Restaurants)*

| | | | |
|---|---|---|---|
| 4½ | cups milk | 8 | ounces cheddar cheese |
| ½ | yellow onion (medium size) | 4 | ounces Monterey Jack cheese |
| 1 | teaspoon ground mustard | 8 | ounces Velveeta cheese |
| 1 | teaspoon granulated garlic | 5 | 10-ounce boxes frozen chopped spinach |
| 1¾ | teaspoon crushed red pepper | | |
| ⅛ | pound + 1 tablespoon melted butter | 1½ | cups grated Monterey Jack cheese (for topping) |
| ⅜ | cup flour | | |

Heat milk and spices in a 4-quart saucepan on medium heat to just below a boil (190 degrees). Then reduce heat and simmer. Finely chop the onion, sauté in 1 tablespoon of butter on medium heat for 5 to 8 minutes, add to sauce pan. Combine the ⅛ pound melted butter with the flour in a small sauté pan. (This is the first step of making a roux that will thicken the sauce.) Mix until completely blended, cook on low heat 3 to 4 minutes to make roux. Add roux to saucepan and mix well. Continue to cook until sauce thickens. Cut the Velveeta, cheddar & Jack cheese into small cubes, add to saucepan. Continue to mix until all the cheese is completely melted and blended into the sauce (be careful not to burn the sauce while the cheese is melting). Remove from heat. Allow to cool for 15 minutes. Slow thaw spinach in the refrigerator for 24 hours. Squeeze as much excess water as possible out of the spinach. Add spinach to cheese sauce, mix until completely blended. Transfer to a 11x9x2 casserole pan and top with grated Monterey Jack cheese. Bake at 350 degrees for 12 to 15 minutes.

Yield: 12 servings

## CRAB BISQUE

*(Available at Chesapeake's & Copper Cellar)*

| | | | |
|---|---|---|---|
| 1 | gallon water | 2 | medium carrots, quartered |
| 1 | pound medium shrimp | 3 | celery ribs, quartered |
| 1 | pound raw white fish fillet | 1 | clove |
| 1 | jumbo Spanish onion, peeled and quartered | 2 | bay leaves |
| | | 2 | sprigs fresh thyme |
| | | 1 | cup clam juice |
| | | 1 | cup white wine |

Peel and de-vein the shrimp and reserve the meat. Combine the shrimp shells and all of the other ingredients and bring to a boil. Reduce heat and simmer until stock is reduced by one-half. Add ice to replenish and reduce again. Strain the stock through a fine sieve and reserve. Steam the shrimp and combine with one cup of cream in a food processor. Blend until a smooth paste is achieved. Reserve.

### ROUX

Blend 2 cups clarified butter and 3 cups all-purpose flour. Cook whisking occasionally until roux is deep golden brown. Blend with shrimp and cream mixture. Combine the roux and the stock together stirring vigorously until a thick rich paste is formed.

**Combine in a double boiler:**

| | | | |
|---|---|---|---|
| 1 | gallon milk | 1 | cup tomato juice |
| 1 | quart whole whipping cream | 1 | cup white wine |

Raise the temperature of the milk mixture to 160 degrees. Blend the mixtures together in a double-boiler stirring well. Cook until a creamy consistency is achieved. Add one pound fresh lump blue crab meat. Season with salt and white pepper.

## BAKED MUSHROOMS STUFFED WITH CRAB IMPERIAL

*(Recipe used at Chesapeake's & Copper Cellar)*

| | | | |
|---|---|---|---|
| 1½ | tablespoons chopped parsley | ½ | tablespoon lemon juice |
| ⅛ | teaspoon cayenne pepper | ¾ | cup mayonnaise |
| 1 | teaspoon ground mustard | 1 | egg |
| ¼ | teaspoon baking powder | 1 | pound blue crab meat |
| ¼ | teaspoon Worcestershire sauce | 45 | large fresh mushrooms |

Place all ingredients except crab and mushrooms in a mixing bowl. Mix with a whisk until completely blended. Pick shells from crab meat and add to mixing bowl and gently mix with a large spoon so that the crab meat will not break apart excessively. Remove the stems from mushrooms. Fill each mushroom cap with approximately 1 tablespoon of the crab imperial mixture, top with grated fresh bread crumbs. Grease the bottom of a large casserole dish with softened butter. Arrange the stuffed mushrooms in the casserole dish so that the mushrooms do not touch each other. Bake at 350 degrees for 15 to 18 minutes (crab mixture needs to be at least 165 degrees).

Yield: 45 mushrooms as appetizer

## SPINACH ARTICHOKE DIP

*(Recipe used at all restaurants)*

| | | | |
|---|---|---|---|
| 4½ | cups milk | 4 | ounces Monterey Jack cheese |
| ½ | medium size yellow onion | 8 | ounces Velveeta cheese |
| 1 | teaspoon ground mustard | 2 | 6-ounce jars artichoke hearts |
| 1 | teaspoon granulated garlic | 3 | 10-ounce boxes frozen chopped spinach |
| 1¾ | teaspoons crushed red pepper | 1½ | cups grated Monterey Jack cheese (for topping) |
| ⅛ | pound & 1 tablespoon melted butter | | |
| ⅜ | cup flour | | |
| 8 | ounces cheddar | | |

Heat milk and spices in a 4-quart sauce pan on medium heat to just below a boil (190 degrees). Then reduce heat and simmer. Finely chop the onion, sauté in 1 tablespoon of butter on medium heat for 5 to 8 minutes, add to saucepan. Combine the ⅛ pound melted butter with the flour in a small sauté pan. (This is the first step of making a roux that will thicken the sauce.) Mix until completely blended, cook on low heat 3 to 4 minutes to make roux. Add roux to saucepan and mix well. Continue to cook until sauce thickens. Cut the Velveeta, cheddar and Jack cheese into small cubes, add to saucepan. Heat over low heat and slowly stir until all the cheese is completely melted and blended into the sauce (be careful not to burn the sauce while the cheese is melting). Remove from heat. Allow to cool for 15 minutes. Drain the artichokes and gently squeeze the excess water out of them. Cut the artichoke into ¼ inch strips. Set aside. Slow thaw spinach in the refrigerator for 24 hours. Squeeze as much excess water as possible out of the spinach. Add spinach and artichokes to cheese sauce, mix until completely blended. Transfer to a 11x9x2 casserole pan and top with grated Monterey Jack cheese. Bake at 350 degrees for 12 to 15 minutes. Serve with warm tortilla chips, salsa and sour cream.

## WHITE CHILI

*(Recipe used at Calhoun's & Copper Cellar Restaurants)*

| | | | |
|---|---|---|---|
| 1 | cup diced yellow onions | ½ | tablespoon cilantro, chopped, fresh |
| 1 | teaspoon oregano | | |
| 1 | tablespoon olive oil | ¼ | cup chopped green chilies (canned) |
| 4 | cups water | | |
| 4 | cups low fat chicken broth | 1 | pound chicken breasts, boneless, skinless |
| 1 | teaspoon granulated garlic | | |
| 1 | teaspoon ground cumin | 6 | cups northern beans (canned) |
| | | ½ | cup cornstarch |
| | | ½ | cup cold water |

Trim all fat and cartilage from the chicken breasts. Place on a baking pan. Bake at 325 degrees for 20 to 30 minutes or until chicken is cooked throughout. Allow to cool, then hand pull into small pieces. Set aside. Sauté diced onions, oregano and olive oil together in a soup pot. Cook for about 5 minutes. Combine water, chicken broth, garlic, cumin, cilantro and green chilies. Add to the sautéed onions. Bring to a boil, reduce heat and simmer. Add chicken and great northern beans, stir often, simmer for 15 minutes. Blend the cornstarch with the cold water and add to chili. Continue to simmer until chili thickens, then remove from heat. Garnish with fresh grated cilantro, low fat Monterey Jack cheese and low fat sour cream.

## BREWMASTER SUBMARINE

*(Recipe used at Smoky Mountain Brewery)*

| | | | |
|---|---|---|---|
| 1 | each sub roll | ¼ | cup + 1 tablespoon sour cream |
| 7 | ounces thinly sliced chicken meat | | |
| | | 3 | slices Swiss cheese |
| 1 | cup sauerkraut | | |

Heat thinly sliced chicken in 1 teaspoon of olive oil in a pan on top of stove (medium heat) or on the griddle for 3 minutes or until chicken is thoroughly cooked. Add sauerkraut. Continue to heat for 1 minute until sauerkraut is hot. Add ¼ cup of sour cream. Mix well with the chicken and sauerkraut until the sour cream is warm and blended in. Spread the remaining 1 tablespoon of sour cream on the sub roll. Fill roll with chicken mixture and top with the Swiss cheese. Place sub in the oven to melt the cheese. Serve with a pickle spear.

## TWICE BAKED POTATO CASSEROLE

*(Recipe used at Calhoun's & Copper Cellar Restaurants)*

| | | | |
|---|---|---|---|
| 7 | 70-count potatoes (baked the day before and chilled) | 8 | ounces grated cheddar cheese |
| | | 8 | ounces bacon bits |
| 4 | ounces melted butter | 4 | ounces chopped green onions |
| 8 | ounces sour cream | ½ | teaspoon salt |
| 8 | ounces ranch dressing | ¼ | teaspoon white pepper |

### TOPPING

| | | | |
|---|---|---|---|
| 2 | cups corn flakes | 2 | ounces clarified butter |

Cut potatoes in half lengthwise and scoop out pulp. Place pulp and melted butter in food processor with blade attachment or mixing bowl with paddle attachment. Mix until pulp is smooth with only a few small lumps. Add remaining ingredients and mix until blended. (Do not overmix.) Using a rubber spatula, empty the contents into a casserole dish and spread evenly throughout. Mix the corn flakes with the clarified butter in a separate bowl. Spread on top of the casserole. Bake at 350 degrees for 20 minutes. Uncover and cook an additional five minutes. Serve.

## BEER CHEESE

*(Recipe used at Calhoun's & Smoky Mountain Brewery)*

| | | | |
|---|---|---|---|
| ½ | pound white American cheese | ½ | tablespoon dry mustard |
| ½ | pound Jack cheese | 1 | teaspoon Dijon mustard |
| ½ | cup milk | | |
| ½ | cup your favorite dark beer | ¼ | teaspoon Tabasco brand hot sauce |
| ½ | tablespoon Worcestershire sauce | | |

Cut white American cheese and Jack cheese into small pieces. Place in the top portion of the double boiler along with the milk. Heat until cheese is melted. Mix well with a wire whip. Place the beer, Worcestershire sauce, dry mustard, Dijon mustard and Tabasco sauce in a small mixing bowl. Mix until completely blended. Add to the melted cheese and mix well with a wire whip. Remove from heat and serve with French fries, tortilla chips or hot pretzels.

Makes approximately 3½ cups.

## COLE SLAW

*(Recipe used at Calhoun's restaurants only)*

| | | | |
|---|---|---|---|
| ¼ | cup granulated sugar | 2¼ | pounds shredded green cabbage |
| ¼ | cup white vinegar | ½ | cup shredded carrots |
| 1 | teaspoon celery seed | ½ | cup chopped green onions |
| 2 | cups mayonnaise | | |

Place sugar, white vinegar and celery seed in a mixing bowl. With a whisk, mix until completely blended. Add mayonnaise, again mix until completely blended. Add thinly shredded green cabbage and chopped green onions, mix with a rubber spatula. Then add the carrots last so that the orange color will not bleed into the slaw.

Yield: 10 servings

## BISCUITS

*(Recipe used at Calhoun's restaurants only)*

| | | | |
|---|---|---|---|
| 1 | 6.25 ounce package White Lily brand buttermilk mix | 1 | cup buttermilk |

Place buttermilk in a mixing bowl. Add biscuit mix with a rubber spatula, mix until a moist dough is formed. Do not overmix. Biscuits will not rise very well if overmixed. Place dough on to a well floured cold surface. Knead 3 times and roll out to ½ inch thickness. Cut with a 3 inch biscuit cutter and place on a pan with a baking sheet. Place in a preheated 400-degree oven and bake for 12 to 15 minutes or until golden brown (rotate pan halfway through cooking). After biscuits are removed from the oven, glaze top of biscuits with melted butter. Serve with butter and honey.

Yield: 8 to 10

# CUMBERLAND GRILL

## BIG ORANGE PIE

*(Recipe used at Calhoun's Restaurants only)*

### CRUST

| | | | |
|---|---|---|---|
| 6 | tablespoons butter | 1 | tablespoon sugar |
| ¾ | cup Graham cracker crumbs | | |

Melt butter and mix with crumbs and sugar until moist enough to press into 9" or 10" pie pan. Chill crust for at least 30 minutes.

### FILLING

| | | | |
|---|---|---|---|
| 2 | cans (14 ounces each) sweetened condensed milk | | A few drops of Wilton Orange Paste (available at party supply store) |
| 8 | large egg yolks | | Use enough to color as desired |
| 3 | ounces fresh lime juice | | |
| 3 | ounces fresh lemon juice | ½ | teaspoon diced orange zest |

Place condensed milk into mixing bowl. Add yolks. Whip until smooth. Add lime and lemon juices. Whip until well mixed. Add orange paste. Mix and check color, adding more if needed. Do not add too much. Add orange extract and zest. Mix. Pour filling into chilled crust. Bake in 350 degree preheated oven for 14 minutes. Turn oven off. Leave door closed. Leave pie in oven for an additional 25 minutes. Chill for at least 2 hours. Pie can be made a day or two in advance. Serve with sweetened whipped cream. Garnish with an orange twist or slice.

SMOKY MOUNTAIN BREWERY & RESTAURANT

## PUMPKIN CHEESECAKE

*(Recipe used at Calhoun's, Chesapeake's & Copper Cellar Restaurants)*

### PECAN GRAHAM CRACKER CRUMB CRUST

| | | | |
|---|---|---|---|
| 1½ | cups graham cracker crumbs | ⅓ | cup sugar |
| ½ | cup chopped toasted pecans | ⅓ | cup melted butter |

### PUMPKIN CHEESECAKE FILLING

| | | | |
|---|---|---|---|
| 2 | 8-ounce packages cream cheese (room temperature) | 1 | 16-ounce can solid pack pumpkin |
| 4 | extra large eggs | 1 | teaspoon ground cinnamon |
| 1 | cup sugar | ½ | teaspoon ground nutmeg |
| ¼ | teaspoon salt | | |
| ¼ | cup almond flavored liqueur (Amaretto) | | |

Combine all ingredients in a bowl and mix well. Press into bottom and sides of a 9 inch springform pan that has been coated with nonstick vegetable spray. Preheat oven to 350 degrees. Using an electric mixer, place the cream cheese into bowl. Use a beater to cream the cheese. Scrape the sides of the bowl with a rubber spatula. Add sugar, salt, cinnamon and nutmeg. Beat well, scrape again. Add Amaretto and eggs. Beat well and scrape again. Add pumpkin and mix until smooth. Pour batter into prepared crust. Bake 55 minutes or until cake is almost set (center will still be soft). Allow to cool, cover and place in refrigerator overnight before serving.

Yield: 1 cheesecake

## TURTLE CHEESECAKE

*(Recipe used at Calhoun's, Chesapeake's & Copper Cellar Restaurants)*

| | | | |
|---|---|---|---|
| 2 | pounds cream cheese (room temperature) | 1 | teaspoon vanilla |
| | | 1 | teaspoon butter |
| 4 | extra large eggs | ½ | cup graham cracker crumbs |
| 1¾ | cups sugar | | |

Preheat oven to 325 degrees. Beat cream cheese till smooth. Scrape, beat again. Add eggs, one at a time. Beat until mixed. Scrape sides of bowl, beat again. Add sugar and vanilla. Beat until mixed. Scrape and

beat again until smooth. Line bottom of 10x4 inch springform pan with waxed paper. Rub sides and bottom of pan with butter. Dust pan with graham cracker crumbs. Pour batter into pan. Shake or stir to level. Bake for 1 hour plus 10 to 15 minutes. Cake will increase in volume until it is as high as the top of the pan. Do not undercook. It's better to bake a little too long than to undercook. However, cake will still be wiggly in the center when done. Cool cake to room temperature. (Approximately 5 to 6 hours.)

Yield: 1 cheesecake

### TOPPING

| | | | |
|---|---|---|---|
| 9 | ounces milk chocolate | 3 | ounces toasted pecans |
| 2¼ | ounces milk | 12 | ounces caramel apple dip |

To toast pecans, bake at 350 degrees for 7 to 8 minutes or until lightly browned. Add milk to chocolate and melt over low heat, while stirring. Place caramel dip on top of cooled cake and spread evenly. Sprinkle toasted pecans on top of caramel. Pour milk chocolate and milk mixture over this and spread. Refrigerate overnight.

## STRAWBERRY SHORTCAKE

### STRAWBERRY

| | | | |
|---|---|---|---|
| 2 | quarts strawberries | 1 | cup granulated sugar |

### SHORTCAKE

| | | | |
|---|---|---|---|
| 5¼ | cups Bisquick | 6 | tablespoons melted butter |
| 6 | tablespoons granulated sugar | 1¼ | cups milk |

Cut strawberries into quarters. Allow 2 to 3 hours for strawberries to bleed before using. Mix the Bisquick, milk, sugar and butter in a mixing bowl. Roll out to ½ inch thickness, use a 4 inch biscuit cutter. Bake at 425 degrees for 8 to 10 minutes.

**To serve:** Cut shortcake in ½, place ½ in a bowl, top with ½ cup of strawberries (with plenty of juice), then top with whipped cream. Place other ½ of shortcake on top, then ½ cup of strawberries (with plenty of juice), top with whipped cream.

# ITALIAN MARKET & GRILL

## 9648 Kingston Pike (Located in Franklin Square) Knoxville, TN 37922

*This Casual Contemporary Italian Restaurant features fresh Italian food, Prime Ribs, Fresh Seafood, Steaks, Veal, Wood Fired Pizzas and Fresh Pasta. The restaurant has an extensive wine list.*

## SAUTÉED CALAMARI

| | | | |
|---|---|---|---|
| 1 | ounce extra virgin olive oil | 2 | tablespoons IMG oreganata butter |
| | Pinch of crushed red pepper | 1 | tablespoon fresh lemon juice |
| 1 | tablespoon chopped garlic | | Pinch of salt and pepper |
| | Fresh squid | | Fresh lemon wedge |
| 1 | ounce white wine | | Chopped parsley for garnish |

Sauté squid in extra virgin olive oil, garlic and crushed red pepper on medium heat for 4 minutes. Deglaze with white wine, add oreganata butter then pepper and salt and cook for 3 minutes. Garnish with parsley and lemon wedge.

Yield: Single serving

# TENDERLOIN MARSALA WITH SHRIMP

| | | | |
|---|---|---|---|
| 2 | to 3 ounces tenderloin medallions | 1 | tablespoon Marsala wine |
| 4 | shrimp | 1 | ounce sliced mushrooms |
| 3 | ounces fresh spinach | 2 | ounces extra virgin olive oil |
| 8 | ounces IMG roasted rosemary potatoes | | Salt & pepper |
| 2 | teaspoons rough chopped garlic | 1 | tablespoon butter |

Sauté medallions in 1 ounce extra virgin olive oil to just under temperature desired, add mushrooms. Deglaze pan with Marsala wine and Marsala sauce and add butter. In separate pan sauté shrimp and spinach in garlic with salt and pepper. Serve medallions with IMG roasted rosemary potatoes and prepared sautéed spinach with shrimp.

Yield: Single serving

## TENNESSEE GRILL

### 900 Neyland Drive
### Knoxville, TN 37916

*Projected opening date: August, 2000. The Tennessee Grill will serve American Grill specialties such as steaks, chicken, fish, shrimp, oysters and pasta.*

## ROASTED SPRING VEGETABLES IN WHITE WINE GARLIC ALFREDO SAUCE

### MARINADE

| | | | |
|---|---|---|---|
| ½ | cup olive oil | 1 | tablespoon coarse ground pepper |
| ⅓ | cup balsamic vinegar | 2 | teaspoons kosher salt |

### VEGETABLES

| | | | |
|---|---|---|---|
| 1 | each red, yellow and green bell peppers (large dice cut) | 1 | yellow squash (large dice cut) |
| 1 | zucchini squash (large dice cut) | 1 | medium red onion (large dice cut) |

Mix marinade, then add vegetables for 30 minutes to 1 hour. Roast in a 350-degree oven for 10 to 12 minutes.

### PASTA

Boil 12 ounces Cappellini pasta in salted water for 5 to 6 minutes (stirring regularly) and drain. Toss with 1 tablespoon of olive oil then add to sauce. (recipe below)

### SAUCE

| | | | |
|---|---|---|---|
| 1 | cup dry white wine (Chardonnay) | 2 | tablespoons chopped garlic |
| 1 | cup chicken broth | | Salt & pepper to taste |
| 1 | cup heavy cream | | |
| ½ | cup grated Romano cheese | | |

**Sauce directions:** Sauté garlic in 1 tablespoon of olive oil for 30 seconds. Add white wine, chicken stock and heavy cream (stirring all the time) and bring to a boil. Reduce for 2 minutes then add Romano cheese, vegetables and pasta. Salt & pepper to taste. Yield: 4 servings.

**Optional:** You can add sliced grilled chicken breast or sautéed shrimp and scallops to this dish if you would like.

*World's Fair
Knoxville, Tennessee*

## CARSON SPRINGS BAPTIST CONFERENCE CENTER

### 1120 Carson Springs Road Newport, TN 37821

**Dori McKinney, C.C.C., Executive Chef**

*Carson Springs Baptist Conference Center (formerly known as Camp Carson) is nestled on the side of English Mountain in Newport, Tennessee. Since its beginning in 1949, Carson Springs has served countless children, youth, and adults in a mountainous Christian retreat setting. Dori has served as Food Services Manager since 1994. Her responsibilities include management of two dining rooms and numerous employees. She achieved her Chef Certification from the American Culinary Federation in June 2000.*

## SUNSHINE VEGETABLE MEDLEY

| | | | |
|---|---|---|---|
| 1 | cup white onion, medium dice | 2 | cups yellow corn |
| 1 | cup red bell pepper, medium dice | 2 | cups white, supersweet corn |
| 2 | cups butternut squash, ½" dice | 4 | tablespoons butter |
| | | | Dash nutmeg |
| | | | Salt & pepper to taste |

Melt butter in large skillet. Sauté onions and peppers lightly for 2-3 minutes over medium heat. Add corn and squash. Sauté until cooked through yet still slightly crisp. Add nutmeg and salt and pepper.

Makes 10 – ½ cup servings

## HOLIDAY PECAN PIES

| | | | |
|---|---|---|---|
| | Pie crusts for 2 pies | 1 | teaspoon butter flavoring |
| 6 | eggs | 2 | cups white corn syrup |
| ¾ | cup sugar | | |
| ¾ | cup all-purpose flour | 1 | cup dark cane syrup |
| 1½ | tablespoons vanilla extract | 3 | cups chopped pecans |

Line two 9-inch pie plates with crust, crimp edges and place in refrigerator until ready to use. Thoroughly beat together sugar and eggs, blend in the flour and vanilla. add syrups and pecans and mix well. Pour half of mixture into each chilled pie shell. Bake at 375 degrees for 45 to 50 minutes or until filling is set. Cool on rack before serving.

## CHRISTOPHER PLACE

### 1500 Pinnacles Way
### Newport, TN 37821

**Drew Ogle, Owner**
**Karen Valentine, Chef**

*Christopher Place is an elegant luxury inn in the Smoky Mountains created especially for romantic getaways. It was named one of the 10 best romantic inns in America and is AAA rated 4 Diamonds. This private mountain estate sits on 200 acres, with suites featuring whirlpools, woodburning fireplaces and panoramic views. One seating nightly at 7 PM.*
*Reservations: 1 800 595-9441*

## A ROMANTIC VALENTINE DINNER

### THE WAY TO THE HEART SALAD

| | | | |
|---|---|---|---|
| 2 | bunches of arugula with the coarse stems discarded | 2 | celery ribs, cut long and thin, like ribbons |
| 1 | small head of radicchio, thinly sliced | 1 | zucchini, cut long and thin, like ribbons |
| 2 | large Belgian endives, cut cross-wise into ½ inch pieces | 1 | can hearts of palm, cut into ½ inch rounds |
| | | | Dressing of choice |

Mix all ingredients together with dressing of choice, for a salad that is sure to win the hearts of many.

Yield: 4 servings

### TOMATO SOUP WITH PARMESAN CREAM HEARTS

| | | | |
|---|---|---|---|
| 1 | cup peeled and diced potato | 2 | 14-ounce cans whole tomatoes (no salt added) undrained and coarsely chopped |
| 1 | cup water | | |
| ½ | cup chopped onion | | |
| 2 | cloves garlic, halved | ½ | cup milk |
| 1 | teaspoon sugar | ¼ | cup plain low fat yogurt |
| ½ | teaspoon dried rosemary, crushed | 2 | tablespoons freshly grated Parmesan cheese |
| ½ | teaspoon salt | | |
| | Dash of pepper | | |

Combine potato, water, chopped onion and garlic in a large saucepan and bring to a boil. Reduce heat and simmer uncovered 10 to 12 minutes until vegetables are tender. Add sugar and rosemary, salt, pepper and tomatoes and bring back to a boil. Cover, reduce heat and simmer for 15 minutes. Purée soup in a blender and strain through a sieve. Add milk to the mixture and stir well. Cook over low heat, stirring constantly until heated. Mix yogurt and cheese and stir well.

Yield: 4 servings

### VALENTINE CONFETTI RICE

| | | | |
|---|---|---|---|
| ¾ | cup long grain rice, uncooked | ¼ | teaspoon salt |
| 2 | tablespoons butter | 1 | medium red pepper, seeded and diced |
| 1 | cup sliced green onions | ¼ | cup water |
| 1 | teaspoon cumin | 11 | ounces chicken stock |
| ½ | teaspoon oregano | | |

Heat skillet over high heat, add rice and cook 3 to 4 minutes until browned. Remove rice from skillet and set aside. Melt butter in skillet over medium high heat. Add onions, cumin, oregano, salt, diced red pepper and sauté for 3 minutes. Add water, stock and rice. Bring to a boil. Cover and reduce heat. Simmer until rice is tender and liquid is absorbed.

Yield: 4 servings

# RED WINE & ROSEMARY ROASTED RACK OF LAMB

## FOR THE LAMB

2  racks of lamb (8 to 9 ribs) with bones frenched and fat trimmed

Salt and ground black pepper

2  tablespoons vegetable oil

Preheat oven to 425 degrees and place a shallow pan in oven to heat. Season lamb with salt and pepper. Heat oil in skillet over high heat. Place lamb in skillet, meat side down with ribs facing outward. Cook until well browned and a crust has formed on the surface, probably 4 to 5 minutes. Use tongs to stand ribs up against each other to brown bottoms. Transfer lamb to preheated roasting pan and roast 12 to 15 minutes (retain 2 tablespoons of fat for use in sauce). Remove and cover meat loosely with foil and let rest 10 to 12 minutes. Carve into individual chops and serve immediately with sauce.

Yield: 4 servings

## FOR THE SAUCE

2  medium shallots, minced

1  cup dry red wine

2½  teaspoons minced rosemary leaves

1  cup low sodium chicken broth

2  tablespoons butter
Salt & ground black pepper to taste

Pour off all but 2 tablespoons of the fat from the skillet where you browned the lamb. Sauce shallots over medium heat in same skillet used for browning until soft. Add red wine and rosemary, increase heat to medium high and simmer until dark and syrupy. Add chicken broth and reduce until about ¾ cup is left. Remove from heat, add butter to blend. Season with salt and pepper.

# GLAZED MEDALLION CARROTS

2  fresh bunches of carrots, peeled

3  tablespoons butter

2  tablespoons honey

1  tablespoon Dijon mustard

2  tablespoons white wine

Slice carrots into ¼ inch rounds. Steam in a small amount of water, drain and reserve the liquid. Return liquid to pan and heat with remaining ingredients. Stir until well mixed. Add carrots and cook to reduce liquid to a glaze.

Yield: 4 servings

# COEUR À LA CRÈME WITH RASPBERRY SAUCE

## FOR THE DESSERT

8  ounces mascarpone cheese

1¼  cups heavy cream

1  teaspoon vanilla extract

1  tablespoon fresh lemon juice

1  tablespoon raspberry liqueur

½  cup sifted confectioner's sugar

Cut a piece of cheesecloth into 4 six-inch squares. Dampen and wring out lightly. Press one square into each of four perforated heat-shaped ceramic molds and set aside. Whip the cheese, ¼ cup of the cream, vanilla, lemon juice and the liqueur until well blended and refrigerate. Whip the remaining 1 cup cream and sugar until the cream forms stiff peaks. Fold the whipped cream into the cheese mixture and spoon into molds. Fold the edges of the cheesecloth over the tops and refrigerate for 3 hours.

## FOR THE SAUCE

1  pint of fresh raspberries

1  tablespoon sugar

1  teaspoon fresh lemon juice

Purée all ingredients. Taste for sweetness. Strain and refrigerate.

**To serve:** Unfold cheesecloth and invert molds onto serving plate. Lift off mold gently. Smooth with back of spoon and remove cheesecloth slowly. Spoon sauce onto plate around the hearts and garnish with more fresh raspberries.

Serves 4.

# THE PARSON'S TABLE
## 102 West Woodrow Avenue Jonesborough, TN 37659

**Debra Myron, Owner**

*Historic Jonesborough, Tennessee holds a culinary surprise: the 1874 First Christian Church, nestled on a hill overlooking the town. A lovely Gothic structure, the church outgrew its original use and because there was no room to expand, the building was vacated. In 1972 the building was completely renovated and a balcony added. It opened as The Parson's Table. In 1986 Debra Myron purchased the restaurant and made extensive repairs to enhance the church's Victorian origin. The menu was also changed from country cuisine to delicious Continental fare. The menu includes Rack of Lamb Dijoinaise, Roast Duckling a la Orange, veal variations, specially procured beef and an array of fresh seafood and shellfish.*

## WALNUT CRANBERRY ORANGE TORTE

| | | | |
|---|---|---|---|
| 1½ | cups flour | 2 | tablespoons plain |
| ¾ | cup chopped | | gelatin |
| | walnuts (for crust) | 1 | cup chopped |
| ¼ | lb. butter | | walnuts |
| 1 | quart cranberry | | |
| | orange relish | | |

Place walnuts in food processor with knife attachment and blend until crumbs. Mix walnut crumbs, flour and butter. Press into springform pan. Bake crust 10 to 15 minutes at 350 degrees. Let cool. Heat to loosen the relish. Soften the gelatin and add to relish. Let come to a low boil. Cool mixture and pour into pan with crust. Refrigerate.

## SHELLFISH MEDLEY

| | | | |
|---|---|---|---|
| 1 | to 2 tablespoons clarified butter | 3 | ounces crab meat, picked clean |
| 1 | teaspoon minced garlic | 2 | tablespoons dry vermouth |
| 1 | teaspoon minced shallots | ½ | cup heavy cream Pinch saffron |
| 1 | small lobster tail (about 2 ounces of meat) | 2 | pastry Pepperidge Farm puff pastry shells baked according to |
| 6 | medium scallops, large muscle removed | | package directions, or 4 ounces cooked angel hair pasta |
| 8 | large shrimp, shelled and deveined | ⅛ | cup grated Swiss or dill Harvard cheese |

Heat clarified butter in non-stick frying pan. Add garlic and shallots and sauté until soft. Do not let brown. Cut lobster tail into 4 pieces. If using large scallops, cut into quarters. Add lobster, scallops, shrimp, crab meat and vermouth. Raise heat to high and reduce vermouth to an essence. Add cream and saffron. Mix and reduce to sauce consistency over low heat. Preheat boiler. Pour seafood into a puff pastry shell or over angel hair pasta. Sprinkle with grated cheese and glaze briefly under the broiler.

**Note:** To clarify butter, slowly melt butter over low heat in a small saucepan. Pour off the clear liquid (this is the clarified butter) and discard the heavy, milky solids.

Yield: 2 servings

## FRUIT SALSA

| | | | |
|---|---|---|---|
| 1 | pint strawberries | 1 | tablespoon white wine |
| 4 | kiwi | | |
| 1 | cup pineapple | 1 | tablespoon cracked black peppercorns |
| 1 | cup chopped red onion | | |
| 2 | tablespoons balsamic vinegar | 1 | tablespoon dill |
| | | 2 | tablespoons olive oil |

Slice strawberries, dice kiwi, dice pineapple. Mix all ingredients together. Great with seafood!

# GENERAL MORGAN INN & CONFERENCE CENTER

## 111 North Main Street
## Greeneville, TN 37743
## 1-800-223-2679

**Ken Cleveland, General Manager**
**Jarvis K. Wynn, Executive Chef**

*Nestled in the Appalachian Foothills in Northeast Tennessee, the historic General Morgan Inn & Conference Center is located in downtown Greeneville between Knoxville and the Tri-Cities area. Rich architectural accents reflect an elegant past, accommodations feature luxurious modern amenities. The landmark property, located in Tennessee's second oldest town, boasts 51 elegantly appointed guestrooms and one lavish Presidential Suite. A complimentary Grand Continental Breakfast Buffet is provided to all guests. The General Morgan Inn also has a full-service restaurant and lounge, spacious meeting and banquet facilities, and a breathtaking outdoor Garden Terrace that is perfect for private parties and weddings. The Inn is only blocks from the President Andrew Johnson Historic Site and Home, the Federal Courthouse and just 10 miles from the birthplace of Davy Crockett.*

## KEY WEST CHIX

6-ounce chicken breasts, boneless & skinless
Seasoned flour
Orange sauce
Mandarin oranges

Corn oil
Roasted pecan halves (roasted in preheated oven for 7 minutes at 300 degrees)

### SEASONED FLOUR

| | | | |
|---|---|---|---|
| 1 | cup flour | 1½ | teaspoons granulated garlic mix |
| 1 | teaspoon Spanish paprika | | |
| 1½ | teaspoons salt | | |
| 1½ | teaspoons white pepper | | |

### ORANGE SAUCE

| | | | |
|---|---|---|---|
| 1 | pint orange juice concentrate | ¼ | cup sugar |

Mix orange juice and sugar and cook over medium heat and reduce by ¼. Add ⅓ cup cornstarch and mix with ⅓ cup of white wine. Cook about 6 more minutes on medium heat stirring constantly to finish orange sauce.

Sauté chicken breasts (dusted with seasoned flour) on both sides in corn oil till done. Pour warm orange sauce over chicken. Garnish with roasted pecan halves and mandarin oranges.

Serves 10.

## APPLE BREAD PUDDING WITH JACK DANIEL SAUCE

| | | | |
|---|---|---|---|
| 10 | cups diced bread (no dark bread) | 1 | tablespoon of vanilla flavoring |
| 1¼ | cups raisins | 1 | tablespoon cinnamon |
| 8 | eggs | | |
| ½ | quart heavy cream | 4 | sliced peeled apples (no seeds) |
| 1½ | cups sugar | | |

Mix all of the above ingredients thoroughly and place in a greased pan in a preheated oven. Cook for 40 to 50 minutes at 300 degrees. Cool before cutting. Serve with warm Jack Daniel Sauce.

Serves 8 to 10.

### JACK DANIEL SAUCE

| | | | |
|---|---|---|---|
| 1½ | cups sugar | 2 | tablespoons flour |
| ½ | cup butter | 1 | cup heavy cream |
| 3 | ounces Jack Daniel whiskey | | |

Put butter in pan then add sugar, stirring constantly until starting to brown (do not burn). Stir in flour and cook on low heat for about 3 minutes. Add heavy cream and cook on low heat for 10 to 12 minutes until smooth. Add Jack Daniel whiskey and cook about 3 more minutes. Put on bread pudding warm.

## THE PEERLESS RESTAURANT

### 2531 North Roan Street Johnson City, TN 37601

**Jim Kalogeros, President**
**Gary Kalogeros, Vice-President/C.O.O.**

*The original Peerless Restaurant opened in 1938 in Johnson City. Now, The Peerless Restaurant, Inc. is eagerly looking forward to celebrating a "legendary 62 year independent tradition" this year! The newest Peerless opened in 1990 with a seating capacity of 675 seats; featuring multi-theme dining, including three dining rooms, 12 private dining rooms and a ballroom facility seating 275. The Peerless Restaurant takes pride in serving Black Angus beef – specifying origins of the mid-western states, then properly aging and hand cutting each steak by the in-house butcher. The seafood is federally inspected using only fresh No. 1 grade products. The restaurant features lighter dishes, made from scratch sauces for the pastas and fresh chicken items. Past awards for the restaurant include being voted with the local 1998 Taste of Johnson City Restaurant Award, Best Seafood in Tri-Cities by Kingsport Peoples Award, and recipient of one out of six "Tennessee's Restaurateur of the Year Award 1997."*

## SLOW ROASTED PRIME RIB

Standing Rib Roast – fresh aged Midwestern beef of high grade USDA choice or trim USDA Prime Roast approximately twelve to thirteen pounds. Steam with two cloves of fresh garlic, black fresh ground pepper, two tablespoons of granulated onion powder and place in a 225-degree oven. Place rib on a wide rack with a drip pan.

Place in a preheated oven and slow roast for about two hours. Check with a meat thermometer for an internal temperature of 125 degrees, a nice medium-rare. Continue to cook if needed, 135 degrees internal temperature for a medium texture.

Let the roast rest for at least twenty minutes. It may be kept in a 135-degree warm oven for several hours. Do not keep in a hotter oven, because the rib will continue to cook. Slice the meat with a seared knife at 9 to 12 ounces just before serving. In the bottom of the drip pan add one-third cup of water to the au jus and stir over heat. You may add sliced prime rib in au jus for one to two minutes to raise the degree of meat from medium to well done.

Whole rib serves 12 to 16.

## TRADITIONAL HORSERADISH SAUCE

*(To Serve With Prime Rib)*

| | | | |
|---|---|---|---|
| 1 | cup sour cream | ½ | tablespoon white pepper |
| 1 | tablespoon hot sauce | ½ | tablespoon salt |
| ¼ | cup straight horseradish sauce | | |

Serves 4 to 8.

## GALLOWAY'S

### 807 North Roan Street
### Johnson City, TN 37604

*Unlike today's theme restaurants, Galloway's is a unique dinner experience reminiscent of a cozy European cafe. Tucked into what was once a charming home in the historic district of Johnson City, Tennessee, Galloway's offers you a blazing fireplace to warm you in the winter or a breezy patio to relax you in the summer. Their expert chef along with the guidance of the owners, Billie Galloway and Bobby Smith, have put together an eclectic lunch and dinner menu featuring only the freshest of ingredients and spices. Among their awards, Galloway's has received "Best of Show," "Most Romantic" and Best Overall" at recent culinary events.*

## GARLIC CHEESE STUFFED MUSHROOMS

| | |
|---|---|
| 2 ounces Swiss cheese, grated | 2 tablespoons butter, softened |
| 1 hard boiled egg, finely chopped | 1 pound fresh mushrooms 1" to 1½" in diameter |
| 3 tablespoons fine dry bread crumbs | 4 tablespoons butter, melted |
| ½ clove garlic, minced | |

Combine cheese, egg, crumbs, garlic and butter. Blend thoroughly. Place stemmed mushrooms rounded side up, on baking pan. Brush with butter and broil a few minutes. Do not brown. Stuff with cheese mixture. Brown under broiler just before serving.

## FILET OF BEEF WITH MUSHROOM PATÉ

10   5-ounce beef filets (all fat removed)

Place in freezer for 20 minutes. Brush chilled filets with oil, sprinkle with salt and pepper and refrigerate.

| | |
|---|---|
| 3 tablespoons butter | Salt & pepper to taste |
| 1½ pounds mushrooms, chopped | ½ lemon, juiced |
| 3 tablespoons instant minced onion | ½ cup fine bread crumbs |
| 2 green onions, chopped | 5 frozen patty shells (i.e. Pepperidge Farms) |
| 4 tablespoons fresh chopped parsley | |

Sauté chopped mushrooms in butter until almost dry. Add lemon juice, minced onion, green onion, parsley, salt and pepper. Remove from heat and add bread crumbs. Roll thawed patty shells to 5"x7" pastry. Divide paté evenly and place on pastry. Top paté with beef filets. Fold in pastry and seal. Place seam side down in shallow pan. Refrigerate. Brush with egg wash before baking.

Serves 5.

Bake in 450 degree oven.

| | |
|---|---|
| Rare Bake 10 minutes | Medium 15 minutes |
| Med. Rare 12 minutes | Med. well 18 minutes |

Serve immediately ladled with Madeira wine sauce (recipe follows).

## MADEIRA SAUCE

| | |
|---|---|
| 3 tablespoons butter | 1 teaspoon Kitchen Bouquet |
| 1½ tablespoons flour | ½ cup Madeira wine |
| ¾ cup beef stock | |

Melt the butter, stir in flour and cook for 5 minutes. Add beef stock, Kitchen Bouquet and Madeira wine. Cook until thickened.

Yield: 1½ cups

## CENTRE AT MILLENNIUM PARK

### 2001 Millennium Place
### Johnson City, TN 37604

**George Gonzalez, Executive Chef**

*Chef Gonzalez is the gold medal winner of the 2000 AMERICAN CULINARY FEDERATION NASHVILLE SALON. A six-year veteran and Tennessee District Chef of culinary leader Sodexho Marriott, Chef Gonzalez has already impressed many people with his culinary flair.*

## SPICY SAUSAGE & GARDEN VEGETABLES FRITTATA

10 ounces spicy Italian sausage

Slice and cook until browned.

### EGG MIXTURE

| | | | |
|---|---|---|---|
| 3 | whole eggs | 1 | teaspoon Italian |
| 2 | tablespoons grated | | seasoning |
| | Parmesan cheese | ¼ | teaspoon pepper |

Whisk in medium bowl. Add cheese, seasoning and pepper.

| | | | |
|---|---|---|---|
| 2 | tablespoons butter | 4 | ounces diced green |
| 4 | ounces diced fresh | | peppers |
| | zucchini | 4 | ounces diced |
| 4 | ounces shredded | | cooked potatoes |
| | carrots | | |
| 4 | ounces diced red | | |
| | peppers | | |

Melt the butter in a 10" ovenproof, nonstick sauté pan. Add vegetables to sauté pan. Cook and stir over medium heat until tender. Pour 3 cups of the egg mixture into the pan. Stir gently to combine. Cook over low heat for about 6 minutes without stirring. Top pan with 3 ounces of shredded Swiss cheese, place pan under the broiler and cook until lightly browned.

Yield: 6 portions

## FOX MANOR BED & BREAKFAST

### 1612 Watauga Street
### Kingsport, TN 37664

**Paulette Fox, Innkeeper**

## VIDALIA ONION CASSEROLE

| | | | |
|---|---|---|---|
| 5 | cups onions (quartered and boiled until tender) | ½ | teaspoon salt |
| | | ¼ | teaspoon pepper |
| | | ½ | cup self-rising flour |
| 5 | cups grated cheese (medium sharp) | 6 | tablespoons butter |

Mix onions, 4 cups cheese and other ingredients. Pour into casserole dish. Sprinkle with remaining cheese. Bake for 30 minutes at 350 degrees.

## SKOBY'S RESTAURANT

### 1001 Konnarock Road
### Kingsport, TN 37664

**Brad Smith, Manager**

## SKOBY'S CORN

| | | | |
|---|---|---|---|
| 16 | ounces frozen whole kernel corn | 2 | cups half and half |
| ½ | teaspoon Accent (MSG) | 1 | tablespoon sugar (heaping) |
| 1 | teaspoon salt | 2 | tablespoons flour (heaping) |
| ½ | teaspoon pepper | | |

Mix together. Use microwave. Cook about 20 minutes. Cook 5 minutes at a time (opening and stirring after each 5 minutes). After it's done, add 1 tablespoon of butter. Stir until it melts. Sprinkle bread crumbs on the top. Served as an accompaniment to steak, etc.

# CULINARY TERMS FREQUENTLY USED BY TENNESSEE CHEFS

**Aioli** ~ A garlic mayonnaise from France usually served with seafood.

**Ancho** ~ A fairly mild red chili pepper.

**Andouille (Fr)** ~ A popular sausage served with red beans and rice.

**Anise** ~ An herb that tastes like licorice. It is often used in pastries, cheeses, etc.

**Antipasto** ~ An antipasto is an appetizer that is generally served before pasta.

**Appareil (Fr)** ~ A mixture of ingredients already prepared for use in a recipe.

**Arborio rice** ~ An Italian medium-grain rice that is used frequently for risotto.

**Arugula** ~ A leafy salad herb that has an aromatic peppery flavor.

**Bain-marie** ~ (Water bath) consists of a bowl placed over a bowl of boiling hot water to gently cook the sauce, etc. without over-cooking.

**Balsamic vinegar** ~ Balsamic vinegar is a very fine aged vinegar made in Modena, Italy. It is expensive but is the favorite vinegar of most Tennessee chefs because of its sweet, mellow flavor.

**Basil** ~ An aromatic herb widely used in Mediterranean cooking. It is used in pesto sauce, salads and cooking fish.

**Basmati rice** ~ A long-grain rice with a nutty flavor.

**Bay** ~ Dried bay leaves are used frequently in poultry, fish and meat dishes as well as stocks and soups.

**Béarnaise** ~ One of the classic French sauces. It is made with emulsified egg yolks, butter, fresh herbs and shallots. It is often served with poultry, grilled fish and meat.

**Béchamel** ~ It is also one of the basic French sauces. It is a sauce made from white roux, milk or cream, onions and seasonings.

**Beignet** ~ A French word for batter dipped fried fritters, usually sweet like a doughnut.

**Beurre blanc** ~ It is a white butter sauce made from shallots, white wine vinegar and white wine that has been reduced and thickened with heavy cream and unsalted butter. Salt and ground white pepper to taste.

**Beurre manié** ~ A paste of flour and butter used to thicken sauces.

**Bisque** ~ A thick seafood soup usually made from oysters, shrimp or lobster and thickened with cream.

**Blanch** ~ The purpose is to loosen the skin on a fruit or vegetable by placing it in hot water for a few minutes and then into cold water to stop the cooking process.

**Braise** ~ The slow cooking of food in a tight container with a flavoring liquid equal to about half the amount of the main ingredient.

**Brie** ~ A soft cows' milk cheese made in the French region of Brie.

**Brûlé** ~ A French word for "burnt" and refers to a caramelized coating of sugar, such as a topping for crème brûlée.

**Bruschetta** ~ Toasted bread slices rubbed with garlic and drizzled with new green olive oil.

**Cannelloni** ~ Italian pasta tubes filled with ricotta cheese, chocolate, etc.

**Caper** ~ The pickled bud of a flowering caper plant. It is found on the Mediterranean coast. Capers are often used as a condiment in salads, used in making tartare sauce and as a seasoning in broiling fish.

**Capon** ~ A castrated male chicken.

**Caramel** ~ Sugar "caramelizes" when dissolved in water and boiled to a golden brown color.

**Cardamom** ~ A member of the ginger family. It has a spicy flavor and is used in Indian and Middle Eastern dishes.

**Cayenne pepper** ~ Red chili pepper that is dried and ground fine for home use.

**Chaurice** ~ A highly spiced sausage used in Cajun cooking.

# CULINARY TERMS FREQUENTLY USED BY TENNESSEE CHEFS

**Chervil** ~ An herb belonging to the parsley family. It is best used fresh because of its delicate flavor.

**Chiffonade** ~ Leafy vegetables such as spinach and lettuce cut into thin strips.

**Chipotle** ~ A brownish-red chili pepper that has been dried and smoked and sometimes canned. This chili pepper has a smoky flavor and is very hot.

**Chive** ~ A member of the onion family used in flavoring foods.

**Chutney** ~ A sweet and/or sour seasoning that can be made from fruits and vegetables and flavored with many kinds of spices.

**Cilantro** ~ A fresh coriander leaf.

**Clarified butter** ~ Butter that has been heated to remove the impurities.

**Clarify** ~ To remove all impurities.

**Condiment** ~ Any seasoning, spice, sauce, relish, etc. used to enhance food at the table.

**Consommé** ~ A clear strained stock, usually clarified, made from poultry, fish, meat or game and flavored with vegetables.

**Coriander** ~ A member of the carrot family. Fresh coriander is also called cilantro. This herb is prized for its dried seeds and fresh leaves and is used in similar ways to parsley.

**Coulis** ~ A thick sauce or purée made from cooked vegetables, fruits, etc.

**Couscous** ~ Traditional couscous is generally made from coarsely ground semolina, a wheat flour used for pasta. It is popular in the Mediterranean areas of Morocco and Algeria. It is often served over vegetables or meats along with sauces.

**Crème Brûlée** ~ A custard made from eggs and covered with a "burnt" layer of sugar which has caramelized in the oven.

**Crème fraîche** ~ It is often made from unpasteurized cream with an additive such as yogurt which gives it a distinctive flavor.

**Crevette** ~ It is a French word for shrimp.

**Cumin** ~ A spice from the seeds of the cumin plant. It is often used in making pickles, chutneys and especially in curries.

**Currant** ~ A delicious fruit used to make jams and jellies. It is also used as a glaze for meats. The red variety is widely used.

**Curry** ~ A mixture of spices widely used in preparing and cooking meats and vegetables. It is often used in Indian cooking.

**Daikon** ~ A large radish.

**Deglacer** ~ A process of dissolving cooking juices left in a pan where meats or poultry have been cooked. This is achieved by adding liquids such as stock or wines to the sediment and then reducing it to half the volume. The sauce is then strained and seasoned.

**Demi-glace** ~ A brown sauce boiled and reduced by half.

**Dente, al** ~ Vegetables cooked until they are firm and crunchy.

**Dijon mustard** ~ Mustard made from a white wine base.

**Dill** ~ An herb used with vinegar to pickle cucumbers. It is also used to flavor foods.

**Dredge** ~ To coat food with a dry ingredient such as breadcrumbs, cornmeal or flour.

**Dungeness crab** ~ A large rock crab found in the Pacific Northwest.

**Fagioli** ~ The Italian word for beans.

**Farfalle** ~ "Butterfly"-shaped pasta.

**Fennel** ~ A vegetable bulb or herb with a spicy flavor. It is often used in soups and salads.

**Feta cheese** ~ A soft and crumbly goat's milk cheese often used in salads and Greek dishes.

**Filé powder** ~ Sassafras leaves that have been dried and used in the final stages to thicken gumbo. Okra can also be used to thicken gumbo instead of filé powder.

# CULINARY TERMS FREQUENTLY USED BY TENNESSEE CHEFS

**Filo** (phyllo) A very thin dough that contains little fat and is used for strudel, baklava and other pastries.

**Flan** ~ An open custard tart made in a mold. Caramel cream custard is a popular flan dessert.

**Foie gras** ~ The enlarged liver of a fattened or force-fed goose.

**Frais, fraîche** ~ Fresh.

**Fraise** ~ Strawberry.

**Fumet** ~ Liquid that gives flavor and body to sauces and stocks. Fish fumet is used to poach fish fillets. It is made from dry white wine, fish stock, and bouquet garni.

**Garde manger** ~ Pantry area where a cold buffet can be prepared.

**Garnish** ~ A small amount of a flavorful, edible ingredient added as trimmings to compliment the main dish and enhance its appearance

**Ginger** ~ A spice from a rhizome of a plant native to China. It is used fresh in Chinese cooking, but can also be used dried or ground.

**Glace** ~ (Fr) ice cream; also used for cake icing.

**Glaze** ~ It is used as a coating to give a shiny appearance to roasts, poultry, custards, jams and jellies.

**Glutinous rice** ~ Sticky rice used by the Japanese to make sushi and rice cakes.

**Gorgonzola** ~ A strong Italian blue cheese.

**Guava** ~ A tropical fruit shrub. It makes delicious jellies.

**Gumbo** ~ A Cajun or Creole soup thickened with okra or filé powder. Gumbo is an African word for okra.

**Habañero** ~ An extremely hot chili pepper, oval-shaped and smaller than the jalapeno. The color changes from green to orange and red upon ripening. It is used in stews and sauces.

**Haddock** ~ It is closely related to a cod but smaller and thin-skinned. It is excellent broiled in butter.

**Halibut** ~ The largest member of the flounder family. It can be smoked, broiled or grilled.

**Hoisin sauce** ~ It is used in Chinese cooking to flavor sauces and marinades. It is a thick brown sauce made from soybeans, garlic, sugar and salt.

**Hollandaise** ~ It is one of the classic sauces in French cooking. It is made from an emulsion of hot clarified butter and eggs lightly heated until it begins to have the consistency of a smooth custard. It also contains lemons and shallots.

**Haricot vert** ~ Green string beans.

**Infuse** ~ To soak spices, herbs, or vegetables in a liquid to extract their flavor.

**Jalapeño** ~ A very hot green chili pepper generally used fresh, but also available canned.

**Jambalaya** ~ A Cajun dish of rice, shrimp, crawfish, sausage, chicken and beans, seasoned with Creole spices.

**Julienne** ~ Vegetables and meats cut into thin strips.

**Kalamata** ~ Kalamata are large black Greek olives.

**Kale** ~ A frilly, leafy vegetable of the cabbage family.

**Leek** ~ A member of the onion family. Leeks are used in soups, casseroles, etc.

**Loganberry** ~ Similar to a blackberry and raspberry. It can be served with cream as a dessert, a filling for tarts or as a cream pudding.

# CULINARY TERMS FREQUENTLY USED BY TENNESSEE CHEFS

**Mandoline** ~ A tool use to cut vegetables evenly into thick or thin slices.

**Mango** ~ A delicious, sweet tropical fruit served as desserts and also used in cooking preserves and chutneys.

**Marinade** ~ A liquid, including seasonings, to flavor and tenderize fish, meat and poultry before cooking.

**Marinara** ~ A tomato sauce flavored with herbs and garlic, usually served with pasta.

**Merlot** ~ A red-wine grape that produces a fruity flavor.

**Mesclun** ~ A mixture of wild salad leaves and herbs. They are generally served with dressing containing walnut or olive oil and wine vinegar.

**Mirepoix** ~ A mixture of cut vegetables – usually carrot, onion, celery and sometimes ham or bacon – used to flavor sauces and as a bed on which to braise meat.

**Mirin** ~ A sweet and syrupy Japanese rice wine used for cooking.

**Mornay** ~ A classic French sauce; béchamel sauce to which egg yolks, cream and cheese are added.

**Oregano** ~ Oregano is an herb very similar to marjoram but more pungent. It is widely used in Greek and Italian cooking.

**Orzo** ~ Rice-shaped pasta.

**Panache** ~ French to describe something mixed or multicolored such as salads, fruit or ice cream.

**Pancetta** ~ Italian bacon that is sometimes rolled into a solid round.

**Paprika** ~ A variety of red bell pepper that has been dried and powdered and made into a cooking spice. It is used in making Hungarian goulash, etc.

**Penne** ~ tube-shaped pasta cut on the diagonal.

**Peperonata** ~ An Italian dish of bell peppers, tomatoes, onions and garlic cooked in olive oil. It can be served hot or cold.

**Pepperoncini** ~ A hot red chili pepper served fresh or dried.

**Pepperoni** ~ An Italian salami of pork and beef seasoned with hot red peppers.

**Phyllo** ~ See filo.

**Picante Sauce** ~ Hot spicy tomato-based sauce.

**Piccata** ~ Veal scallop.

**Plantain** ~ A tropical fruit similar to the banana.

**Poisson** ~ French for fish.

**Poivre** ~ French for pepper.

**Pomodoro** ~ Italian for tomato.

**Porcino** ~ Italian for a wild mushroom.

**Portobello mushroom** ~ A large cultivated field mushroom which has a firm texture and is ideal for grilling and as a meat substitute.

**Prawn** ~ A large shrimp.

**Prosciutto** ~ Italian ham cured by salting and air drying.

**Purée** ~ Food that is pounded, finely chopped, or processed through a blender or strained through a sieve to achieve a smooth consistency.

**Quiche** ~ A custard-filled tart with a savory flavor.

**Radicchio** ~ A reddish member of the chicory family used as a garnish or for salad.

**Ratatouille** ~ A mixture of tomatoes, eggplants, zucchini, bell peppers and onions cooked in olive oil. It can be served hot or cold.

**Reduce** ~ To boil down a liquid to thicken its consistency and concentrate its flavor.

**Relleno** ~ Stuffing.

# CULINARY TERMS FREQUENTLY USED BY TENNESSEE CHEFS

**Remoulade** ~ One of the classic French sauces. It is made from mayonnaise seasoned with chopped eggs and gherkins, parsley, capers, tarragon and shallots. It is served with shellfish, vegetables and cold meats.

**Rice wine** ~ Distilled from fermented rice.

**Ricotta** ~ The word ricotta means "recooked" in Italian. It is a soft cheese made from whey. It has a slightly sweet taste.

**Rigatoni** ~ Italian macaroni.

**Risotto** ~ An Italian arborio rice dish simmered slowly.

**Roghan josh** ~ A spicy lamb dish from India, red in color and served with rice.

**Roulade** ~ French for a rolled slice of meat or piece of fish filled with a savory stuffing.

**Rosemary** ~ A shrub with aromatic needle-like leaves. It is used fresh or dried as an herb, especially with lamb, pork and veal.

**Rouille** ~ A spicy red pepper and garlic mayonnaise.

**Roux** (Fr) ~ A mixture of flour and fat (usually butter or shortening) cooked together slowly to form a thickening agent for sauces, gumbos, and other soups.

**Sec** ~ Means dry.

**Shallot** ~ A sweet member of the onion family. It has a more delicate flavor than regular onions. It is used extensively in French cooking.

**Shiitake** ~ It is a dark brown mushroom with a meaty flavor. It is available both fresh and dried. ~ It was originally from Japan but is now cultivated in both America and Europe.

**Sommelier** ~ (Fr) Wine Steward.

**Sorrel** ~ A leafy plant often used in salads, soups, omelets, purees and sauces. It has a distinct lemon taste.

**Sweat** ~ To sauté in a covered vessel until natural juices are exuded.

**Tartare** ~ Tartare sauce is made with mayonnaise, egg yolks, chopped onions, capers and chives. It is often served with fish, meat and poultry.

**Tasso** ~ A highly seasoned Cajun sausage made from pork or beef.

**Thyme** ~ A herb with a pungent smell that belongs to the same family as mint. It is used in soups, stocks, casseroles and stews.

**Timbale** ~ (Fr) Metal mold shaped like a drum.

**Tofu** ~ It is a white Japanese bean curd made from minced soy beans boiled in water then strained and coagulated with sea water. It is soft and easily digested.

**Tomatillo** ~ Mexican fruit related to the tomato. It is often used in salsa, salads, sauces, etc.

**Toufflé** ~ Similar to soufflé.

**Tournedos** ~ A trimmed cut of beef or veal fillet.

**Veal** ~ The meat of milk-fed baby beef.

**Vermicelli** ~ A thin Italian pasta.

**Vinaigrette** ~ A basic dressing of oil and vinegar with salt, pepper, herbs and sometimes mustard.

**White sauce** ~ Béchamel or velouté sauce, both made from roux.

**Zabaglione** ~ A rich Italian custard made of egg yolks beaten with Marsala wine and sugar until very thick.

**Zest** ~ The outer skin of citrus where the important oils have accumulated.

## REGIONAL INDEX

**PLEASE SEND ME:**

_____ copies of **Fine Dining Tennessee Style** @ $29.95 each $ _____

_____ copies of **Fine Dining Mississippi Style** @ $29.95 each $ _____

Tennessee residents add sales tax @ $ 2.62 each $ _____

Add shipping & handling @ $ 6.50 each $ _____

Total Enclosed $ _____

Mail cookbook(s) to:

Name _____

Address _____

**(NO PO BOX NUMBERS PLEASE)**

City _____ State _____ Zip _____

**Make checks payable to Starr★Toof.**

Charge to ☐ Visa ☐ MasterCard Valid thru _____

Account Number _____ Signature _____

Mail to: Toof Cookbooks
Starr★Toof
670 South Cooper Street
Memphis, Tennessee 38104

---

**PLEASE SEND ME:**

_____ copies of **Fine Dining Tennessee Style** @ $29.95 each $ _____

_____ copies of **Fine Dining Mississippi Style** @ $29.95 each $ _____

Tennessee residents add sales tax @ $ 2.62 each $ _____

Add shipping & handling @ $ 6.50 each $ _____

Total Enclosed $ _____

Mail cookbook(s) to:

Name _____

Address _____

**(NO PO BOX NUMBERS PLEASE)**

City _____ State _____ Zip _____

**Make checks payable to Starr★Toof.**

Charge to ☐ Visa ☐ MasterCard Valid thru _____

Account Number _____ Signature _____

Mail to: Toof Cookbooks
Starr★Toof
670 South Cooper Street
Memphis, Tennessee 38104

Belle Meade Mansion, Nashville, Tennessee

Covered Bridge, Elizabethton, Tennessee